IN THE SERVICE OF PEACE

MEMORIES OF LEBANON

FROM THE PAGES OF AN COSANTÓIR

Edited

by

COMDT BRENDAN O'SHEA

PUBLISHED IN ASSOCIATION WITH

AN COSANTÓIR

THE DEFENCE FORCES MAGAZINE

MERCIER PRESS

MERCIER PRESS
5 French Church Street, Cork
16 Hume Street, Dublin 2

Trade enquiries to COLUMBA MERCIER DISTRIBUTION,
55a Spruce Avenue, Stillorgan Industrial Park, Blackrock, Dublin

© An Cosantóir, 2001

ISBN: 1 85635 376 1

10 9 8 7 6 5 4 3 2 1

The fact that an article appears in this book does not indicate official
Defence Forces approval for the views of the author.

Printed in Ireland by Colour Books Ltd.

CONTENTS

AN COSANTÓIR
THE DEFENCE FORCES MAGAZINE

The phrase 'end of an era' is bandied about with such ubiquity that it has almost lost its meaning, but in the case of the Irish Battalion's withdrawal from Lebanon, that epithet is justifiably applied. When 89 Irishbatt pulls out of our Area of Operations in south Lebanon in October 2001, a continuous period of twenty-three years of Irish Battalions serving with UNIFIL will come to a close.

Part valediction, part commemoration, *An Cosantóir* has collected this compilation of previously published articles about Irish involvement in Lebanon during that time. Mainly written by military personnel – with the odd 'civvie' reporter getting a look-in – what links them all is that they were written by first-hand witnesses and participants, people who were at the heart of the action earmarking the conflict at various points during that quarter of a century.

Even though a general theme runs through all these pieces, a range of subjects is covered, from, say, Capt Ray Murphy's definitive article on the Battle of At Tiri, through to Lt Maoliosa Ó Culcháin's reflections on the imported art of dry stone walling in the hills of south Lebanon. We hope that the reader is left with the impression that this was a multi-dimensional mission, encompassing both peacekeeping objectives and humanitarian operations over the course of its twenty-three years – as indeed it was.

With Lebanon being so much part of the military climate for such a long period, it is sometimes hard to remember what life was like in the Defence Forces before 1978. However, since its foundation in 1940, *An Cosantóir*, The Defence Forces Magazine, has reflected all aspects of that life, whether it be the very latest news from the army, naval service and air corps, or features on operations, new equipment, training, technology, sport, history, overseas service, humanitarian work, travel and weapons, while not forgetting day-to-day comment on general service corps and unit activities.

In the years ahead the plan is to stick with this tried and tested formula, and who knows, perhaps twenty years from now we may find ourselves celebrating the success of yet another historic mission.

Sgt Willie Braine
Editor
An Cosantóir

GLOSSARY

ADC	Aide de Camp
ADL	Armistice Demarcation Line of 1949 between Israel and Lebanon
AE	Armed Element (AMAL, Hizbullah, etc.)
AFV	Armoured Fighting Vehicle
AHQ	Army Headquarters (also known as DFHQ – Defence Forces Headquarters)
AK-47	Standard Soviet issue Assault Rifle
AMAL	Political Party led by Nabbih Berrie (also a paramilitary resistance group)
AML 60	Panhard Armoured Car armed with a 60mm mortar
AML 90	Panhard Armoured Car armed with a 90mm gun
AO	Area of Operations
APC	Armoured Personnel Carrier
ATk	Anti-tank (missile)
BMR	Battalion Mobile Reserve
Bn	Battalion (500 troops approx.)
Chalk	Group or part of the battalion being rotated. Irishbatt was generally rotated in three Chalks
Cherokee	US made Landrover
Christian Militia	The Forces of Maj Saad Haddad in the early 1980s. Later became the DFF (SLA)
CO	Commanding Officer
Col	Colonel
Comcen	Communications Centre
COMIRCON	Officer Commanding all Irish troops in UNIFIL (Irishbatt, FMR, and UNIFIL HQ)
Coy	Company (150 troops approx.)
CP	Check Point
Cpl	Corporal
CQMS	Company Quartermaster Sergeant
DCOS	Deputy Chief of Staff
DFC	Deputy Force Commander (UNIFIL)
DFF	De Facto Forces (also known as South Lebanon Army [SLA])
DFR	Defence Forces Regulations
Druze	Minority Religious Group in Lebanon
DSM	Distinguished Service Medal
Echo (Point)	Term used to identify IDF/DFF positions in the eastern sector of the Security Zone
Echo 219	IDF Artillery Position (formerly known as Gate 12)
EOD	Explosive Ordnance Disposal
Fatah	Core element of the PLO led by Yasser Arafat

FC	Force Commander (UNIFIL)
FCÁ	Forsa Cosanta Áitúil
FMR	Force Mobile Reserve (UNIFIL)
Gen	General
GOC	General Officer Commanding
GPMG	General Purpose Machine Gun
Half-track	Small armoured personnel carrier (wheels front – tracks back)
Hamas	Islamic Resistance Group based in Israel
Hizbullah	The Party of God. Political movement and main military resistance group in Lebanon
HMG	Heavy Machine Gun
HQ	Headquarters
IAF	Israeli Air Force
ICA	Israeli Controlled Area (also known as The Enclave or The Security Zone)
IDF	Israeli Defence Forces
IR	Islamic Resistance (umbrella term for Hizbullah, AMAL, Lebanese Squads, etc.)
Khakis	Cream coloured tropical uniform
LAW	Light Anti-tank Weapon
LT	Local Time
Lt Col	Lieutenant Colonel
M113	Tracked Armoured Personnel Carrier used by IDF and DFF
Maronite	Main Christian grouping in Lebanon
Maj	Major
MBT	Main Battle Tank
Mingy	Also Minghi – term used by Irish troops to describe items of inferior quality (mingy man is a seller of cheap goods)
MIO	Military Information Officer
MMG	Medium Machine Gun
MNF	Multi-National Force
Muktar	Village Leader
NBC	Nuclear Biological Chemical
NCO	Non Commissioned Officer
NVE	Night Vision Equipment
OC	Officer Commanding
OGL	Observer Group Lebanon
OIC	Officer in Charge
ONUC	Organisation Nations Unis Congo (United Nations Mission to the Congo)
OP	Observation Post
OPS	Operations (room or officer)
PFLP	Popular Front for the Liberation of Palestine.
Phalange	Military arm of Beirut-based Christian political party
Pl	Platoon (34 troops approx.)

Pol Log	Polish Logistics Unit
PLO	Palestine Liberation Organisation
PX	Welfare-shop or canteen
QMG	Quarter Master General
RAP	Regimental Aid Post
Recce	Reconnaissance
RPG	Rocket Propelled Grenade
RSB	Roadside Bomb
Shi'ite	Main Muslim grouping in Lebanon (the other being Sunni)
Shin Bet	Israeli Intelligence Agency
SISU	Finnish-made Armoured Personnel Carrier
SOPs	Standard Operating Procedures
SST	Special Search Team (also known as ESST – Engineer Special Search Team)
Sunnis	The second Muslim Grouping in Lebanon
TOW	US-made Wire Guided Anti-tank Missile
UN	United Nations
UNDOF	United Nations Disengagement Force (on the Golan Heights since 1974)
UNEF	United Nations Emergency Force (in Sinai)
UNFICYP	United Nations Force in Cyprus
UNIFIL	United Nations Interim Force in Lebanon
UNMO	United Nations Military Observer (unarmed)
UNOGIL	United Nations Observer Group in Lebanon
UNTSI	United Nations Training School Ireland (part of the Military College)
UNTSO	United Nations Truce Supervision Organisation
Wadi	A deep valley
Whiskey (Point)	Term used to identify IDF/DFF positions in the western sector of the Security Zone
Whiskey 134	DFF position overlooking Haddathah village
WO	Warrant Officer

ADDITIONAL TERMS

An Chéad Chath	1 Inf Bn, Irish-speaking, based in Galway
Firing close	Any firing impacting close to Irish or other UN positions
Letter of Assist	UN procedure for purchasing equipment
Shootrep	Report of any shooting, seen or heard
Riding Shotgun	Providing armed security

Editor's Note

For twenty-three years, Irish soldiers have worked in the cause of peace in South Lebanon. During that time, many commentators have seen fit to criticise UNIFIL for having taken so long to establish a durable peace, and some have continually disparaged the 'interim' concept contained in the name of the force itself. That it has taken twenty-three years to achieve stability in the region is not an issue – it is a fact. It is also a fact that a United Nations Peacekeeping Force operating under Chapter 6 of the United Nations Charter can only supervise a peace agreement if such an arrangement has actually been worked out between the parties to the conflict in the first place. In 1978, when the first Irish troops were deployed in Lebanon, no such agreement was in place.

In the 'interim', the conflict in south Lebanon continued despite the presence of UNIFIL with the warring factions on occasion inventing new rules by which to conduct their operations. The best (or worst) example of this was the so called 'April Understanding' of 1996 when the only constraints either Hizbullah or the IDF/DFF were actually prepared to accept involved not firing into Israel, not firing at one another from inside villages or from locations within 500m of UNIFIL positions, and not making civilians the object of attack. Everything else was fair game with the presence of UNIFIL apparently providing little deterrent!

That said Irish soldiers know that only for our commitment to hold our positions in the face of adversity the situation on the ground could, and would, have become far worse. In this collection of stories, drawn from the pages of *An Cosantóir* during that time, several authors make precisely this point. It would have been much worse had we not stayed, and the area we know as Irishbatt AO would almost certainly have been turned into a free-fire zone with the civilian population forced to pack some meagre belongings and face life elsewhere either as displaced persons or refugees.

We did not abandon those we came to help, and by staying, when at times the easier option was certainly to pack up and go, the people of south Lebanon today have an economic and social infrastructure upon which they can begin to build their future. That of itself makes twenty-three years of peacekeeping worthwhile; it makes our contribution a success story; and something of which every soldier who served there has a genuine right to be proud.

The collection of stories you are about to read reflects in a unique way what Irish soldiers, from all ranks and services, thought about the contribution both they and their colleagues were making. It is in fact the original 'inside story' and the ranks attributed to the authors are those they held at the time of original publication.

In the summer of 2000, the IDF finally withdrew all their troops from Lebanon and UNIFIL set about verifying their departure and confirming their compliance with UN Security Council Resolution 425 of 1978. It was fitting that an Irish Brigadier General should lead that international verification team and that three other Senior Irish Officers would play integral roles.

This October Irishbatt withdraws from UNIFIL – mission accomplished – and we leave behind a legacy that will live in the hearts of the Lebanese people for years and years to come. For thousands of Irish soldiers this will also be a sad occasion – saying goodbye to 'The Leb' will be hard for us too. And the memories contained in following pages explain why!

The production of this book was possible because down through the years successive editors of *An Cosantóir* saw some merit in publishing what might loosely be called 'stories from Lebanon'. Had a different editorial policy prevailed many of these articles would never have been published at all and as a consequence we would not now have the archive of material from which this collection is drawn. Not surprisingly then my first vote of thanks must go to the past editors of *An Cosantóir* for having had the wisdom to run these stories in the first instance.

Secondly, I am indebted to all those authors who submitted their work for publication over the years and who took the time and effort to write their stories and share their experience with the rest of us. I hope the inclusion of their work in this book will inspire them to keep writing as indeed I hope the inclusion of Sgt Michael Clarke's excellent prints will encourage others with that talent to keep painting.

I am also grateful to Capt Fred O'Donovan, the current manager of *An Cosantóir* for his support when the initial proposal for this work was made, and to Comdt Kieran McDaid, Defence Forces Press Officer, for giving the project an extra push when it was most needed.

Equally I have no illusions that but for the unconditional assistance I received from my team of 'volunteer typists' in Cork we would never had made the first deadline on 17 July. To Theresa Murphy, Charlotte O'Keeffe, Anne Foley, Sgt Richard O'Brien, Sgt Gerry O'Brien, Sgt Paddy Walshe, Sgt Mick Kelleher, Cpl Denis McGee, and Pte Michelle Bramley – I am very grateful to you all.

I am also mindful of the debt I owe to CQMS Gerry White for providing material from his own archives; to Armn John Daly for providing the cover photograph of Pte Christy Cashman on patrol; to the current staff of *An Cosantóir* – Cpl Dave Nagle, Cpl Paul Hevey, Cpl Willie Barr, Armn Wesley Bourke, Mr Gavin Corbett, and Sgt Terry McLaughlin in Lebanon; and to Comdt Joe Casey, Coy Sgt Willie Scott, and Sgt Pat McKee for permitting me to include their three marvellous personal recollections.

However, without any doubt whatsoever the good-natured, enthusiastic support of the current editor of *An Cosantóir* was a critical factor in bringing the project to fruition. Sgt Willie Braine left no stone unturned on the many occasions I asked for assistance, and the procurement and selection of the photographs was essentially his work.

I will be forever grateful to Mercier Press for running with the project almost from the moment it was first suggested. They felt that publishing this book was the right thing to do because twenty-three years in the service of peace in Lebanon should be recognised. All Irish soldiers who served with UNIFIL will thank them for that endorsement.

In conclusion, I wish to thank the Chief of Staff, Lt Gen Colm Mangan, for writing the Foreword. Having commanded Irishbatt himself, he has a personal understanding of the unique contribution Irish troops have made in South Lebanon over the years.

COMDT BRENDAN O'SHEA
September 2001

THIS BOOK IS DEDICATED TO THE MEMORY
OF THE
FORTY-FIVE IRISH PEACEKEEPERS
WHO GAVE THEIR LIVES IN THE SERVICE OF PEACE
IN LEBANON BETWEEN 1978 AND 2001

FOREWORD

LT GEN COLM MANGAN, CHIEF OF STAFF

As Chief of Staff at the time of an Irish Battalion's last involvement with UNIFIL, I am proud to write the Foreword for this compilation of *An Cosantóir* articles concerning the Irish Defence Forces' presence in Lebanon since 1978.

The pieces gathered here will hopefully provide an interesting, informative and varied picture of our involvement in that troubled land over the last twenty-three years, as well as bringing back some memories for personnel who served us so proudly out there.

Reading over these essays, my own mind was transported to the time I spent in Lebanon in the mid-1980s and early 1990s. I know that this book will reflect our men and women as I remember them, and the professionalism and camaraderie displayed as they carried out operations in the midst of one of the most savage and tragic conflicts in recent world history.

As we take this look back on an era, we also remember with great sadness our fallen comrades who gave their lives in the service of peace. They will never be forgotten by the Defence Forces. We think too of Pte Kevin Joyce who is still missing in action, and our thoughts go out to all of them and their families who have made such a sacrifice in the name of peace.

From the beginning of hostilities, *An Cosantóir* has tried to convey events in Lebanon as they were taking place and as told by those who were right there on the front line. I am sure that everyone who served with UNIFIL has a story to tell about their own time in the Middle East. Some of the seismic events that changed the course of the conflict were chronicled by Irish peacekeepers in the pages of *An Cosantóir* over the years. But many lighter moments – little anecdotes or small humanitarian projects that would otherwise have slipped through the grille of history had they not been committed to paper – were also recorded. These articles, reflecting many different points of view and individual experiences, are a distillation of that.

If you are looking for a comprehensive history of Lebanon over the last quarter of a century or so, then please refer to the history books. This, on the other hand, is a story about people, primarily the people representing our Defence Forces, who served with UNIFIL in the cause of peace. Read, enjoy, and treasure.

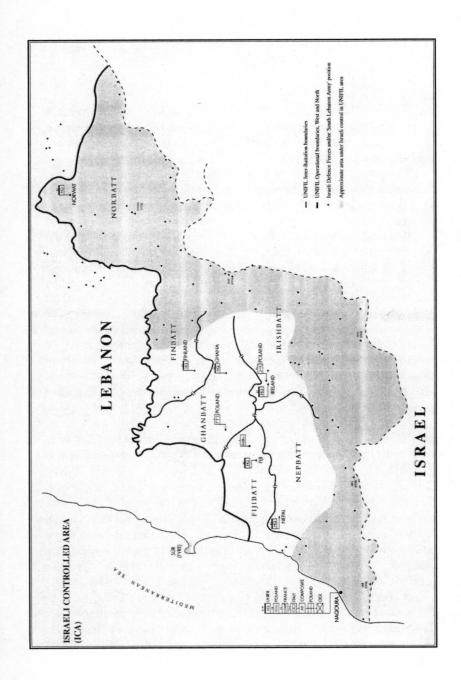

MELTING POT OF THE MIDDLE EAST – RELIGION IN LEBANON

SGT WILLIE BRAINE

Down through the centuries Lebanon has been a refuge for adherents of many different religions. The legacy of this is evident today in the unique – and sometimes volatile – mix of faiths that can be found in a country dominated by two main religions.

The majority of the population practise either the Muslim (54% approx) or Christian (39% approx) faiths. There are four Christian, two Islamic and one Druze group in Lebanon. The Druze are categorised by many westerners as Muslim, although neither they nor most Muslims accept this. They form 5-6% of the population.

Breaking down these religious groups further, we find that the Shi'ite sect of Muslims has about 992,000 (32%) followers in Lebanon; Sunni Muslims number 697,500 (22.5%); the Druze, 170,500 (5.5%); Christians, comprised of various sects, 1,209,000 (39%); and other religions make up 31,000 (1%) of the population.

THE MUSLIM FAITH

The Muslim faith has its origins in the teachings of the Prophet Mohammed, to whom God made his revelations (assembled later as the *Koran*) on the so-called 'Night of Power', or Ramadan, in the early seventh century AD. To this day, Ramadan is still the principal festival in the Muslim calendar, and the scene of those revelations to Mohammed, Mecca, is the sacred site of pilgrimage for all Muslims.

Mohammed's first converts were his wife and members of his household, followed some time later by various uncles and cousins. At the beginning, the majority of his converts were from the lower classes and from minor tribes affiliated with the Quraish tribe. When they first practised their new faith in public they were ridiculed for the most part by the wealthy classes. At this stage, they were tolerated, as they did not constitute a threat.

Gradually the new faith took root in the locality in spite of many difficulties. In 622 Mohammed and his followers journeyed to Medina which was a Jewish stronghold in northern Arabia. Over the following eight years, a series of battles took place which strengthened his following so that he returned to his stronghold of Mecca in 630 as a powerful leader. At this time, numerous smaller tribes were flocking to him to embrace the new faith and when he died in 632, Arabia was united under one leader for the first time.

Mohammed was succeeded by a Caliph ('Khalifa' = successor) Abu Bakr (632-634), followed by a second Caliph Umar (634-644). On his death, Umar appointed a committee of six to choose his successor. The choice lay between Uthman of the Umayyad tribe, who was married to two of the prophet's daughters, and Ali the prophet's first cousin, who was also married to his daughter Fatima. Uthman won the vote for the third Caliphate but his position was immediately contested by Ali and his followers. It was here that the seeds were sown for the sectarian divisions, which persist to this day.

The religion of Islam (meaning 'submission to the will of God') as laid out in the *Koran*, consists of five 'pillars' of faith all of which must be obeyed. The first of these is the 'Shahda', or profession of faith, which dictates that there is no God but Allah and Mohammed is the messenger of Allah. The *Koran* clearly identifies Allah as the same God worshipped by Jews and Christians alike, although the Christian concept of 'the Son of God as one with God' is specifically and repeatedly repudiated in the *Koran* which describes Jesus as a prophet and no more. The *Koran* says in Sura 112, 'He begot none nor was he begotten. None is equal to him.' Throughout history, God revealed his power, his oneness and his commands to men through various prophets and books. Muslims believe that the last of these prophets was Mohammed of Mecca, and the last revelation, the *Koran*, is the written record of the words spoken by God to Mohammed, through the Angel Gabriel. The succession of prophesies ends with Mohammed, because the *Koran* reveals all that need be known and synthesises all that went before.

The second pillar, prayer, is a duty incumbent on the faithful. The timings are not specified in the *Koran*, but in practice they are recognised as occurring five times daily: at dawn, midday, afternoon, evening and night. The exact times vary from country to country and even in large countries from town to town, according to the time of sunrise and sunset. The believer may say his prayers wherever he is, alone or in a group, as long as he faces Mecca. The call to prayer in Arabic is sounded from the minaret or tower of every mosque. Each prayer ritual is marked by a change of position: standing, bending to put hands on knees, kneeling with palms on thighs, and kneeling with forehead on the floor. At the mosque, worshippers align themselves in rows, spaced so that they may kneel and bow without touching those in front of them.

All Muslims have an equal relationship with God. In large mosques, the leader of the prayers may be an 'Imam' (an individual with religious training who is learned in the *Koran*) who gives a sermon on Fridays. A mosque is not a church. God is no more present there than he is anywhere else. There is no altar, no tabernacle, no baptismal font, no statues and no choir loft. Because all men are equal before Allah, mosques have no reserved places or pews for dignitaries. It is customary to take off footwear upon entering and the function of the mosque as a social and economic leveller can be seen in the racks of varying qualities of footwear outside any mosque.

The third pillar of the faith is the Zakat, or 'Alms Tax', a mandatory donation to charity. The obligation to share what one has with those less fortunate is stressed throughout the holy book. The *Koran* does not specify how much should be given or how the requirement to pay the tax should be enforced. In practice, the most common measure is 2.5% of the amount of cash an individual holds in savings or investments for a year. In addition, a tax of one day's food for one person per day is to be paid on 'Eid-Al-Fitr', end of Ramadan.

The fourth pillar of the faith is the fast of the month of Ramadan. Ramadan is one of the twelve months of the lunar calendar, used by the Muslims since the seventh century of the Islamic era. Because it is set according to the lunar calendar, Ramadan occurs on different dates in each year of the Gregorian calendar. It is the month in which the first Koranic verses were revealed to Mohammed and in which Mohammed's small band of followers achieved their first important military success at the 'Battle of Badr' in 624 AD.

During Ramadan, Muslims are obliged to refrain from eating, smoking, drinking and pleasures of the flesh from first light to last light, unless they are ill, travelling or pregnant. The time of fasting begins, according to the *Koran*, when it becomes possible to tell a white thread from a black one in the first light of dawn. At the end of the month, Muslims celebrate 'Eid-Al-Fitr', after which life returns to normal.

The fifth pillar, the pilgrimage, which all Muslims are obliged to make once in their lives, is the unifying force of Islam. It brings together in the experience of faith, people of different race, colour and origin. All sects within Islam participate side by side in the event. The spiritual objective of the pilgrimage is to put off worldly concerns and things of the self, to commune with God and contemplate his oneness. The central place of devotion is the 'Ka'aba', the chief shrine of Islam, which stands in the courtyard of the great mosque at Mecca. 'Ka'aba' is a stone structure 40 feet wide, 30 feet long and 50 feet high, which is usually covered by a cloth. Nothing in its appearance is inspirational. Its religious significance lies in its history. A door leads to the interior of the Ka'aba, where the pilgrim will find a black stone about eight inches in diameter. This stone is believed by Muslims to be a fragment of the original temple of Abraham.

SUNNI MUSLIMS

In addition to revealing God's will through the *Koran*, Mohammed laid down laws and principles, which serve as a model of behaviour. These are contained in a body of traditional sayings ascribed to Mohammed, known as the 'Hadith'. The 'Hadith' and other Islamic traditions together provide the basis for the 'Sunnah'. The largest of the main Muslim groups adhere to the traditions of the Sunnah and are called 'Sunnites'. Estimates indicate that Sunni Muslims comprise more than 20% of Lebanon's population. Clustered in the coastal cities, especially Beirut and Tripoli, they are found in all professions and trades.

Leadership of the Sunni Muslim community in Lebanon is based on principles and institutions deriving partly from traditional Islam and partly from French influence. Under the French mandate, a Supreme Islamic council was established at national level, headed by a Grand Mufti and a national Directorate of Awqaf (religious endowments). The French also established local departments of Awqaf, which staffed and maintained hospitals, schools, cemeteries, and mosques. In addition, they managed the funds which supported these operations. The funds were obtained partly from direct donations and partly from the income derived from real property given to the community as an endowment.

Traditional types of Islamic leaders include, 'Imams', 'Muftis' and 'Qadis'. Muftis are Muslim scholars who are the final arbiters in matters of religious law. Qadis are the judges of the Sharia courts in which personal matters of the Sunni community are adjudicated. Sheikh is an honorary title given to a doctor of theology.

SHIA MUSLIMS

The split between the two main branches of Islam first appeared soon after the death of Mohammed in 632 AD, when Umar and Ali contested the appointment of third Caliph. The term *Shi'ite* is derived from 'Shiat Ali', or the party of Ali. The Shi'ites, unlike the Sunnites, believe that Mohammed's real successors were not only temporal rulers, but also spiritually guided Imams, mediating between God and man. These Imams are considered to be the source of hidden truth. There are twelve Imams, of whom Ali was the first, although some Shia groups outside Lebanon recognise only seven Imams. Shia Muslims impose the same basic requirements on believers as do the Sunnites, but have their own set of traditions.

THE DRUZE

A close-knit, well-organised community, the Druze are mainly farming people, and share the rugged slopes of Mount Lebanon with the Maronites. Independent to the point of fierceness when outsiders threaten them, hard-working and hospitable when left alone, they occupy an important place in the country's pattern of religious coexistence.

Their religion is, in part, a historical derivative of Shia Islam, but they do not regard themselves, nor do others regard them, as Muslims. They reject part of the most important article of the Islamic faith – the supreme prophet-hood of Mohammed. The Druze believe not only in the divine character of the prophets and Imams but also that God became incarnate in man in a series of ten successive divine manifestations. The most perfect of these was the ninth-century Fatimid Caliph Al-Hakim. In addition, they believe that God's revelations have both open and hidden meanings, and that only a handful of select men may know all of God's will. The remainder of the faithful live in relative ignorance of doctrine and conform to their commands. The Druze also believe in the transmigration of souls.

The moral system of the Druze religion differs completely from that of the Muslims. The Druze took from the Shi'ites, however, the practice of 'taqiya', which not only permits but also even encourages an individual, for his own protection, to adhere to the religion of the ruling group under which he lives. For example, under the Ottomans, Druze often claimed to be Muslims, giving their sons the name of Mohammed, but secretly remained Druze. The spiritual leader of the Druze in Lebanon bears the title Sheik Al-Aql.

CHRISTIANITY

The Christian community of Lebanon includes a small number of Roman Catholics; a majority of Roman Catholic Uniates whose Churches are in full communion with Rome but are organised separately; a substantial number of adherents of various Churches of the east, orthodox or schismatic; and a few thousand Protestants. However Roman Catholics and Protestants have no formal organisation in Lebanon.

When doctrinal controversies split Christianity between east and west, most Arab Christians allied themselves with Orthodox Churches. After the Crusades (1096–1291), however, some returned to full communion with Rome. The so-called Uniate Churches, which then came into being fully, accepted the Catholic faith and, in matters of doctrine, fully agreed with the Holy See. Rather than adopt the Latin rite, however, they retained their own ancient rites in various languages. Uniate groups in Lebanon today represent the largest number of Christians in the country, about 39% of the population.

The Maronites are by far the largest of the Uniate groups, estimated at 24.5% of the population. The Maronite Church is indigenous to the country, tracing its beginnings to St Maron, a fifth-century hermit, and to the later teaching activities of monks who built retreats in the valleys and along the coast. In the seventh century, its leaders accepted a doctrine relating to the nature of Christ, which was regarded as heretical by the main body of Christendom. Thereafter, other Christians persecuted the Maronites and, as a result, they retreated far into Mount Lebanon to worship as they pleased. Union with the Roman Catholic Church came in the twelfth century, but the bond was broken some time afterwards and not formally re-established until the sixteenth century.

Under Ottoman rule (1515–1914) and the 'millet' system, which permitted non-Muslim groups to administer their affairs under their own religious laws, the Maronites were able to maintain extensive control over their own community. The principal event in modern Maronite history was the conflict with the Druzes in 1860, which prompted France to send a military expedition to Lebanon and which culminated, after the First World War, in the French Mandate over Lebanon and Syria. Since 1860, the Maronites have had a strong affiliation with France.

The greatest concentration of Maronites continues to be in the valleys and on the slopes of Mount Lebanon, the same region that provided sanctuary many centuries ago. Most of them are farmers, but they also make up a significant proportion of the professional, middle and upper-class segments of Beirut society. The Church has rich land possessions and numerous schools. Its monasteries and convents are among the largest landholders in the country. Many Maronites have also emigrated, especially to the United States.

The Maronites principally follow the Syriac liturgy of St James, but the lessons and some prayers are in Arabic, the use of which is increasing. The highest official of the Church is the Patriarch of Antioch and All the East who, traditionally, is elected by the bishops and confirmed by the pope. He resides at Bkirki, near Beirut, in the winter and at the Deman Palace at Al Qannabah, in the mountains about twenty miles south-east of Sidon, in the summer. Among his rights and responsibilities are the appointment and consecration of bishops, the convening of synods, receiving appeals from lower confessional (religious) courts of the Maronite community, and the review of religious publications.

In 1968, the patriarch of the Maronite Church was Cardinal Paul Peter Meouch. He was the first Maronite patriarch to attend the

Ecumenical Council at the Vatican and the first Maronite to be appointed a cardinal. The Church has divided the country ecclesiastically into the archdioceses of Beirut, Tripoli, Tyre and Sidon with the subordinate dioceses of Sarba, about fifteen miles south-east of Sidon, and of Baalbeck and Jubayl, which reaches from the Bekaa valley to the Mediterranean coast north of Beirut.

Greek Catholics are the second-largest Uniate community, estimated to include about 4% of the population. They emerged as a distinct group in the early eighteenth century when, at the height of the Uniate movement, they split from the Greek Orthodox Church and gave their allegiance to Rome. Although fully accepting Catholic dogma as asserted by Rome, they have generally remained close to the Greek Orthodox Church, retaining more of its ancient rituals and customs than have the Maronites. They use Arabic and follow the Byzantine rite. Sometimes they are called Melkites (a historical term meaning 'king's men') to distinguish them from European Catholics of the Byzantine rite, whose traditions are quite different. In Lebanon, when someone speaks of Catholics, he is referring to this group, not to the Roman Catholics or the Maronites.

The highest official of the Church is the patriarch of Antioch, who resides at Ain Traz, about fifteen miles south-east of Beirut. Archdioceses have been established at Tyre, Marjayoun, Tripoli, Sidon, Baaleck, Zahlah, and Al Furzul. The patriarch is elected by the bishops in synod and confirmed by the pope in Rome, who sends him the 'pallium' (a circular band of white wool worn by archbishops) in recognition of their communion. The patriarch and the bishops live simply, as do the clergy and most of their parishioners. Greek Catholic churches, like those of the Greek Orthodox, contain paintings of sacred subjects (icons) but no statutes. Religious leaders are highly respected and the faithful have a reputation for piety and devotion to their rites.

Greek Catholics live primarily in the southern and eastern parts of the country, dispersed in many villages. Less western-oriented than the Maronites, the Greek Catholics are proud of their Arab cultural heritage. However, the intellectuals and businessmen among them prefer association with the west, especially the United States.

Besides the Maronites and the Greek Catholics, three smaller Uniate groups are also represented, the Syrian Catholics, the Armenian Catholics, and the Chaldeans, although none of these groups is believed to have more than 25,000 adherents.

The Eastern Churches not in communion with Rome include the various Orthodox Churches and several small schismatic Churches that broke away in the fifth century in controversy over the nature of Christ. The largest Orthodox Church found in Lebanon is the Greek

Orthodox Church, whose adherents form the fourth largest of the country's groups, an estimated 6.5% of the population. They are found mainly in Beirut and the nearby Al Matn area, as well as in Tripoli and the nearby Al Kurah area. The community includes persons of varying social origins, ranging from urban upper-class families, who have been prominent for generations, to village peasants. Between these two groups are middle-class persons whose immediate forbearers were villagers but who have themselves achieved prominence in the urban professions.

The Greek Orthodox of Lebanon belong to one of the four original Byzantine patriarchies, that of Antioch. Their patriarch resides in Damascus, Syria. He is equal in rank to the other three Middle Eastern patriarchs, who reside, respectively, in Istanbul, Jerusalem, and Alexandria. Below the patriarch in rank are a number of archbishops, bishops and priests, among whom Arabs, not Greek nationals, predominate. Arabic is the liturgical language, and there are about a dozen monasteries and several convents.

Members of the Armenian Church, a schismatic Orthodox Church, make up an estimated 4%. Most are refugees, or descendants of refugees, who fled actual or feared persecution in Turkey after the First World War. The supreme ecclesiastical figure in the Church lives in Russia.

The Nestorians, whose Church is variously known as the Eastern or Assyrian Church, were once a large group, but centuries of persecution have diminished their number to tiny communities scattered throughout various Middle Eastern countries. A few adherents of this faith are found in Lebanon. Another small religious group, numbering no more than a few thousand members, is the Syrian Jacobite community, mostly found in Beirut.

A Short History of Lebanon

Armn Wesley Bourke

To us Lebanon is a troubled land, always in the news after a bomb attack or an artillery strike along its borders. To a foreigner it would seem that the country has never known peace since it gained its independence 80 years ago. But Lebanon's history, like our own, is long and complex. At one stage, it was the cultural centre of the known world, but over the centuries was subjected to invading armies, foreign rule, and suffered at the hands of so-called liberators. All of this has left the country with vast religious and cultural differences, which have led to some of the problems its people are dealing with today.

The first recorded history of Lebanon is 3000 BC. At that time, it was no more than a string of fortified coastal cities, all independent of each other. The majority of the population lived along the coast as most of the hinterland was heavily forested and the mountains in the east prevented expansion in that direction. They were a Semitic people, the Canaanites, known to the Greeks as the Phoenicians. They were sea-going and engaged in trading with other Mediterranean tribes. Cities like Tyre and Gubla became important cultural and trading centres. Their development of the art of navigation allowed them to set up colonies in Crete and Carthage, to circumnavigate Africa, and spread their culture and riches wherever they went.

However, their prosperity was checked as a series of invasions brought the cities under foreign control. The Assyrians, Babylonians, Persians and Alexander the Great, at one time or another besieged all or parts of the country. In 64 BC, Syria and Lebanon became part of the Roman Empire. Under Roman rule economic and intellectual activities flourished. Berytus (Beirut) became famous for its law school and university. It was known as the intellectual centre of the Roman Empire. In the sixth century AD, a great earthquake levelled Berytus, destroying its temples and schools killing 30,000 people.

The Arab conquests of the mid-seventh century, brought the Muslim religion to Lebanon and under the rule of the Umayyads and the Abbasids, Lebanon became a place of refuge for different religions and ethnic groups, thus setting a pattern for the eventual emergence of a modern Lebanese state.

The Arabs were tolerant to both Christians and Jews, who were assessed by religion for special taxes. They also developed the system of administrating non-Muslim groups separately called 'millets'. Some of the first Christians to come to Lebanon were the ancestors of the modern day Maronites and the Melkites.

Another religion also found its way into Lebanon. It was founded by the Fatimid Caliph of Egypt, Al Hakim (985–1021) and he proclaimed himself an incarnation of God. One of his followers, Darazi, came to south Lebanon to preach and his followers became known as the Druze.

From 1096–1291, the Middle East endured the bloody battles and sieges of the Crusades, which were launched to take back the Holy Land from the Muslims. Even though the Crusades failed, western civilisation left its mark on Lebanon. The Maronites formed links with religious orders in the west and the French, who had played such a major role in the Crusades, would now influence the course of Lebanese history from this period onwards.

But Lebanon was never given a breathing space. Mongols from the Steppes and the Mamlukes from Egypt all sought to rule the region. The Mamluke rule lasted until the early sixteenth century. It was during this period that the Shi'ites, a branch of the Islam faith, settled in the Bekaa valley north of Beirut.

After the Mamlukes came a long period of Ottoman rule which lasted until 1914. During this period, Lebanon was given semi-autonomous status. The Ottomans brought stability to the country, links were formed with the Dukes of Tuscany and Florence, and life improved for the people as advances were made in agriculture, architecture, engineering and irrigation.

However, during the nineteenth century some of the seeds of today's troubles were sown. In 1840, the Ottoman Sultan proclaimed Bashir III as prince of Mount Lebanon (as Syria and Lebanon were known at the time). Bitter conflicts broke out between the Christians and the Druze. The Sultan replaced the prince in 1842 with governor Omar Pasha but this only flared up into more violence. The European powers then decided to step in and partition the country with Christians to the north and Druze to the south. The Beirut–Damascus road became the partition line but animosities and foreign interests only served to transform political and social tension into bitter conflict, all of which led to a massacre of the Maronites by the Druze in 1860.

The First World War saw the collapse of the Ottoman Empire and in 1920 Syria and Lebanon were placed under French control. The Lebanese were allowed to establish their own government and to write a constitution, but the scars from the First World War continued to show in the politics of the region as religious groups who had allied themselves with the opposing sides during the war now sought to assert themselves politically.

On 1 September 1920, Greater Lebanon was established within its present-day borders and with Beirut as its capital. In 1926, the first constitution was adopted and Charles Debbas was elected the country's first president. The constitution still placed the French governor as head of state and this did not go down well with nationalist groups.

By the time the Second World War broke out Emile Edde was president but was forced to resign when Vichy French control was established. This did not last long however as Vichy forces were unable to repel Allied armies moving into Syria and Lebanon.

On 26 November 1941, Lebanon was granted independence and in 1943 a new government was set up with Bishara El-Khoury as its president. The constitution was amended removing all reference to their former governors. The French authorities still operating in the region had the senior members of the government arrested and exiled, but international pressure mounted for their reinstatement and the full withdrawal of French from the area. By the end of 1946, all French troops had pulled out.

Lebanon didn't waste any time obtaining international recognition. In 1945, it joined the Arab League and later the United Nations, but the new state still had hidden problems. In 1952, the Nationalist and Socialist Front emerged demanding the eradication of sectarianism and corruption in the government. The front was headed by some of Lebanon's most prestigious figures such as Camille Chamoun, a former ambassador to Great Britain, Emille Bustani, a self-made millionaire, and several other influential figures.

In May 1952, the front held a rally at Deir El-Khamar. Fifty thousand people attended. They threatened rebellion if the president didn't resign, and called for a general strike. This was met with popular support and most of the major cities were brought to a standstill. Tensions mounted and President El-Khoury called on General Feud Shihab, the army Chief of Staff, to intervene. When the general refused, the president had no choice but to resign. The Chamber of Deputies elected Camille Chamoun as president.

Soon discontentment grew within the government at the performance of the new president in that it was felt he was reverting to traditional politics and overlooking the disproportionate representation of religions in the parliament. Then the late 1950s brought pressure on Lebanon as a general state of unrest developed in the Arab world, with the evolution of Pan-Arabism, symbolised by Gamal Abdel Nasser of Egypt, who had become a leading figure in the Arab world since the Suez crises and the forging of an alliance between Egypt and Syria.

Lebanese Muslims looked to Nasser for inspiration as rivalry among clans and religious groups mounted in the ideological struggle between nationalism and Pan-Arabism. President Chamoun would not bow to Pan-Arab pressures, believing that Lebanon's Christian links to the west guaranteed its independence, but tension continued to grow when Chamoun changed the constitution so he could run for a second term of office.

In the elections of May–June 1957 Chamoun secured his second term but pro-Nasser support grew in numbers and in violence. The crises became worse when on 14 July a revolution in Iraq overthrew the monarchy. There was jubilation in the streets of Lebanon with the people chanting that Chamoun and his government were next. The president realised his position was in danger and he called upon France, Great Britain and the United States for immediate assistance. American troops were deployed to contain the situation.

As part of the response, the UN also established UNOGIL (United Nations Observer Group in Lebanon). The group consisted of 600 unarmed officers from twenty-one countries, and Ireland committed 50 personnel. Their main task was to prevent arms being smuggled across the Syrian border. As hostilities ceased, the government knew it could not let one religion dominate the other and it also realised that they could not isolate themselves from either the Arab or western worlds. Nevertheless, these problems would constantly recur in Lebanese politics. That said the 1960s were a prosperous time for Lebanon. Beirut was hailed as the 'Monte Carlo of the Middle East'. The chamber of deputies elected Charles Hilu as president in August 1964, a journalist, jurist, and diplomat well-known for his moral and intellectual qualities. But the economic boom only hid the social, religious and ethnic problems.

Critical here was the case of the Palestinians, 114,000 of whom had fled to Lebanon after the declaration of the state of Israel. Now the PLO was becoming organised and a force to be reckoned with, especially since the Cairo Accord had effectively given the Palestinians in Lebanon a number of quasi-legal rights and when a further group arrived following expulsion from Jordan during 'Black September', they turned out to be battle-hardened fighters.

Then during the early 1970s, the PLO began launching raids into Israel and attempts were made by the Lebanese to control this, but they failed. In 1975, a Maronite Militia group called the Phalange engaged in a number of fire-fights with the Palestinians. Soon the whole country erupted into civil war, with the Muslim groupings in the government supporting the Palestinians and the right wing parties backing the Christians. To prevent a Palestinian victory, Syria deployed troops in Lebanon and later the Arab League set up a multinational deterrent force.

The civil war officially ended after the election of President Elias Sarkis and changes were made to the Constitution, but negotiations between opposing parties were difficult because the Shi'ite Muslims were now the dominant force in Lebanon. Fighting continued in the south and when Syrian forces started to deploy into the area, the Israelis threatened stern action if they advanced any further. The Lebanese government tried desperately to get the situation under control but the army had become ineffective and local clans and villages had set up their own militia units for protection.

By 1978, the PLO had commenced launching commando raids into Israel and pressure mounted on the Israeli government to do something about it. On 11 March, the PLO claimed responsibility for an indiscriminate commando raid near Haifa that left 37 dead and 76 wounded. Israel had had enough and, on the night 14/15 March 1978, its armed forces invaded south Lebanon.

Within a short time, the IDF had occupied most of the area south of the Litani river, and the Lebanese government, under President Elias Sarkis, worked frantically to conjure up international support to put pressure on the Israelis to withdraw.

In March, they submitted a strong protest to the UN Security Council stating that Lebanon was not responsible for Palestinian activities along its borders. Having considered the situation, the Council passed Resolution 425, calling for an immediate withdrawal of Israeli forces and the establishment of a UN interim force in south Lebanon.

The situation remained tense and volatile as the PLO withdrew into the Tyre pocket and north of the Litani river. There they were able to regroup and with their heavy equipment intact established strongholds in Nabatiyah and at Chateau Beaufort.

Lt Gen Erskine was appointed commander of UNIFIL and a headquarters was temporarily set up in Naquora. Observers were detached from UNTSO and to make the force operational troops were deployed from the two existing UN missions in the Middle East – a company came from the Iranian contingent in UNDOF, a Canadian logistics unit from UNDOF, and a Swedish company was relocated from UNEF 2 in Sinai.

Initially the force was to be 4,000 strong, but later it was decided to increase this to 6,000. By mid-June 1978 the force consisted of infantry battalions from France, Fiji, Nepal, Iran, Ireland, Nigeria, Norway, Senegal and three logistic support units from Canada, France and Norway. In addition, 42 observers from UNTSO were permanently assigned to UNIFIL and became Observer Group Lebanon.

In April and June of the same year, Israeli forces conducted a phased withdrawal from south Lebanon. There were several exchanges of fire between UNIFIL and units of the PLO, and also between UNIFIL and the new players on the scene – the De Facto Forces of Major Saad Haddad. In the final phase of their withdrawal, the Israeli forces turned over control of the border area to the DFF thus forming a 'security zone', which in time became known as 'The Enclave', and later simply the Israeli Controlled Area, the ICA. Ironically, enough Haddad and his cronies proclaimed the area to be 'Free Lebanon' but it was nothing of the kind.

Meanwhile clashes had also been occurring between the Arab Deterrent Force and Christian militias further north. To help stop the fighting an Arab Follow-Up Committee was set up by Lebanon, Saudi Arabia, Syria and Kuwait. However, when the Saudi Arabian ambassador was wounded in December 1978 that put paid to the committee, which did not meet again until 1981.

At this point, the Lebanese government did try to establish control over the south and with UNIFIL's assistance several attempts were made to deploy a Lebanese army battalion in the area. After some initial success, the plan failed when fighting between Israel and the PLO intensified.

Sporadic fighting between IDF/DFF, the PLO, and other militia units continued until July 1981 when Philip Habib, the special envoy for US President Ronald Reagan, orchestrated a cease-fire, between Israel and the PLO, to take effect on 24 July 1981. Over the next ten months, the situation generally remained calm, but PLO cross-border attacks continued and in 1982 Israel returned to Lebanon in an operation known as 'Peace for Galilee'. Their objective this time was to destroy all terrorist bases in south Lebanon but by mid-June, the IDF had linked up with Phalangist Militia and thereby cut off West Beirut laying siege to the Palestinian and Syrian forces within the city.

Over the next three months, there was intense air, naval and artillery bombardments of Beirut and Philip Habib worked tirelessly to come up with a settlement. In August, he was successful in bringing about an agreement in which Syrian and PLO troops were able to withdraw from the city. The agreement also provided for a Multi-National Force to be sent to Beirut to oversee the withdrawal and by late August US marines, and French and Italian troops had deployed in the city.

Throughout the Israeli invasion, the Lebanese government continued to function, even though it had lost control over the majority of the country. In August, elections were held and Bashir Gemayel, son of the founder of the Phalangist party, was elected president. However, on 14 September Bashir was assassinated along with several members of his new cabinet and the next day IDF troops occupied the rest of Beirut. Over the following days Phalangist Militias carried out revenge attacks on Palestinian refugees in the Sabra and Shatilla camps in West Beirut with the death toll eventually estimated at 1,400.

This massacre was a major embarrassment for Israel and after Bashir's brother, Amine, was elected president MNF troops were deployed in Beirut and the force was later augmented by a British contingent. The new government immediately put a major emphasis on the withdrawal of Israeli, Palestinian and Syrian forces from Lebanon and by the end of 1982 negotiations had begun with Israel.

On 17 May 1983, an agreement was signed between Lebanon, Israel and the US, on the withdrawal of Israeli troops from Lebanon, and although Syria boycotted the negotiations and refused to withdraw its troops the Israelis went ahead anyway and began a phased withdrawal shortly afterwards – but more problems ensued.

As the IDF started to withdraw from the Shuf Mountains overlooking Beirut a power struggle erupted between Lebanese Christians, the Lebanese army and Syrian-backed Druze. Throughout the reminder of the country the situation was little different and as the IDF and DFF forces moved southwards both Amal and Hizbullah militia harassed them continually.

In October 1983, sixty-two Lebanese government officials were brought to the Saudi Arabian resort of Taif where in conjunction with the Arab League and the US they struck an accord to end the civil war. However opposition to the negotiations, and to continued US support for Amine Gemayel's government, had led in April to the bombing of the US embassy killing sixty-three people. Now in October it resulted in a suicide car bombing of the US marine headquarters near the airport and killed a further 298. Not surprisingly, the MNF pulled of Beirut in March 1984.

This latest Israeli invasion, and the intermittent civil war, had left the country in ruins. There were thousands of casualties; the government was practically ineffective; the Taif Accord had left the Shuf in Druze control; and many Druze and Muslim units of the Lebanese army had defected in February 1984 to form their own militias. The government then came under pressure from Syria to cancel the 17 May 1983 agreement with Israel, thus straining political ties even further. However by June 1985 most IDF and DFF troops had withdrawn from Lebanon, except for an area known again as the 'security zone' in the south. They believed this was necessary as a buffer against further attacks and up to a point they were right. The problem was that none of the parties operating in the area had much respect for the only armed troops actually authorised to work there – UNIFIL.

When the IDF rolled into south Lebanon in 1982 the UNIFIL AO was quickly over-run as its troops were in no position to prevent the invasion being armed only with light defensive weapons. UNIFIL could only offer humanitarian assistance within its own limits and although the Secretary General had recommended in February 1982 that the force strength be increased, by June 1982, when the invasion took place, the strength of UNIFIL had risen to just under 7,000.

The composition of the force at that time was infantry battalions from Fiji, France, Ghana, Ireland, Nepal, Netherlands, Nigeria, Norway and Senegal, supported by logistic units from France, Italy, Norway, and Sweden.

Between mid-1982 and 1985, the force had undergone several changes. The French government requested that 482 personnel from their contingent be withdrawn and redeployed as part of the MNF in Beirut while at the end of 1982 the Nepalese were also withdrawn and replaced by a Finnish battalion. Over the next two years the Nigerian, Dutch and Senegalese battalions all pulled out but were replaced by the returning French and Nepalese. After that, UNIFIL set about trying to keep what in reality was never more than a very uneasy peace!

Statue of Major Haddad

RESOLUTION 425 (1978)
Adopted by the Security Council at its 2,074th Meeting, 19/3/78

The Security Council

Taking note of the letters of the Permanent Representative of Lebanon (S/12605 and S/12606) and the Permanent Representative of Israel (S/12607).

Having heard the statements of the Permanent Representatives of Lebanon and Israel.

Gravely concerned at the deterioration of the situation in the Middle East, and its consequences to the maintenance of international peace.

Convinced that the present situation impedes the achievement of a just peace in the Middle East.

1. **Calls for** strict respect for the territorial integrity, sovereignty and political independence of Lebanon within its internationally recognised boundaries;

2. **Calls upon** Israel to cease immediately its military action against Lebanese territorial integrity and withdraw forthwith its forces from all Lebanese territory;

3. **Decides**, in the light of the request of the Government of Lebanon, to establish immediately under its authority a United Nations Interim Force for South Lebanon for the purpose of confirming the withdrawal of Israeli forces, restoring international peace and security and assisting the Government of Lebanon in ensuring the return of its effective authority in the area, the force to be composed of personnel drawn from State Members of the United Nations;

4. **Requests** the Secretary General to report to the Council within twenty-four hours on the implementation of this resolution.

RESOLUTION 426 (1978)
Adopted by the Security Council at its 2,075th Meeting, 20/3/78

The Security Council

1. **Approves** the report of the Secretary General on the implementation of Security Council resolution 425 (1978) contained in document S/312611 dated 19 March 1978.

2. **Decides** that the Force shall be established in accordance with the above-mentioned report for an initial period of six months and that it shall continue in operation thereafter, if required, provided the Security Council so decides.

MEETING CAPTAIN DOYLE

COMDT JOE CASEY

We touched down at Ben Gurion Airport near Tel Aviv early on the morning of 7 June 1978 and the usual chaos attached to the organisation of any new mission prevailed. As the sun scorched down we were loaded onto French trucks and headed north for Lebanon. Crossing the border presented lots of difficulties but we eventually arrived in the small village of Haris towards late evening with the light fading.

Both A and HQ Companies had their designated areas but B Company was to be held in reserve and nobody knew exactly where. Somebody said it was over the hill in the Tibnin area but the French transport people refused to bring us any further. There was nothing to do but walk, in the old soldier fashion, so I fell in the company on the roadside and with myself at the head, our packs on our backs, and my blackthorn stick in hand, we headed off into the fading light across the hill. After a while we met Capt Colm Doyle, the company second-in-command who had been sent out before us, and he directed us into a bombed-out house at the entrance to the Norwegian Maintenance Company's Camp. Somehow all one hundred and eighteen of us found a spot on the floor.

We remained at this location for a number of days but soon the overcrowding became a real problem. Battalion headquarters was experiencing similar problems in the village of Haris so I had to find an alternative location for my company. I saw this village called Bra'shit south of us near the Israeli lines and I told the battalion commander that I intended to occupy it. He agreed and told me to make all the necessary arrangements myself. Capt Doyle and Company Quartermaster-Sergeant Seán Foley undertook a reconnaissance of the area and having found a suitable location we began to build Bra'shit Camp.

We had exciting times after the Israeli withdrawal from the so-called 'Charlie Line' on 13 June. Christian militia forces now occupied the zone previously occupied by Israel and contrary to what we were led to believe on arrival, our efforts were concentrated not on reporting or preventing PLO infiltration from the north but on countering harassment from the Christian militia to the south. Close firing became almost a nightly occurrence and we had some narrow escapes but no casualties. Despite ongoing harassment, we held our line.

On the Ground with the 43rd

Comdt George Kerwin

43 Irishbatt is deployed about one hour's drive from UNIFIL head-quarters based in Naquora which is on the coast and very beautiful. In this area, UNIFIL plans to open a rest camp for its troops. A fertile strip of land hugs the coastline where the tomato crop is being harvested and the long green hanks of bananas are gradually changing colour.

This rich agricultural belt, however, quickly gives way to the starkly contrasting parched hilltops and winding valleys that disappear eastwards as far as the eye can see. Children gave flowers and sweets through the widows of our jeeps, and local people emphasised to me repeatedly that the Irish were especially welcome in their area. One man suggested that because of the troubles in Ireland, Irish troops knew and appreciated the importance of peace and were therefore most welcome in his country.

While it is early days yet for UNIFIL operations on the ground there are very definite indications that it is succeeding in stabilising the situation in south Lebanon and allowing the people there to return to a normal way of life. In the areas most affected by the recent conflict, neglected crops are once again being tended to in the fields and goat herds and their shepherds are reappearing in the valleys.

In Tibnin, a town sprawled across the top of a hill and dominated by the crumbling walls of an old Crusader castle, the population has risen from five to ten thousand since the arrival of UNIFIL. The hospital has reopened and children have returned to school. The headquarters of the Irish Battalion is now located in its own tented village on the outskirts of this town which is in fact one of the bigger and more important towns in south Lebanon.

The full deployment of the 43 Irishbatt had not taken place before I left on 16 June but should by now be well under way. With the possible exception of A Company, each of the other companies knew their present locations were only temporary. While men spoke with misgivings at leaving locations where they were already settling in very well they were at the same time anxious to get properly deployed in their own areas of responsibility and to get on with the job of peacekeeping.

No doubt, when the men from Donegal, under Lt Colm Cox, move from their present location they will take with them the sign they have suspended between two palm trees and which reads 'Barnsmore Gap'.

The men of A Company, mostly 'Dubs', are all under canvas perched on a hill about a mile from the town of Shaqra. Here women in their brightly coloured costumes can be seen making their way to and from the watering hole with their shining utensils on their heads. A Company guards what is regarded as a very possible infiltration route in this area. A mile across the valley a platoon from the company operates a post that was held by the Israelis up to 13 June. Another Crusader castle standing on a neck of land jutting into the valley gives testimony to the strategic importance of this stretch of terrain in years long gone by.

To succeed in their mission Irish peacekeepers must gain a thorough knowledge of the terrain in which they are operating. This, they are well on their way to doing through intensive patrolling. Likewise, they must get to know the local people and win their support and confidence. The experience the Irish soldier has gained in our own internal security operations will stand him in good stead in this mission.

43 Irishbatt has arrived in Lebanon with a high reputation. It is generally regarded as the best-equipped and most mobile unit in the mission. Previous UN service and security operations at home have ensured that we are regarded as being among the best and most experienced in the UNIFIL force. Our troops, no doubt will play their part and live up to their reputations.

As far as equipment is concerned, nothing has been spared but wear and tear will be heavy. In order to ensure that the high standard which has been set is maintained a proper back-up and resupply programme from home will be essential because no such system exists within UNIFIL at this time leaving Irishbatt largely to fend for itself.

The mission is interesting and demanding, and one in which there is every indication that Irish troops will play a major role. Very soon, names like Tibnin and Shaqra will take their place beside those of Elizabethville and Katima whenever Irish soldiers gather and stories of UN service abroad are recounted.

GOING TO 'THE PARK'

COY SGT WILLIAM SCOTT

On 11 March 1978 a PLO raiding party landed in Israel by sea and hijacked a bus on the Tel Aviv–Haifa road which resulted in 37 dead and 76 wounded. Nine of the eleven PLO raiders were also killed. On 15 March the IDF announced that a 'mopping-up' operation had commenced in Lebanon. It was called Operation Litani and would ultimately involve 30,000 troops.

Four days later, on foot of a US proposal, the Security Council of the United Nations passed Resolution 425 – and as they say, the rest is history! General Erskine from Ghana was appointed as the new UN force commander and UNIFIL HQ was established in Naquora just across the border.

There was great excitement within the Defence Forces on hearing that troops were required to serve in Lebanon under the Blue Flag as we had been out of peacekeeping since 1974. Volunteers were immediately sought and such was the response that two battalions could easily have been filled. Led by Lt Col Eric Guerin 43 Irishbatt returned to peacekeeping on 6 June thanks to a huge airlift supplied by US Air Force DC10s.

A lasting memory for everyone would be the welcome we received from the local people with tears in their eyes and joy in their hearts. They had peace of mind under the protection of the Blue Flag and it was apparent from the massive destruction of the villages, and the poverty of the villagers, that this had been an unhappy occupation by unwelcome forces. UNIFIL now offered hope for the future.

Work immediately started on erecting tents, cookhouses, defensive positions, shelters, and 'long drops'. It was not long before the company and platoon headquarters were all established and then we started manning our observation posts at places like the Black Hole, Fraggle Rock and Hill 880.

The provision of water was a major problem as our supply had to be drawn by water trucks from the Litani river, which was a considerable distance from our positions. The entire battalion was accommodated under canvas. The troops slept on 'safari beds' with the additional luxury of an air mattress (known to all as the 'wobbly bed').

Once the pattern of operational activities was established, thoughts turned towards providing recreational facilities. B Company discovered a flat field near its company headquarters in Bra'shit village. This was a rarity in the mountains of south Lebanon. Work immediately began on clearing the field. Work parties under the guidance of our chaplain Fr Michael Kelly (himself a keen sportsman) set about clearing this field, with armoured cars being used to remove a few large boulders.

Within a couple of weeks, the field was ready and goalposts were erected. All that remained was the selection of a suitable name for our sporting arena and what better name than Páirc Uí Caoimh? For the lads from B Company 'going to the park' took on a whole new meaning! The park was put to good use and many a tough hurling and football match was played there. 43 Irishbatt had the honour of hosting the first UNIFIL inter-contingent sports, which were held at Páirc Uí Caoimh.

The first Irish UNIFIL soldier to die in Lebanon was a member of the 43 Irishbatt. He was also a member of the garrison of Collins Barracks, Cork. Private Finbarr Moon was a native of Fair Hill in Cork city. He enlisted in the army on 30 September 1976 and having completed his recruit training was assigned to the 4th Infantry Battalion. He was serving his first engagement when he volunteered for service with UNIFIL. He died on 25 August 1978 because of injuries sustained in a road traffic accident. When Finbarr Moon's remains were brought back to Cork he was buried with full military honours.

The 43rd was an excellent unit. Like our predecessors in the 32nd Battalion, who were the first out to the Congo, we were proud of the fact that we paved the way for subsequent Irish units who were to serve in Lebanon. No matter how tough things got during our tour of duty, morale always remained high within the whole battalion. The ultimate satisfaction for every officer, NCO and private of the battalion was the fact that we were in a position to help those less privileged than ourselves. This was sufficient reward for all concerned.

IN THE BEGINNING

COL E. D. DOYLE

By 1978, it was four years since we had troops overseas. The with-drawal symptoms had not become less painful. In 1977, when the Senegalese left the Sinai, I was Chief Observer. A senior general told me that the Irish contingent had left an important area of the Sinai in 1973 at a crucial time and he would not be asking for their return.

SETTING UP A FORCE

Whatever views have since been formed or expressed the army was very keen indeed to become involved in UNIFIL in March 1978. How-ever, we were not asked for troops in the initial stages, but some months later, when the force was expanded. Considerable contingency plan-ning was done, nevertheless. The composition of peacekeeping forces is determined at UN HQ in New York by a series of hypothetical queries.

The secretariat say to a diplomat, 'If your government were to be asked for a battalion and some staff officers, and if your contingent proved acceptable to the disputing parties, would your government supply them?' The diplomat says he will check. The secretariat also approach the diplomats representing the parties to the conflict and say, 'If the government of X is willing to supply troops would they be acceptable you?' These diplomats say they will also check. Some dip-lomats, of course, may be able to give some answers based on their knowledge of their governments' policies. So, the cables fly to and from governments, and it is some time before a force is finally con-structed in a series of parallel discussions.

Simultaneously, there are negotiations on the selection of the force commander, transportation to the mission area, strength of the force, estimates of cost, etc. The Secretary General keeps the members of the Security Council informed as he goes along. Although he carries out the day-to-day upper-level direction of peacekeeping forces, he never forgets that he is doing it on behalf of the Security Council.

THE PROCESS

The process can be diagrammatically, if somewhat incompletely, sum-marised as follows:

1. The Security Council passes a RESOLUTION to set up a peace-

keeping force and requests the Secretary General to report back on implementation.

2. He then conducts the negotiations outlined above and submits a REPORT giving the terms of reference, proposed strength, estimated costs, proposed contributing countries, etc.

3. The Security Council pass further RESOLUTIONS accepting Secretary General's report.

4. The General Assembly votes the funds.

5. The Secretariat issues 'Guidelines for Troop-Contributing Countries', and finalises requests for troops, transportation, etc.

As the UNEF 2 operation showed in Sinai, the above procedure can be gone through very rapidly when necessary. Indeed Henry Kissinger said that no army could have reacted faster than the UN did in 1973.

In negotiations, the Secretary General tries to get a wide geographical spread of troop contributors. In practice, this means at least one contingent from each continent. Apart from the obvious reasons – avoiding political, racial or colour bias – a wide spread of troop contributors helps ensure a wide spread of continuing support for the peacekeeping operation, both in the Security Council and the General Assembly. There are disadvantages to this policy also, of course.

THE BACKGROUND

It is hard to believe it now, but UNIFIL was the result of an American initiative in the Security Council. It was an American draft that later became Security Council Resolution 425. Lebanon as the host country clearly welcomed the resolution and wanted the peacekeeping force. Israel did not.

Indeed, many of the subsequent actions against UNIFIL were really aimed at the US. They were part of the cat and mouse defiance Israel seems to feel it can and should show to her great supporter, as a reminder of internal American political and financial realities. And, indeed American failure to support the force it had sponsored was a consequence of those realities.

There were some voices which cautioned that the conditions for an effective peacekeeping operation did not fully exist in the Lebanon, but few were disposed to listen to them.

CONTINGENCY PLANNING

For the early contingency planning carried out an appreciation was made which enabled us to draw some general conclusions as to the probable employment of our battalion, its likely problems, and arising from these, its organisation. The general conclusions were:

The battalion to be sent should be strong in support weapons.
The new battalion organisation and equipment tables, which had
been recently drawn up, should be followed as far as possible.
We should have a welfare/administrative radio link to home.
(This had been forbidden in earlier operations, but such links
had been common in other contingents by this time).

We had considerable knowledge of the UNIFIL area at that time with
several observers recently returned from there – including Capt Hayes,
who had been wounded in one of the various ambushes which had
been occurring since the beginning of 1978.

Law and order had been failing. Armed teenagers had been holding up UN vehicles going to and from UNTSO OPs, stealing radios,
food, personal belongings and even vehicles from the unarmed observers. Posts were sometimes marooned for up to two weeks. Clearly,
unarmed observers alone were no longer appropriate. We saw armoured vehicles as necessary to ensure reliefs, amongst other things.

We knew that the Israelis had given the Christian Militias captured Soviet artillery (mainly 122mm D.30 gun-howitzers) and had
trained the gun teams. There was no possibility of bringing artillery
so the best we could do was to plan on bringing 120mm mortars. It is
generally accepted that UN forces cannot win, and should not even
enter an arms race with any parties in dispute. The fact that Israel later
gave American tanks to the Christian Militias illustrated this. The
PLO, in turn, got Soviet tanks.

THE GUIDELINES
UN HQ issued a set of 'Guidelines for Troop-Contributing Countries'
an early stage. UNIFIL was the first operation for which so comprehensive a document was compiled. It gave much information on
the area of operations and on the requirements. Each infantry battalion was to have:

A strength of 600 all ranks.
A Headquarters Company and three rifle companies of 130 all
ranks each. Companies were to be capable of mounting patrols,
staffing OPs and checkpoints, and providing escorts.
HQ Company was to be capable of providing second-line support.

It can be seen that the UN envisaged the HQ Company as having about

210 all ranks – more than one-third of the strength of the battalion. The reason for this emerged when the other requirements were read.

The transport platoon was to have the capability of lifting the battalion (whether in one or more lifts was not stated). It was also to have petrol and water tankers and a refrigerated truck. The platoon was also to have a second line repair capability. It should carry six months' spares and be able to do vehicle recovery, generator and refrigerator maintenance.

The battalion engineer platoon was to be capable of limited mine clearing and demolitions. It should be able to maintain water, sewage and electricity supplies and do some limited construction. It was indicated to us that most of the force would be in tents initially.

There was detailed advice about immunisations and about the medical platoon and the medical stores we were to bring.

As far as equipment was concerned, the guidelines specified defensive weapons only. At a later stage contingents were actually asked to bring APCs when by then it was clear that advantage was being taken of the traditional UN concept of a force of lightly armed 'rifle' battalions. Now we saw that unsupported units were very vulnerable.

Communications were to be 'one up', i.e., platoons should have company-level radios, companies should have battalion-level ones, and so on. This advice harked back to the Congo days where subunits had to work over vast distances. It was not necessary in the comparatively small area we have in UNIFIL, but the principle is generally sound. If a UN force has not got good communications, it cannot do its job.

We were also told to bring 25 kms of cable per company and enough radios to mount three patrols per company. Four refrigerators per company were suggested, as well as laundry, ablution and sanitary facilities. A jerry can per man for water was suggested as well as 60 days compo rations. This was later cut to 30 days, I think. Even 30 days compo rations for 600 men takes a great deal of transport. Measure a ration and work it out – or ask the quartermaster of our initial battalion!

The Cutting Problem

Now we had been planning on a normal battalion with a support company. The then 'new' battalion organisation had a strength of 768 all ranks – to which we were adding Legal and Welfare Officers, etc. We now had the problems of dispersing the support company and of cutting the overall strength. We put some armoured vehicles, signals and medical personnel into the companies, but the HQ Company remained very large and administratively unwieldy. There was also the danger that company commanders in referring to 'my APCs', 'my signals', etc., might consider them truly their own. Support platoons should be grouped in the HQ Company under their own platoon commanders, for allocation by the battalion commander as he judges the needs of the situations which confront him.

Cutting the overall strength was another problem. We were faced with the difficulty that the UN's advice about having an independent maintenance capability could only be met by cutting into the infantry. We were very reluctant to do this, indeed we wished to increase the rather minimal 130 figure referred to above. Lt Col Jack Gallagher and Lt Col Pat Ronayne who went over it all very carefully put considerable thought into this. Despite these difficulties, the 'Guidelines' document was invaluable. It showed that the UN was seeking to get its act together, literally and metaphorically, because previous guidance had been embodied in a stream of separate documents.

RECCE PARTY

A formal request for a battalion finally arrived and was approved by the government. A Recce party under the then Col Louis Hogan was dispatched immediately, but the commands were also provided with a provisional establishment. We protested to the UN that the upper-level battalion strength restriction would make it very difficult to supply a balanced unit and pointed to the UN's own stipulations about maintenance troops. We knew, however, that we could not win. We were latecomers, so to speak, and the upper level had been set for the force as a whole.

A stream of recommendations came back daily from Col Hogan's party, often via Gen Callaghan in Jerusalem. Where necessary, procurement action was initiated immediately by the QMG's branch and the civilian side co-operated very well in speeding up the normal purchasing procedures. Such abnormal items as refrigerated vehicles, washing machines, refrigerators, additional water tankers, water coolers and pack rations were obtained.

The Recce party returned and reported in writing within one day of arrival. Our general outline of the battalion seemed satisfactory, although there were additional items such as tents to be added to the equipment tables.

THE CORPS

The corps was required to put in bids based on the requirements in the 'Guidelines' and to nominate one staff officer per corps to discuss the bids. Lt Col Gallagher and I took half each of the cavalry, artillery, signals, engineers, ordnance, medical and military police directorate representatives. Everyone's bids had to be cut down to practical figures, having regard to the strength limitations, while ensuring that the essentials were adequately covered. An early decision was taken to crew the APCs with cavalry personnel's expertise and training which were not adequate in the infantry corps at that time. The artillery would crew the 120mm mortars.

AN EXISTING BATTALION?
At a very early stage, we looked carefully at the possibility of making a break with the past and sending out an existing battalion, or at least basing the unit on an existing battalion. This proved impractical for a diverse set of reasons, but the examination was a useful and necessary exercise.

PREPARATION
The UN pressed very hard for the immediate dispatch of the battalion, which they said was expected on the ground in a week. The commands were making good progress in nominating and processing personnel, but it was firmly decided to delay dispatch for about a month. Purchases could only be started when the government had given approval to the UN's troop request and everything from tropical kit to new vehicles had to be bought. There was a mountain of stores to be assembled, packed and weighed. The processing and kitting could not be skimped – we had learned these lessons from the Congo.

Both the commands and ourselves (ops sec.) were rusty on procedures – we had not sent out a unit for some years and we had never before sent one so well-equipped. There were also the training and briefing aspects to be dealt with, range practices to be completed, and troops to be formed into and exercised as sub-units. We were able, however, to concentrate the battalion into one place – Gormanston Camp – something that subsequently proved impossible. Some odd things showed up. Administration had been faulty – many soldiers' army numbers proved to have been incorrect on their documents for a number of years.

Once operations section got out the basic operation order document with establishment, equipment and armament tables, the task of 'filling in the faces' and providing and issuing the equipment got underway. Then training section produced a training directive and intelligence section and operations section provided all the briefings, but equipment continued to be delivered up to the very last day before departure. Now it only remained to figure out how we were going to get there.

The American Air Force had already been moving troops into the Middle East from Africa and Asia. A young officer was sent to Dublin. He seemed to us to exemplify that apparently casual, but actually smooth and flexible efficiency that we have always found in the US Air Force during these air lifts. It emerged that we needed more cargo space than any other battalion they had so far lifted to Lebanon. Meeting this caused considerable re-staging of aircraft in many parts of the world, but it was done without fuss. One watched armoured cars, trucks, APCs and troops vanishing into the maws of the great aircraft as if they were toys.

ON THE GROUND

The battalion got away. Much of its mountain of stores remained on the ground at Tel Aviv airport for several weeks, because of the sheer difficulty of moving it. Being the best-equipped battalion in the force had its difficulties. I have always had sympathy for the adjutant, the OC HQ Company and the QM of that battalion.

Shortly afterward, we were asked for various specialist units – a force signal company and an engineer company – but we had to decline having consulted the corps' directors. We were then asked for about one hundred all ranks for the force HQ Company, about half of whom were to be clerks, storemen, mess staff, and transport personnel. The other half was to be a large defence platoon commanded by a commandant.

This platoon had attractions. It required the most basic soldiers of all, with the ability all trained soldiers have – the ability to do guard duty. Therefore, it could have a mixture of troops and various types of men such as the military college company personnel, who might otherwise find it difficult to get to UNIFIL at that time.

Commands saw this point and co-operated in providing the men. After a few rotations, one command had difficulty in raising its infantry company. In order to make that company up we had to tell the UN we could no longer provide the defence platoon. The Ghanaian battalion was becoming available from the Sinai so Ghana took over the task. Indeed, the UN reduced the overall strength of our battalion on several rotations after the initial battalion although from the beginning our military police seemed to do well and we were asked to provide more and more of them for the HQ, including senior NCOs and those trained in investigations.

CO-ORDINATING

It can be seen that raising an initial unit and its subsequent replacement is divided between AHQ staff branches and directorates, as well

45

as the commands. AHQ Ops section had a co-ordinating function and the main instrument for this after dispatch of the initial unit was the monthly report. This became particularly important as regards spare parts. The UN has a system whereby spares can be supplied by the contingents' home countries on repayment by the UN. In the case of the smaller countries, these have to be sent out during rotations.

It was necessary to get spares requests in the monthly reports and ensure that depots set them aside, or got purchase action ready, so that there would not be a last minute rush just before rotation. At the UNIFIL end a requisition was initiated, processed and sent to New York. Only when the 'Letter of Assist' from New York arrived here could final action be taken, so it was vital that the paperwork should be handled expeditiously. We could co-ordinate the work at this end but it became clear that the procedure was tortuous at the UNIFIL end and the Letters of Assist were arriving late or arriving at the last minute.

I recall asking the force signal officer to draw up a flow chart of the procedure. He had to visit the various field service offices to do this and when it was finally drawn up, it was so complicated that the people concerned immediately started to simplify the procedure. We finally got a more rational one, which worked smoothly and rapidly.

The format of the monthly report was standardised at an early stage. These reports were also of considerable value to the battalion commander because it gave him an overall picture of the statistics and activities of his unit for the previous month. When any battalion staff officer or support sub-unit commander made a request or a recommendation (and there were many such in the first year) the battalion commander was required to give his comments – especially where personnel increases were sought. Because of the fixed ceiling on strength we had to get the battalion commander to say where a balancing saving could be made if he supported the increase.

Many recommendations were, of course, invaluable on training, employment, preparation and equipment. To avoid a build-up of unrepaired equipment towards the end of a unit's tour (something the writer had often seen in many nationalities in UNFICYP) we got tabulations showing the flow of equipment into and out of workshops. As the replacement battalion commander and his staff had access to these reports there was an incentive on the battalion in UNIFIL not to accumulate repair work, but to spread the load as evenly as possible over the tour.

CO-ORDINATING SOPs

From the beginning, a need was felt for a ready reference to procedures for raising and processing units. When procedures are not written down, they become almost 'folkloric', with uncertainties, arguments and thumbing through files. We were fortunate to have Lt Col Johnny White available – he had been involved in much of this work in the past. Hand-overs in the field were disclosing losses of tools, service manuals, etc. A need to standardise arrangements for troop control during rotations also arose. All this prompted the compilation of a set of SOPs covering various aspects of co-ordination. By their very nature, such SOPs need considerable amendment and updating, as conditions and requirements change. The reader will appreciate that this article covers no more than the details of staff-work at home. Operations in the field were a very different matter.

Recce Company leaving on patrol

1980

AT TIRI REMEMBERED
6–13 APRIL 1980

'THOSE WHO WERE THERE'

At Tiri village is located at the forward edge of Irishbatt's Area of Operations in the UNIFIL AO. It is situated in a valley running east to west and dominated to the north by a range of hills, the highest being Hill 880, and by a smaller range to the south. In 1980 the population of the village was some 2,000 persons, exclusively Muslim. By local standards, it had a large population.

It controlled the only road leading north onto Hill 880. From this hill, the towns of Haddathah, Tibnin, Haris and the fertile Tibnin Valley could be easily dominated by direct fire. The village was under UNIFIL control and jutted southwards into the area controlled by the Israeli backed and supported De Facto Forces of Major Saad Haddad – the so-called 'Christian Enclave'. This is an area of south Lebanon between the Israeli border and the limit to which UNIFIL was allowed to deploy.

Irishbatt had four UN posts established in that enclave. Because of their isolation and vulnerability within the DFF controlled enclave, these posts became commonly known as 'Hostage Posts'. They were of little strategic value to UNIFIL but were considered politically important. Requests to have them closed down had been denied.

The following article has been compiled by a number of personnel who were on the ground in At Tiri from 6 to 13 April 1980 and is dedicated to the memory of Pte Stephen Griffin of 46 Irishbatt, Pte S. Sornaivalu of Fijibatt and those other members of UNIFIL who were injured during the 'Battle of At Tiri'.

Sunday 6 April dawned clear over south Lebanon. Having celebrated the religious rites of Easter, off-duty personnel of Irishbatt settled down for an entertaining afternoon at the battalion sports. This was the last notable event that would take place before rotation so morale was very high. At the dusty pitch next door to the Total Garage competition, as well as the heat, was intense. The 10,000m runners were back after their gruelling ordeal. The sprint finals were completed and the novelty events had brought light relief from the seriousness of competition.

The inter-company tug-o-war was just beginning. HQ Company had pulled Recce Company and both teams were 'on the rope' for the second pull. A familiar cry 'Recce turn out' rang out across the pitch. Immediately the rope was dropped and all ran to the waiting armoured vehicles. The time was 1545hrs.

At the briefing, the situation was made clear. The De Facto Forces of Major Haddad had broken into the village of At Tiri and the Battalion Reserve (which consisted of Recce Company plus some other other elements) was to move immediately to the village by way of Hill 880 in order to assist C Company. By 1550hrs, all vehicles were mobile and heading for the Hill – even before many down at Total fully realised what was happening.

The DFF had approached At Tiri from the direction of Kunin. With the physical assistance of a 'half-track' and despite the best efforts of the checkpoint (CP) personnel, they had forced their way through. Once through they took up a position at the end of the avenue leading to the UN position, and having commandeered local houses, they set up further defensive positions.

Having crossed Hill 880 Recce Company deployed near the CP. Reconnaissance was completed and all available information was gathered from the CP personnel. At 1632hrs, more DFF and some local villagers approached the CP in order to discuss the situation. They were not permitted to pass the tank stops and after some pushing and shoving a deputation of unarmed personnel were allowed to come forward.

The UN policy from the outset was simply that the DFF would have to withdraw from the village. The DFF argued that the inhabitants had invited them into the village, which from the attitude of the locals was patently untrue. A simple solution was not readily apparent and a prolonged stay (stand-off) was now expected.

In the meantime, an APC from C Company was sent to the west end of the village in order to pick up one of our patrols which had been stationed there. The DFF sent personnel there also and they managed to isolate and cut off the APC after it had picked up the patrol. In spite of this, the tactic at this time was still to try and resolve the situation through discussion and negotiation.

At 1725hrs an APC from Recce Company was ordered to move to the west end and to help extricate the stranded APC and its crew. The APC moved by a ring route to the north of the village, later to be known as the North Circular Road. The DFF meanwhile reinforced their position by infiltrating more personnel across country from the south and then into the village. As the rescuing APC made its way into the west end it encountered a DFF position at a location to be subsequently

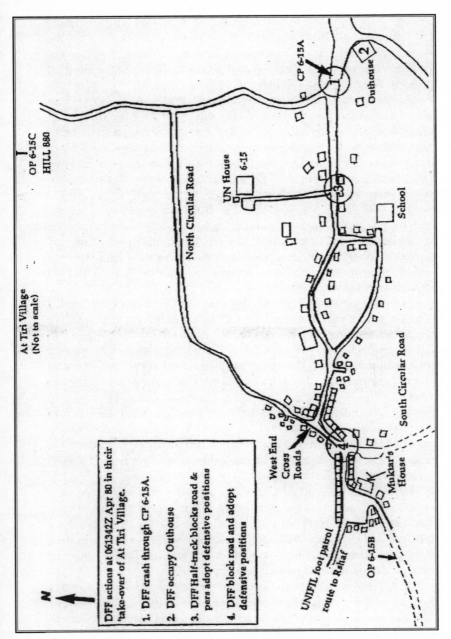

At Tri Village
(Not to scale)

N

OP 6-15C
HILL 880

North Circular Road

UN House
6-15

CP 6-15A

2
Outhouse

3

School

South Circular Road

West End
Cross
Roads

Muktar's
House

UNFIL foot patrol
route to Rshaf

OP 6-15B

DFF actions at 061342Z Apr 80 in their
'take-over' of At Tri Village.

1. DFF crash through CP 6-15A.

2. DFF occupy Outhouse

3. DFF Half-track blocks road &
   pers adopt defensive positions

4. DFF block road and adopt
   defensive positions

called 'The Junction'. The time was 1735hrs and the attitude of the
DFF was now decidedly hostile and aggressive. Rather than aggra-
vate a delicate situation the APC was ordered not to push forward but

instead to just hold its ground.

Back at the UN CP, at the east end, more DFF personnel were arriving from Saff al Hawa in civilian cars and in another 'half-track'. This 'half-track' attempted to ram the UN APC blocking the road but at the last moment it backed off and switched off its engine. The DFF, with a strength of approx. 150 now in the village, set up two mortar positions near an outhouse. A large crowd of anxious villagers gathered near the CP and as the tension increased the DFF fired approx. twenty rounds of small arms fire near the CP.

Hearing the shooting at the CP the DFF personnel at the west end also joined in and opened fire. As it was now dark, the rescuing APC began to inch forward by blinding the DFF with its searchlight but there was a danger here of this APC being cut off. Reinforcements were called for and another APC arrived at 1908hrs. The DFF also reinforced their position and after further scuffling, it was agreed to make no further moves by either side. The situation in both locations then 'stabilised'.

That night a wedding reception was taking place in the muktar's house at the west end. A blue Datsun car from the village tried to get through the UN position at the junction but was blocked by a UN APC. Some very angry personnel in militia uniform got out and one in particular was most upset. The villagers later identified him as Maj Haim – a DFF leader. A scuffle broke out and his spectacles were accidentally broken when his chin came into contact with a UN fist. After some further discussion, the tension eased and the status quo was restored.

To show good faith to all, the UN personnel were invited to the reception. Despite many cups of *shi* (tea), and a multitude of cigarettes, the most welcome event was the opportunity to have a wash. To the vast amusement of the local women, the soldiers gleefully washed in their helmets and then danced and sang in the courtyard. The reception itself was a sombre affair, despite the best efforts of the Irish to enliven the proceedings.

Meanwhile, plans were being prepared to rescue the stranded APC. It was first necessary to reconnoitre the area and to do this the DFF were engaged in conversation whilst an Irishbatt foot patrol slipped quietly into the dark to have a look. It was also time to try to get some sleep in the APCs. With changes of sentry, intermittent DFF calls for more *shi* drinking, there was still more than a slight apprehension of what the morrow would bring, and sleep was difficult to come by.

The plan was that one APC would move forward at dawn to make contact with the stranded APC whilst the second APC held position at the junction. A diversion would be created at the east end by all the vehicles starting and revving their engines. At the west end, however, there was a small problem. A DFF jeep was now blocking the narrow alley-way to the stranded APC.

At approx. 0500hrs UN personnel asked the DFF if they could buy some coffee. The DFF readily agreed to sell and one of their members was detailed to go back into the village to get some. Once he had passed through the junction in his jeep, he was not allowed back until the rescue operation was completed.

At 0525hrs, the rescuing APC moved forward and immediately the DFF came into the alley-way and stood in front of the APC. The driver was instructed to continue driving slowly. The DFF were brushed to either side of the vehicle and they immediately opened fire on the APC. The APC moved on into a small square and immediately came under more fire from another DFF patrol. Directions were passed to the stranded APC as it negotiated its way back along a twisty lane. The DFF attempted to immobilise the rescuing APC but the driver kept the vehicle moving forward and back in the confined space while the vehicle commander threatened to return fire.

After what seemed like an eternity the APC made its way back to the junction from where it was sent via the North Circular Road to the UN CP at the east end. The junction was then blocked, using both APCs. Concertina wire had been requisitioned and was now delivered and in position at the Junction by 0615hrs. By 0620hrs, however, the DFF, were in an extremely angry mood and arrived in force at the junction. While the UN personnel were diverted by negotiations and scuffles, the DFF attached a jeep to the concertina wire and pulled it away.

During the ensuing negotiations, the DFF claimed that one of their men had been seriously injured by the APC moving down the narrow alley. UN personnel countered this by describing how the so-called 'injured' man had run after the APC firing his rifle from the shoulder. On advice from another DFF man, he then suddenly lay on the ground and complained that he was unable to walk or move his shoulder. The DFF carried him away on a stretcher and subsequently claimed that he had suffered a fracture of the thigh and shoulder. Later still they were to claim that he died from loss of blood!!

Reinforcements were sent to the junction and at 0715hrs a DFF man put a round up the breech of his rifle and aimed it at a UN sentry. This escalation in tension eased when the DFF began to realise that the Irish were serious about returning fire if they were fired upon.

About 0725hrs, the DFF said that they would bring up a tank to the village at 0800hrs that morning. At the east end, the second 'half-track' moved behind an outhouse and the DFF proceeded to sandbag the position. At 0735hrs, a tank was observed on the move from Saff al Hawa, followed by five Mercedes cars. Single rounds of small arms fire were being fired indiscriminately by the DFF from all positions.

At 0820hrs, the tank arrived at the CP from the direction of Kunin. Permission to engage it was sought by the commander of an AML 90 but this was refused. However, the rate of indiscriminate fire increased and all UN vehicles in the area were hit. At 0838hrs, an Irish soldier was hit by rifle fire. He was immediately evacuated under cover to Haddathah and from there was flown by helicopter to the UN hospital at Naquora. Fire and movement by the DFF continued and at 0846hrs a number of Irish personnel were captured by the DFF.

At 0925hrs, a ceasefire was negotiated and UN reinforcements were held at Haddathah. Talks continued with the DFF as the villagers began to leave the village and at 1030hrs DFF personnel were observed at the half-track in the village wearing Irish combat and flak jackets. At the same time reports were coming in of the captured Irish being moved to the Brown Mound area south of the village. By this stage, Major Haddad had arrived and was allowed to enter the village in order to conduct negotiations.

At approx 1115hrs, a number of DFF personnel approached the junction from the village and engaged in a heated discussion with the UN troops. They attempted to drag further coils of concertina wire from the position but were prevented from doing so. Rifle butts were freely used to convince them that they had no authority to have freedom of movement. A number of DFF forced an entry into the APC and threatened to destroy it if the other APC did not move back off the road.

Amidst heightened tension, discussions took place on the spot. Shortly afterwards the APC was handed back to the UN and the DFF were given limited freedom to pass the junction. By 1140hrs, the situation had calmed somewhat and a meeting was called between the deputy force commander (DFC) of UNIFIL, the officer commanding Irishbatt, Major Haddad and Abu Amile, at the village of Bayt Yahun. After the meeting, the DFC was permitted to reach the junction and efforts continued to calm the situation and to retrieve equipment taken from the APC and the soldiers.

At 1214hrs, the DFF again opened fire at the junction but on the spot negotiations quickly brought the situation back to what might be called 'reasonable normality'. Nevertheless, at 1225hrs, an APC coming over Hill 880 was fired on by the half-track and at 1227hrs a message was received from the DFF to the effect that they would kill an Irish soldier every fifteen minutes (and they now held nine of them), if any more vehicles came over the hill.

At 1200hrs, the Irish at the junction were withdrawn, via the

North Circular Road, to the rear of the UN house in order to rest and recuperate. At the same time as the meeting at Bayt Yahun was taking place troops from Dutchbatt were being deployed in the area and a platoon from Fijibatt took over the junction position.

At 1400hrs Dutch APCs were seen coming over the hill and immediately came under heavy machine gun fire from the half-track. Nevertheless, one Dutch APC reached the CP and at approx. 1410hrs took up a position facing the tank. The DFF then set up another mortar position near the half-track but after discussion this was later stood down.

Throughout that afternoon, the DFF used the forward slopes of Hill 880 for target practice, possibly in the hope of deterring other vehicles from coming over. At 1645hrs, the Dutch APC left the CP and returned to the rear slope of Hill 880. As the APC climbed the slope, it again came under heavy machine-gun fire and at 1710hrs it was forced to begin returning to the CP under cover of a smoke-screen.

At 1725hrs, three more Dutch APCs were seen manoeuvring slowly down the slope of Hill 800. The three APCs came under fire and all were hit. The tank aimed its gun on the Irish AML 90 and the gunner of the AML 90 traversed his barrel onto the tank. Once again, the tension heightened and at 1752hrs the Dutch APC returned to the CP. Shortly afterwards, information was received that the UNIFIL Force Reserve had deployed their TOW missiles on Hill 880. Then the ration car began the journey down from Hill 800 and shortly afterwards at 1820hrs it too was fired on and hit. Thereafter an APC was used to bring in the supplies and began its twice-daily run, at midnight and at mid-day.

Early on Tuesday 8 April, the Irish were ordered to re-take the junction. At 0630hrs, three APCs from Recce Company once again moved back and re-established control over the junction. The Fijibatt platoon remained on as part of this now reinforced unit who deployed in 'all round defence' with the rooftops being utilised to give observation and better fields of fire. Others took up position on the roads leading to the junction and at the CP itself. [These positions were to be held without relief until the operation ended on Saturday.]

As a gesture of goodwill, three of the captured Irish were returned that morning by the DFF but that did not stop intermittent heavy machine gun fire from the direction of the 'Brown Mound' as well as from all the half-tracks in the area.

At 1240hrs, Major Abu Amile arrived at the junction from the south. Four jeep loads of personnel and some Israelis accompanied him. They demanded to be allowed to pass through the junction and into the village. This was denied them so an RPG 7 was loaded and aimed at

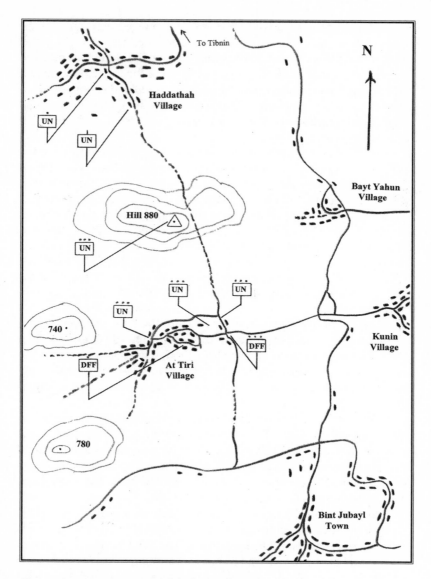

the rear door of an APC blocking the road.

Threats and counter-threats were passed. An 84mm anti-tank gun was deployed by UN personnel from a rooftop and aimed at the DFF. Discussion continued and eventually Amile and his party withdrew and the UN troops breathed a sigh of relief.

Shortly afterwards firing broke out at the east end CP and continued for about an hour. At 1414hrs, a landrover taking an injured

UN soldier (sprained ankle) from the junction was fired on near the crossroads at the east end. First reports indicated that two personnel were injured in this burst of firing and in fact one soldier had received a shrapnel wound. Both were evacuated out of the area to Haddathah and throughout the afternoon the situation remained extremely tense as all kinds of rumours spread throughout the area. The DFF brought media people from the Israeli side, gave interviews, and posed for photographs at the east end CP.

At 1735hrs, the DFF attempted to re-supply their positions and personnel with ammunition through the west end. They were denied entry. Immediately they took up firing positions and threatened to throw hand grenades. One in fact pulled out the pin and threw it at the APC. After more negotiations the situation once again calmed down and the DFF man holding the hand grenade with no pin casually put a nail into it and tossed it into the wadi. The DFF then re-treated and entered the village across country from the south. At 1930hrs, UNTSO observers were brought on a conducted tour of the area and shortly after this the remainder of the captured Irish were released.

That night it was peaceful, apart from the tank moving back to Kunin. To the delight of all the rations arrived shortly after midnight. Sleeping-bags were also distributed, although only 50% could sleep at any time because the remainder had to stay alert. In any case, the only place to sleep was 'on the job' – either on a rooftop, in the roadway, or in an APC.

Next morning, Wednesday 9 April, there was considerable movement by the DFF. The hillside opposite the village (to the south) was being patrolled by a number of personnel in uniform and it appeared that positions were being selected. A number of tanks and half-tracks were observed digging in, whilst an armoured bulldozer was observed preparing positions south of Bayt Yahun.

With no confrontations most of the day was spent observing and reporting but in the afternoon Major Haddad arrived at Bayt Yahun accompanied by four IDF landrovers. The UNIFIL Reserve drawn from Ghanbatt personnel was dispatched as reinforcements to the area but in their enthusiasm and zealousness they sped into the area and nearly overshot the CP. Then with the sudden braking of the first driver the unfortunate APC commander (sitting up top) was unceremoniously dispatched from the turret of his vehicle and landed in a heap at the CP. Thereafter, and apart from the normal routine of changing sentries and cooking rations, that evening and night passed very quietly with no activity reported by either side.

However early next morning, Thursday 10 April, Israeli Defence

Force APCs were observed on the move from Saff al Hawa to Kunin and there was general apprehension as to the IDF's intentions. The APCs, identified as M113s, did not come forward of the village of Kunin but instead took up position in the prepared sites.

At 0820hrs, a UN convoy was observed coming over Hill 880. Immediately the DFF opened fire on it. The personnel in the convoy were observed to 'hit the dirt' rather rapidly. The convoy included a number of 'VIPs', amongst whom was an oversize ABC reporter who immediately equipped himself with an undersize flak jacket and attempted to take cover behind a medium sized rock! Negotiations eventually allowed the convoy to continue to At Tiri where the members received a guided tour of the area without further incident.

Around midday, information was received that Major Haddad had entered the village across country from the south. Shortly afterwards he exited the village via the CP and made his way to Saff al Hawa. By now, there were thirteen M113s in the general area. A patrol of sixteen DFF persons made a foot incursion into A Company's area but after being confronted they withdrew. At 1525hrs, Major Haddad once again arrived at the east end CP and was refused entry. Having tried all avenues of negotiation and discussion, the UN were adopting a tougher line in dealing with the DFF incursion. As a result of the refusal to allow Major Haddad to enter the village, retaliation was expected and two tanks from Saff al Hawa were observed coming forward of the Brown Mound. All that afternoon the tanks were heard manoeuvring behind the ridge south of the village and eventually they adopted 'hull down' positions from where they could engage UN positions.

At 1700hrs mortar fire from Saff al Hawa landed in the area, with one round exploding five metres from a UN OP. Fortunately there were no casualties. At 1715hrs, a helicopter was heard flying in the direction of Ayn Ibil. At 1820hrs, the DFF used a loudspeaker system from the local mosque to harangue the villagers into non-co-operation with the UN.

At 2015hrs, a civilian from the village passed through the junction CP with a can of fuel. The DFF stopped him and took the can off him. They emptied the contents and, when the liquid (petrol) was under the UN APC they tried to ignite it with a hand-held flare. The troops on the ground were quick to spread sand over the flame, thus preventing a major incident. The DFF then retreated behind cover and opened fire on the junction. For the first time, and after much aggravation, UN troops returned fire. The DFF disappeared into the night, probably back into the village. The relief of having finally met fire with fire was immense and raised morale very high. With retaliation expected, the situation remained tense but the night passed without further incident.

Friday 11 April began with the usual pattern of the DFF firing at any movement. The UN now adopted a policy of returning fire, round for round. A UN convoy was observed coming over Hill 880. It consisted of one Cherokee with OC Irishbatt and the Chief Logs Officer on board; a second Cherokee with Team Zulu (OGL) and the ADC to DCOS Ops driving; a Dutch APC with DFC UNIFIL, DCOS Ops, the Chief Political Officer, and a number of others inside, and a truck with a 500 gallon water trailer on tow. That was the order of march. When the party/convoy came under fire, the second Cherokee went behind the APC for cover, the driver of the water-truck applied his hand brake and also dived for cover. Unfortunately, the hand brake did not hold the truck and trailer continued and squashed the Cherokee into the back of the APC, converting it into something like a mini minor.

The rest of the convoy then proceeded on and arrived at the east end CP safely. There was now considerable DFF activity on the road between Kunin and Saff al Hawa. In the early afternoon the locals reported that there was going to be shelling and that they were going undercover. The shelling did not take place. However at around 1500hrs villagers were led by the DFF to the outhouse position and there at 1530hrs Major Haddad gave an interview to the Israeli media. The ages of the villagers in attendance ranged from six to about sixteen years of age.

In the meantime, UN foot-patrolling of the west end and junction had commenced. This was a further development in the UN re-asserting its influence on the village. On the first patrol, there was no contact with the DFF and the reaction of the villagers was one of delight. The DFF were not happy when they heard of this occurrence and they assaulted the village muktar for allowing the UN to patrol. The DFF, however, did not attempt to encounter the UN patrols at this stage.

From first light, on Friday morning 11 April, the DFF manoeuvred their tanks. One of the tanks appeared to be giving trouble and a recovery vehicle was called up to the tank position. At the east end, the village dominating patrols continued. At 1100hrs, the inevitable confrontation took place. Both sides immediately took up firing position and after much discussion and negotiation the DFF tank withdrew threatening revenge. Shortly afterwards the DFF tank in the Cuckoo's Nest position away to the west opened fire and the rounds landed in the vicinity of the Caltex garage back in Tibnin village, the home of Recce Company.

At around 1443hrs the DFF brought a truck-load of youths and women from the village to the outhouse position. These people were equipped with tyres and a can of petrol. They were made to fill the tyres with petrol and light them. Once lit, they rolled the tyres down the hill at the APC blocking the road at the UN CP. The DFF, meanwhile, continued with their sporadic firing. They also warned that they 'would hold the UN enclave personnel hostage if any of the children were hurt'. (The enclave personnel operated other UN positions in the Israeli controlled DFF area as well as At Tiri). The DFF also warned that they would fire for effect if their warnings were not heeded.

More civilians were observed approaching the east end CP from the Kunin direction. The DFF were behind them firing shots into the road on either side in order to keep the civilians moving. A sniper at the junction opened fire and the UN troops returned fire. At the east end, the civilians, who still appeared hesitant despite the 'encouragement' of the DFF, were throwing stones. At 1520hrs, the half-track in the village opened fire and immediately a UN APC returned fire. In this burst of fire by the DFF a UN Fijian soldier was mortally wounded. He was immediately evacuated, under cover of UN fire to Haddathah. A tank, on the southern ridge then opened fire. One tank round hit the UN house, penetrating through the walls and landing in a room where a number of UN troops were. Luckily, the round was solid shot and not high explosive.

At 1525hrs, an AML 90 was instructed to put the half-track out of action. Personnel at the west end were warned to take cover as they were directly in line between the AML 90 and the half-track. At 1530hrs, the AML opened fire and then returned to its position behind cover having immobilised the half-track. Meanwhile the UNIFIL Reserve from their position up on Hill 880 fired a TOW missile at one of the tanks as a warning. The commander of AML 90 was then instructed to go forward again and take out the HMG of the half-track which was still firing even though the vehicle itself had been immobilised. Under covering fire from UN troops, he did so and at 1543hrs the famous statement was heard on the radio, 'I'm finished firing and he's finished'.

Immediately troops at the west end were ordered to move into the village and to secure it. At 1545hrs, they arrived at the half-track position with two APCs. In the eerie silence the UN troops, both Dutch and Irish dismounted and deployed on all sides. The DFF were seen retreating down the wadi carrying their wounded. A house search was immediately undertaken and after a number of rifle rounds were fired two DFF men were captured and were sent to the UN house under escort. By 1610hrs, the village was in UN hands and consolidation was well advanced.

However, DFF mortar rounds then began to land and explode in the village area. Although morale was exuberant, there was a considerable degree of concern as to where the next round would land. All necessary precautions were taken. Around 1830hrs, a tank came forward and opened fire, but a TOW missile landing to his front soon changed his mind and he retreated behind cover again. By 1900hrs, a search of the entire village had been completed and positions prepared for a tense all-night vigil.

At 0147hrs on the Saturday morning, word was received that an agreement had been reached between UNIFIL HQ and the DFF. Part of the agreement was that At Tiri would remain in UN hands and the situation was to revert to the status quo of the previous week. All extra UN troops were to be withdrawn to the north of Hill 880. At 0500hrs, the convoys started to make their way back up the hill to join the remainder of the UNIFIL Force Reserve. A long day was spent catching up on some much needed sleep, swapping souvenirs with other nationalities of the Force Reserve and hoping there would be no reason to go back over the top again.

At Tiri, on the edge of the Irish Area of Operations

Background to the Battle of At Tiri

A Personal Assessment

Capt Ray Murphy

In April 1980, Irish and other UNIFIL troops made a determined stance against an attempt by De Facto Forces to take over a strategic village in the Irish Area of Operations. The attempt was foiled, but only after a strong show of force and casualties on both sides.

The defence of At Tiri marked a significant change in the policy of Irish UN troops towards DFF incursions and led directly to the UN Security Council adopting Resolution 467 (1980). This resolution was important in that it made specific reference to UNIFIL's right to use force in self-defence and vindicated the stance taken by the military commander at the time. This article sets out to place the At Tiri, and other closely related incidents, into the broader framework of what was happening at the time, in the Middle East and on the wider political stage.

Introduction

In early 1980, the Irish President and the Minister for Foreign Affairs paid an official visit to Bahrain. At the end of the visit, a joint communiqué was issued. Paragraph 6 of this communiqué stated:

> The two sides stressed that all parties, including the PLO should play a full role in the negotiations for a comprehensive peace settlement. In this regard, Ireland recognises the role of the PLO in representing the Palestinian people.[1]

The communiqué increased the tension between Major Haddad's forces and Irish UNIFIL troops. News of the statement soon reached Israel where one newspaper headline declared *Ireland recognises PLO. Is prepared to host Arafat.*[2] In south Lebanon the DFF leader, Major Haddad, threatened to use force to oust Irish troops. He demanded that they be withdrawn because of Ireland's attitude to the PLO.[3] The DFF also resumed shelling of the Irish area and stepped up their policy of harassment. In April 1980, a particularly serious situation developed in the Irish AO. The DFF with the support of the Israeli Defence Forces attempted to take over the village of At Tiri in the Irish sector. UNIFIL was the subject of intense harassment at the time and the level of violence escalated rapidly. There had been a general 'hardening of attitudes' from early in the year and tension was mounting between the DFF and UNIFIL in the weeks immediately prior to the At Tiri confrontation in April.[4]

Strategic Value of At Tiri Village

The village of At Tiri is situated alongside a strategic crossroads. The village itself was at the forward edge of the Irish area and jutted into the area controlled by Major Haddad at the time. It would have been a serious political and military setback to UNIFIL if the village and crossroads fell under the control of the DFF. Control of the crossroads would have given access to high ground to the north and would have allowed Major Haddad to dominate the whole Irish AO. In the words of one Irish officer in Lebanon at the time, had the De Facto Forces taken over the village 'then Irishbatt and the rest of UNIFIL might as well have packed up and gone home'.[5]

UNIFIL had never taken control of the full area intended for its deployment in 1978. Instead of gradually gaining ground since then, it in fact lost territory to the DFF.[6] The official UN maps of the area did not reflect the situation on the ground. The time was now reached where UNIFIL could not afford to lose control of further ground. A firm stance had to be taken if the authority of the peacekeeping force and the UN itself was to have any significance there.

The confrontation over At Tiri is well-documented and reported upon.[7] The level of harassment and shootings escalated to a situation of almost open warfare between UNIFIL and Major Haddad's forces. The DFF used small arms, heavy machine gun, mortar and tank fire against the Irish and other UNIFIL troops. UNIFIL returned fire in a restrained and disciplined fashion.

UNIFIL HQ in Naquora was also subjected to heavy fire, which did not spare the force hospital. There were casualties and many injuries on both sides.[8] At the end of the day a firm and resolute stand by UNIFIL troops led to the withdrawal of the DFF from the village and the area immediately around it.

PLO Attack Misgav Am

While the conflict between the DFF and UNIFIL was taking place in At Tiri, the PLO launched an attack on a settlement in northern Israel. The attack on Kibbutz Misgav Am again brought criticism of UNIFIL by Israel.[9] In this instance Israel responded by sending over 250 heavily armed and supported troops into south Lebanon.

These troops established positions in and adjoining the UNIFIL area of deployment.[10] At the time it was not clear what the IDF intended to do in south Lebanon. It was a large-scale incursion and could have been the preliminary stage of another operation similar to Operation Litani in 1978. Alternatively, it could have been to support, directly or indirectly, the DFF attempted take-over of At Tiri. In any event, it had a profound effect on the morale of UNIFIL troops defending the village.[11]

It was also seen to make the DFF more aggressive and less flexible in negotiations with UNIFIL. These factors had to be taken into account by the military commander in At Tiri when assessing what the appropriate response to the DFF incursion should be.

In the criticism of UNIFIL's failure to prevent the infiltration and attack on Misgav Am, few commentators referred to the attack on the Irish position in At Tiri by the DFF. While this was underway, the PLO attacked the settlement. This was one of the occasions when the Irish battalion and other elements from UNIFIL were almost exclusively involved in resolving problems created by Major Haddad's militia.

In this regard, they were seriously hampered in preventing armed infiltrations through their AO. In fact, the DFF themselves committed men and resources to harassing UNIFIL instead of preventing infiltrations through the area under their control. The Israelis claimed the PLO had infiltrated through the Irish and Nigerian battalion areas and yet produced no proof to this effect. UNIFIL denied these allegations. The situation was aptly summarised by one commentator at the time: 'If the five terrorists did pass through UNIFIL lines, they also passed through Haddad's and Israel's own defence system'.[12] By what logic, it is asked, do the Israelis expect under-strength, multinational, peacekeepers to be more efficient and motivated than the Israelis themselves?[13] The Israelis did finally withdraw the troops in question. This was after discussion between the Force Commander and the Israeli Chief of Staff. The Israelis had also come under significant pressure from the US to end the violation of Lebanese sovereignty.[14] Premier Begin was due to meet President Carter in Washington in mid April and the Israeli incursion would not have been conducive to a successful meeting. The Lebanese government had decided to bring the matter before the Security Council for urgent debate. The US did not support the Israeli action and its anticipated attitude in any Security Council debate on the subject would be embarrassing to Israel and detrimental to its relations with the Carter administration.

Unfortunately, however, US pressure upon Israel was not strong enough to prevent the DFF attempting to take over the village of At Tiri. Once again, UNIFIL was left largely to its own devices in its endeavours to implement the mandate.

CAPTURE AND MURDER OF IRISH SOLDIERS

On 18 April, as the situation in At Tiri appeared to be resolved, another very serious incident occurred. On their way to an observation post in the enclave controlled by Major Haddad's militia, three Irish soldiers were stopped by DFF. One was shot and badly wounded and the other two were taken away and subsequently murdered.[15]

The Secretary General immediately expressed his 'shock and outrage' at the 'murder in cold blood by DFF'.[16] The manner of the deaths at the hands of DFF shocked Irish and international opinion. Irish/Israeli relations, already tense, reached an all time low. The murders focused attention on the difficult role UNIFIL was being asked to perform. The Irish government launched a diplomatic offensive to press Israel to withdraw support from the DFF.

An emergency meeting of the government to discuss the situation in Lebanon ruled out the possibility of withdrawing Irish troops from UNIFIL. A statement said a precipitous withdrawal could have serious consequences at a time of heightened international tension. The statement also supported the Security Council decision that the peacekeeping force should take immediate and total control of its AO.

The Israelis denied that they were in any way responsible for the murders and attributed blame on a so called 'blood feud'.[17] The IDF even went to the trouble of organising a special news conference in Bint Jubayl, a stronghold of Major Haddad in south Lebanon. The murder of the two Irish soldiers had demonstrated to the world the ill-disciplined and criminal nature of Major Haddad's militia. Nevertheless, the Israelis made it clear that they would continue to support the DFF. This was considered 'highly irresponsible' by the Irish ambassador to Lebanon at the time[18] and although not referring to the Israelis by name, he was also reported as having said: 'Those who build up the Frankenstein monster and then say they cannot control it, cannot run away from the consequences'.[19]

WORLD POLITICAL REACTION

The murder of the two soldiers was also strongly criticised by the US administration.[20] The argument, by the Israelis and Major Haddad, that this was the outcome of a traditional blood feud involving Shi'ite members of the local population was not accepted in Washington. Prior to the murders, Major Haddad had demanded a ransom of 40,000 Lebanese pounds (approx. IR£5,500 at the time) for the corpses of two Irish soldiers. This was to be compensation for the killing of one of his men during the At Tiri incident. Major Haddad could not now claim he was not responsible for what happened.

The Irish government did ask the US to put pressure upon Israel to stop supporting the DFF and curb their activities. It was reported that the taoiseach had written personally to President Carter on the matter. The government also sought the support of the European Community in its campaign to place UNIFIL in full control of all its AO, right up to the international frontier with Israel. On 25 April, the nine EC members issued a statement condemning recent developments and supporting the call for UNIFIL to take control of all its intended area.[21]

In New York, the Secretary General had kept the members of the Security Council informed of the unfolding events in Lebanon. A strong statement was issued after the murder of the two Irish soldiers. The statement did not mention Israel by name. The message to Israel was, nonetheless, clear and unambiguous: 'The Security Council condemns all those who share in the responsibility for this outrageous act. The council reaffirms its intention to take such determined action as the situation calls for, to enable UNIFIL take immediate and total control of its entire area of operation ...'[22]

IRISH DIPLOMATIC INITIATIVE
The Irish government held a special meeting on 20 April and issued a statement, which made specific reference to the Security Council's intention to take the necessary action to enable UNIFIL take control of its entire area,[23] and now looked to the Security Council for this action. It did not want the peacekeeping force to adopt a more aggressive stance which would be more appropriate to a peace enforcement mission. The action required, under the circumstances, had to be of a political and diplomatic nature. It required the cessation of the harassment and attacks on UNIFIL by Major Haddad's DFF. To achieve this, they had to be deprived of all outside support. The government also decided to seek to arrange an early meeting at ministerial level with the other troop-contributing countries. The purpose of the meeting was to consider the adequacy of the measures taken by the council in ensuring the effectiveness of the force and the safety of its personnel.

THE FRAMING OF RESOLUTION 467 AND ITS SIGNIFICANCE
In the course of the Security Council debate, two draft resolutions were introduced. In both instances, the US let it be known that if they were put to a vote, they would have no option but to veto. A third and final draft was introduced on 24 April. This was adopted as Resolution 467 (1980). The US abstained on the voting, along with the USSR and the German Democratic Republic but the resolution was significant in several respects.

It commended the force for its great restraint in very adverse circumstances and called attention to the provisions of the mandate that would allow the force to use its right of self-defence.[24] This was a very significant provision of the resolution. It was the first occasion the Security Council found it necessary to make direct reference in this way to the force's right of self defence. It was a retrospective approval of the action taken at At Tiri. It supported the use of force by the Irish troops in defence of themselves and their positions. In this regard, it was also a reminder to all the parties concerned, and the force itself, that this was the appropriate action in the circumstances.

The resolution also condemned all actions contrary to the provisions of earlier resolutions on south Lebanon.[25] In particular it strongly deplored 'the military intervention of Israel in Lebanon' and the 'provision of assistance to the so-called De Facto Forces'. The US abstention on the adoption of Resolution 467 (1980) exemplified its policy and attitude to the problem of south Lebanon at the UN. President Carter admitted that since direct American interest was aroused primarily in moments of crisis, 'a concerted effort to find a permanent solution to the continuing Lebanese tragedy' had never been mounted by the US.[26] The US sought continuously what it perceived to be a balanced perspective in the Resolutions adopted by the Security Council. In this regard, it was echoing similar Israeli demands.

The US permanent representative stated that his country abstained from voting because the resolution did not deal with the problem in a balanced or comprehensive way.[27] In this particular instance the emphasis was on condemnation rather than constructive proposals. In particular, the resolution did not refer to the terrorist attack on the Misgav Am Kibbutz in northern Israel and other attempts by Palestinians to infiltrate into the UNIFIL AO. This was consistent with previous American statements relating to the Middle East question at the UN. The US administration's view was that other parties were also involved in what it termed a 'cycle of violence'. To attribute blame or responsibility to one party reflected an imbalanced and unfair approach. Why should the encroachments by the DFF warrant special attention while the activities of the Palestinians in Lebanon go unmentioned?

INADEQUACY OF US RESPONSE IN THE SECURITY COUNCIL

It can be argued that the US point of view was justified on certain occasions. In this instance, however, it was not. The DFF had instigated the attack on UNIFIL troops in At Tiri. This attack was unprovoked and unwarranted. The only appropriate response now was condemnation. The attack on Misgav Am that the Americans wanted referred to and condemned, did not take place until after the DFF attempt to take over At Tiri. It had no direct relationship with the

66

events surrounding the incident which could have precipitated the withdrawal of the force.

The DFF could not have carried out the attack without the support of Israel. Israel, a member of the UN had chosen to totally disregard the authority of this organisation. The US administration protected it in its actions. If the threat of the American veto had not existed, then the Security Council could have taken action against Israel to ensure compliance with its resolutions. The policy of the US was weak and reprehensible during the whole affair. It did not give the peacekeeping force the support it deserved and it denied the Security Council the opportunity to do likewise.

THE MEETING OF TROOP-CONTRIBUTING COUNTRIES

After the At Tiri incident and the murder of the two Irish soldiers, the Irish government called for a ministerial-level meeting of troop-contributing countries. It was proposed that the meeting be held in Dublin to discuss and assess the situation. Representatives from eleven countries attended. The outcome of the meeting was keenly awaited by the various contingents comprising UNIFIL. After the determined stand at At Tiri and the passing of Resolution 467 (1980), the troops of the force wanted to see an endorsement of the firm policy adopted by the Security Council.[28]

Prior to the meeting of troop-contributing countries, the Minister for Foreign Affairs announced that Ireland intended to rely on diplomatic pressure to persuade the Israelis to cease supporting Major Haddad's militia.[29] This approach was confirmed when the agreed communiqué was released after the meeting. The conference was not very significant as no major decisions were taken there. However, it did rule out any suggestion that the peacekeeping role of UNIFIL be changed to a peace-enforcing one. In the words of Ireland's foreign minister, there was 'absolute unanimity on peacekeeping'.[30] There was also a thinly-veiled threat to withdraw the troops if the situation did not improve. The actual text of the communiqué on this point stated: '... unless rapid progress is made in the creation of conditions in which the force can operate more safely and more effectively, including adequate international protection and immunity for its personnel, its continued viability may be brought into question ...'[31]

This threat could not be taken lightly. At the same time, it was not an ideal means of putting pressure on the Israelis and the DFF. In certain instances, it could be very counter-productive. Major Haddad had often expressed his desire to get the Irish, and UNIFIL in general, out of south Lebanon. If he considered that putting more pressure on the force could precipitate a withdrawal, then he was likely to do just that. Despite this obvious danger, the ministers saw it as the only effective way of putting real pressure on the Israelis to curb the activities of the DFF.

Although the Israelis were often critical of the force, they were also pragmatists. They realised that there were more benefits than disadvantages from UNIFIL's presence in Lebanon. The danger in this premise was once they changed their minds and decided otherwise, then diplomatic pressure and threats to withdraw would mean nothing. There was also evidence within Israel that the diplomatic offensive and bad publicity as a result of the At Tiri incident, was causing certain Israelis to question the official government policy on Major Haddad and Lebanon.[32]

In assessing the response of the contributing countries to the situation, it had to be kept in mind that there was no formal role for this group in the UN framework. They had neither an executive nor consultative role. The lack of a constitutional base meant that they had limited power as a group to influence events. Meetings had to be organised on an ad hoc basis. They certainly had no power to change the mandate.

At the time, the Irish Foreign Minister was questioned regarding UNIFIL taking military action to gain control of the enclave. Significantly, he is reported to have said Ireland would withdraw rather than support action of that kind. Unfortunately, the meeting did not achieve the results hoped for. Soon afterwards the intentions of the Israeli government were made clear when a foreign ministry official stated '... we will use our own influence to alleviate tension between Haddad and the UN Forces, but we can't see our way to removing support for him'.[33]

CRITICISMS AND ASSESSMENT OF UNIFIL'S POLICY AND TACTICS

The minister's remarks probably reflected the surprise and shock of many observers after the conflict between UNIFIL and the DFF at At Tiri. After the initial deployment of the force there were no further major incidents involving UNIFIL and armed elements or DFF. The Irish contingent in particular had done their utmost to ensure there was no escalation of violence during periods of intense harassment by DFF. This in fact had brought criticism by observers of the Irish approach to peacekeeping in south Lebanon.[34]

It was said that if they had taken a firmer stand against action by Major Haddad, they might not have suffered so much harassment. The so called 'kid glove' approach reportedly favoured by the Irish led to timid responses to encroachment by DFF.[35] Other contingents considered this was the reason why so much of the Irish battalion area was taken over by the DFF. A report at the time explained it as follows: 'Because of the strategy adopted by the Irish, in negotiating with the militia instead of shooting at them, the battalion has ceded control of two villages which use to be in the Irish area – Kunin and R'shaf in another village, Bayt Yahun, Irish soldiers and militia men coexist side by side.'[36]

There were other criticisms of the tactics employed by certain contingents, including the Irish. There was a tendency early on in the mission to rely on fixed positions and firepower and to minimise the value of resolute and constant patrolling. The conventional military deployment on high ground and hills was not always the most appropriate method of preventing encroachments. The occupation of such key terrain did not guarantee control of the ground dominated in the conventional manner by these posts. It was often more effective to deploy troops on flat vulnerable ground with the primary purpose of preventing any incursion by the DFF.

The tactics adopted by the Irish battalion defending At Tiri marked a turning point for Irish troops with UNIFIL. In the early years of UNIFIL, certain parties misinterpreted the policy of negotiation and persuasion as weakness. It was not until well into the mission that the reality of south Lebanon and Middle East politics was fully appreciated by the Irish peacekeeping troops. The promised co-operation with UNIFIL from parties to the conflict was never forthcoming. The force was left largely to its own devices. Even the US, which instigated the establishment of UNIFIL, was indifferent to its predicament.

RIGHT TO USE FORCE IN SELF-DEFENCE
The provision of the UNIFIL mandate that allowed the force to use its right to self-defence gave each member sufficient scope to use force when he or she considered it necessary to do so. The Secretary General had stated in his terms of reference that self-defence would include attempts by forceful means to prevent UNIFIL from discharging its duties under the mandate.[37] When debating the events in south Lebanon in the Dáil, certain deputies had expressed concern regarding the UNIFIL guide to the use of force and were reassured by the Minister for Defence as follows: '... the guide to the use of force by UNIFIL personnel issued by the force commander, gives ample power to local commanders to deal with any situation with which they may be confronted. The circumstances in which unarmed or armed force may be used are well defined, and the decision to use force always rests with the commander on the spot'.[38]

Therefore, it was up to each commander to assess every situation and decide what was the appropriate action in the circumstances. Observers, even with the benefit of hindsight, may not be in possession of all the facts. Furthermore, they have no responsibility and will seldom have experienced the circumstances in which a decision is made at first hand.

TACTICS DICTATED BY DEPLOYMENT

The DFF at the time obviously believed there would be no real resistance to their attempted take-over of the village. They were very aware of the presence of isolated Irish UNIFIL troops in observation posts inside the enclave. They still remained acutely vulnerable in any confrontation with the DFF and could be described as the 'Achilles Heel' of this and previous Irish battalions.

The DFF had been led into this false sense of security by the actions, or in this case lack of action, during previous encounters. On this occasion, the response from UNIFIL was not that anticipated. Major Haddad was told there were no grounds for compromise. The negotiations were straight forward and to the point. There would be no acceptance of a DFF presence in or around the village. They had to withdraw completely. Major Haddad initially stated he would never do so.

He allowed his militia to fire on UNIFIL forces in the area and on resupply convoys approaching the village. In the early stages, the UNIFIL commander in the village was unable to return fire. This was not because he had been ordered to refrain from doing so or because the rules regarding the use of force did not permit it. In fact too many Irish and other UNIFIL troops were very vulnerable in the first few days. Some of those in exposed positions were taken hostage for a time.

The Secretary General's report of the incident is misleading in regard to the use of force. It states that often, during intense small arms fire on Irish positions, the force commander 'gave permission to return controlled fire'.[39] In fact, the Irish commander in the area was well aware that he could return fire. He refrained from doing so until his troops were in reasonable positions from which they could return fire and when it became evident there would not be a negotiated solution to the impasse. Then restrained small arms fire was resorted to in self-defence. This escalated to the use of heavy weapons. These were fired on the order of the local UNIFIL commander.

It is interesting to note that the secretariat in New York became quite alarmed by this and after the At Tiri incident, the rules regarding the use of such weapons became more restrictive. The restrained and firm reaction to the incursion proved to the DFF that UNIFIL was committed to the defence of its AO. It focused attention on the predicament of the force and Israel's continued support of the DFF. It helped achieve an uneasy peace for a short period between UNIFIL and those forces.

An unofficial 'understanding' was reached similar to that with the PLO after the clashes during UNIFIL's early deployment. The area occupied by the Irish was very important in political and strategic terms to Major Haddad. The defence of At Tiri was a watershed in relations between UNIFIL and the DFF. When negotiations and persuasion failed, the peacekeeping force was prepared to use the necessary means to defend itself and carry out its duties. However, this did not mean that the response to every act of aggression would lead to a corresponding act of defence.

THE ADOPTION OF RESOLUTION 467 (1980)
The adoption of Resolution 467 (1980) could have brought a change in UNIFIL's policy towards the DFF and armed elements by the Security Council and Secretary General. This resolution differed from those that had previously been adopted in relation to UNIFIL in that it made specific reference to UNIFIL's right to use force in self-defence.[40]

This could have provided UNIFIL with sufficient authority to adopt a more aggressive stance toward the DFF and armed elements. However, the apparent authority to use force in self-defence to implement the mandate was not backed up with the political will to do so. The contributing countries' statement after the meeting in Dublin had made it clear that they would only support stronger diplomatic action.[41]

Within the Security Council, there was insufficient consensus in relation to UNIFIL to support the Secretary General in any bold initiative by the peacekeeping force in south Lebanon. This left him with very little scope when making decisions pertaining to the implementation of Security Council resolutions regarding UNIFIL.

In his report on UNIFIL for the first six months of 1980 the Secretary General found it necessary to refer to UNIFIL's right to use force in self-defence.[42] Despite the reaffirmation of this right in Resolution 467 (1980) and its potentially broad interpretation, he was constrained by the lack of consensus in the Security Council and by a clear message from the contributing countries that they would not support a stronger show of force. Having referred to Resolution 467 (1980) and its reference to the provisions in the UNIFIL mandate that would allow the force use its right to self-defence, the Secretary General went on to state: 'A peacekeeping operation must achieve its major objectives through means other than the use of force, and this consideration certainly applies to UNIFIL ... I believe that the main road to full implementation of the UNIFIL mandate lies in a political and diplomatic effort'.[43]

This policy was primarily the result of practical considerations.

The death or injury of UNIFIL or other personnel did not of itself serve any worthwhile purpose. Its implications were demonstrated when Irish positions were under sustained mortar shelling in June 1980 and the force commander refused permission to return fire.[44]

PROSPECTS FOR A SOLUTION THROUGH CO-OPERATION

In the latter part of 1980, the DFF continued to resist further deployment of UNIFIL and continued their attempts at encroaching upon the area controlled by UNIFIL.[45] Despite the events of the year and the continuous requests by the Secretary General, the co-operation of the parties concerned was not forthcoming. The situation had not changed to any significant extent. It was not surprising that the Lebanese government complained of the lack of progress made by UNIFIL.[46] It called for practical ways and means to render the mandate 'more effective and more implementable'.

This did not mean the Lebanese government wanted the mandate reviewed or redefined. It had consistently held the view that a 'certain measure of "peace enforcing" was not precluded at the very inception of UNIFIL'.[47] The Secretary General's policy regarding UNIFIL was the only one feasible under the circumstances. UNIFIL's effectiveness as a peacekeeping force depended primarily on gaining the cooperation of the parties concerned, while its survival depended on its remaining impartial and uninvolved in Lebanon's factional wars.

In a situation as volatile as south Lebanon, the continued existence of the peacekeeping force reflected the realism and political astuteness of the Secretary General and the military commanders charged with implementing the mandate on the ground. The debacle of the Multi-National Forces involvement in Beirut during 1983 has subsequently vindicated the policy adopted by the Secretary General and enhanced further prospects of continued United Nations involvement in the Middle East peace process.

1980

A Voyage to Lebanon

Lt Cmdr Eamon Doyle, NS

Not so very long ago the prospect of the naval service sending a ship (or the ship) abroad on a modest courtesy cruise seemed as remote as the deep ocean. Then, in 1976, the minesweeper *Gráinne* visited Brest, in France. Every year since then the navy has shown the flag at various times in the waters of all the maritime states of the European Community and also in Norway and Iceland.

These voyages have been made at minimal cost; whether a naval ship operates in foreign or home waters she still requires much the same maintenance effort; her complement must be paid and fed and the fuel consumption will reflect the distances steamed. Aside from any operational mission the real value in a foreign trip is seen in the way morale soars at all levels. Many factors, too numerous and obvious to mention here, contribute to this. Not least is the commitment by all ranks to making a trip a success, and the confidence built upon success. It is no surprise, therefore, that navy men value foreign trips almost as much as their new ships; and the longer and more ambitious voyages of the past year or so may be viewed in this light.

Thus, when the proposal to send a ship to the Middle East was suggested in late October 1979, the excitement was intense. The requirement, from the corridors of power, was to transport military stores to Beirut for the Irish contingent serving with the United Nations Peacekeeping Force in south Lebanon (UNIFIL).

The choice of ship was relatively simple. The demands of the task ruled out the minesweepers and the oil-fired steamer, *Setanta*, could not seriously be considered because of her very high fuel consumption. Of the three patrol vessels, *Aoife,* had only recently entered service and was insufficiently tested for a long endurance voyage. The improvement in *Emer's* design meant she had a significant edge over *Deirdre* in stability and endurance, and so she was selected. (In any case, with *Deirdre*, not long back from a summer cruise to Norway, Denmark, Germany and Holland, the choice of that ship would have ruffled many a feather amongst *Emer's* crew!).

At the time, *Emer* was back in the builder's yard (Verolme Cork Dockyard) at Rushbrooke to catch up on outstanding maintenance and repairs. This work was now pushed ahead with great thoroughness, as indeed were all the other preparations – jobs like storing and victualling the ship (for 35 days), medicals and jabs for all hands, creating a small mountain of paper – in triplicate – to keep the administrative staffs happy, charts and other hydrographic publications for the area, endurance and stability calculations and so on. The list grew endless and all the while a firm decision to go was 'pending'.

A tentative date of departure was set for mid-November. This came and went as did several 'firm decisions', but finally an absolutely firm 'go' was made late evening on 21 November. The news was conveyed by a fairly senior naval officer to one less senior as follows (almost):

'The Lebanon trip has just been confirmed.'

'That's great news! When do we sail?'

'Tomorrow.'

'Tomorrow! You're all bananas up there – sir – with all due respects.'

(Very important that last bit. Many a military career has been stunted by failure to use that phrase tactically).

In the event, *Emer* was to sail within 48 hours. And if steam was let off at the now indecent haste of the operation all on board knew that further delay could make the prospect of Christmas in Biscay a reality.

On the late afternoon of 23 November, all stores and supplies for the 46th Battalion, UNIFIL, were secured on board and the ship was ready for sea. Almost all spare berths were occupied; a few extra ratings here and there; an army officer to take care of the military stores; a *Slua Muiri* (Reserve) officer, who somehow managed to get four weeks off work; and a young ensign who had been admitted to Cork Military Hospital a few days previously, recovered with miraculous speed to rejoin the ship on the day of departure. (Former patients will fully appreciate that latter achievement). Finally, the naval chaplain, Fr Michael O'Brien, came on board to celebrate mass and impart a blessing for a safe voyage.

With a few media people there to record the event *Emer* slipped from the naval base that afternoon. A long salute on the ship's siren passing Cobh bade farewell to families and friends. Once clear of Cork harbour a course was set for Cape Finisterre on the north-western corner of Spain, and the ship settled down to the steady routine of an ocean passage.

Crossing the Bay of Biscay in winter months normally generates some anxiety, but on this occasion perfect weather prevailed. The fair weather held for most of the way to the Central Mediterranean, except for a windy spell approaching the Straits of Gibraltar. This was the 'Levanter', the name given to the easterly wind in the strait, which often reaches, and on this occasion did blow to, gale force.

Although the *Deirdre*-class ships have considerable range, it is unwise to allow fuel to run too low; consequently, the broad plan for the voyage listed refuelling needs on both the outward and homeward trips. These stops would also provide the only opportunities for crew rest and recreation since Beirut would not be a shore liberty port, nor could replenishment of fuel and water there be relied upon. Initially, Malta was designated for the outward call but this was changed *en route*, for Augusta in Sicily, and Gibraltar remained the homeward call.

For most on board, Augusta turned out to be quite a surprise. Arriving there on 30 November, we found the harbour encompassed some of the largest oil terminals about, in addition to the important naval facilities known to us. Augusta is in fact Italy's 'Bantry Bay' on a very much larger scale, catering for mammoth tankers of up to almost 400,000 tons deadweight. Unlike Bantry, the area is dotted with several refineries and related petrochemical industries. It is the most prosperous area in Sicily and as a consequence, the most expensive.

By Monday morning, 3 December, it was time to resume our voyage. We had undertaken to reach Beirut by first light on the sixth, which meant covering a thousand miles in less than three days. Any delay, therefore, would put that beyond reach, particularly as the weather maps now began to show 'instability' – a Mediterranean euphemism for gales. On cue, the wind freshened to meet *Emer* as she cleared Augusta shortly after midday.

For the next nine days, or the 3,000 miles to Gibraltar via Lebanon, strong head-winds would give a most uncomfortable passage; rough weather in the Mediterranean tends to raise comparatively short steep waves which can make life difficult for a small ship. In contrast, similar weather in our western approaches is more likely to create a long heavy sea, or swell, which is not as severe on the stomach. However, by setting a course south of Crete and Cyprus to gain some small lee the schedule was maintained, and we arrived off Beirut on 6 December. By 0700hrs, the pilot had boarded to guide the ship into harbour.

Prior to the civil war, Beirut was probably the busiest port in the Middle East, handling not alone cargoes for Lebanese centres, but also a great deal of trans-shipment cargoes destined for countries like Iraq and Saudi Arabia. But during the intense fighting of 1975/1976 Beirut suffered heavily with widespread destruction of the port facilities and the nearby commercial centre of the city.

Only in recent times has the port returned to a semblance of normality and even this is interrupted from time to time as fighting breaks out close by. On these occasions shipping must clear the harbour and anchor off until things quieten down. It is hardly surprising then to hear that piracy is considered a real threat in this part of the Mediterranean.

Whole cargoes, it seems, have vanished ... and bargains are offered for sale with the explanation that '... it fell off the back of a ship', or so the local gossip has it. Only as we sailed in past the breakwater, towards our berth, did we get some idea of the heavy damage and losses to shipping suffered during the worst fighting at the outbreak of the civil war. There are about five wrecks in the harbour and several other ships, though afloat, are damaged beyond economic repair. It was a sad sight.

Beirut is not an extensive port and by 0720hrs *Emer* was secured alongside her berth. There to meet us were some familiar faces from the 46th Battalion and a group of French officers serving with UNIFIL who had responsibility for clearing UN supplies through the port to the forward area. To signify our peaceful intentions and clarify our status, the United Nations standard (flag) was flown from the masthead – for the first time ever on an Irish ship (a necessary precaution in the war zone where the sudden arrival of a strange warship could provoke agitation amongst the belligerents).

There also to greet us was, the Irish Charge d'Affaires, Mr Seán Whelan. Before long, the convoy of white UN trucks was alongside and off-loading of the supplies was underway. It was interesting to see also in port a supply ship of the Nigerian navy in a similar mission to our own. The Lebanese army maintains security within the docks area, but immediately outside the perimeter the opposing factions hold sway. They are separated by the city centre ruins across which an uneasy cease-fire prevails. Each side has a command of several high-rise buildings which are used for observation posts and sniper positions. That morning sniper fire started at about 1100hrs and continued sporadically for the rest of the day. It was confirmation, if any was needed, that Beirut, on this occasion, was not an attractive liberty post. To have come 3,000 miles and not get ashore was a disappointment indeed, but unavoidable in the interests of personal safety.

By noon, all supplies had been loaded on the trucks, and some odds and ends loaded on board for return to Ireland. Before departure, there was time to relax for lunch with our army colleagues and the Charge d'Affaires, but by 1500hrs we had said our goodbyes and were on our way home.

The unsettled weather we had carried since leaving Sicily was to remain with us more or less all the way to Gibraltar. Predominantly fresh to strong head-winds meant constant spray which didn't at all suit the 'sun worshippers' on board, and acquiring a 'bronzy' for Christmas was now high on the order of priorities.

A different route on the homeward passage took us through the Strait of Messina, separating Sicily and the Italian mainland. This is an extremely busy waterway connecting the Tyrrhenian Sea to the north with the Ionian Sea southward. The density of shipping and small fishing craft, and the currents and whirlpools, famous from antiquity, ensure that navigation in the strait is never dull.

The currents are generated by an unusual phenomenon: high water at the northern end of the Strait coincides with low water at the southern end, and vice versa. Though the difference in tide levels is less than one foot at springs, it is concentrated into such a short distance (about three miles) that currents of four knots are common. This constant intermixing of two different water masses gives rise to an important fishery worked by small open boats, but these boats provide a unique mail service for passing ships.

There is a custom, quite common on the regular traders through the strait, of posting letters and cards in bottles with some cigarettes, or cigars, included. The fishermen recover these and post the mail as soon as they get ashore. It's a marvellous tradition, and amazingly reliable. However, seeing is believing, and only two bottles (the captain's and executive officer's) were chucked over the side; the rest of the crew were too sceptical to risk disposing of their tobacco in such a manner. For the record, the cards 'dispatched' reached Passage West and Monkstown, Co. Cork, within a day or so of letters air-mailed from Gibraltar!!!

A few days later, on 12 December, we were off the Rock, looking forward to a well-earned break. We went alongside our berth at 0845hrs but replenishment of fuel and water had first to be got underway before shore liberty. However, this didn't take long and within an hour or so only the bare duty watch remained on board. Gibraltar has always been looked on by seamen as a 'good run ashore', and even if these days inflation has dulled the image a bit there are still many bargains for those who persevere, particularly in cameras, watches, and electrical goods. It was fortunate that no cruise liners or large naval units were in port, otherwise the traders would have marked their prices to match the demands. Although half the fun of shopping there was in knocking the price of an item down to the lowest possible level. By the time we sailed few on board would need (or could afford) Christmas shopping at home! It was a very hectic two-day visit.

On the afternoon of the fourteenth, we were all set to resume the voyage. There were none more surprised than ourselves that a tentative schedule agreed a month previously was still holding; a long delay in the eastern Mediterranean could easily have materialised. As we sailed from Gibraltar that afternoon we savoured a last flash of sunshine and hoped for a quick passage to Cobh, but the weather maps for the North Atlantic and western approaches painted a tale of woe. If they were right, and a quick radio call to Haulbowline said they were, we were heading into some of the worst winter gales for several years.

Rounding southern Portugal, we met a long heavy swell, but little wind; that was to come on the last day of the trip when we were well into the Bay of Biscay. A westerly gale of force 9 to 10 that day kept us on our toenails (sometimes). However, with the wind and sea on the beam the ship's speed held up well. Of course, this caused some very heavy rolling which, without stabilisers and good stability, could have meant heaving to until the worst of the storm passed. Keeping up a reasonable speed brought us closer to a lee from the land all the time, so that by mid-morning on 17 December, we were in sight of familiar landmarks like the Old Head of Kinsale and Roche's Point. The awful weather conditions ensured that this landfall was even more welcome than it had always promised to be.

When *Emer* was secured to her berth at 1317hrs a voyage of 24 days and 6,281 miles ended. For the Naval Service this had been an historic and unique voyage. It was made all the more so because it signified a taste of things to come, and the sight of the UN standard flying high on *Emer* while alongside in Beirut was a source of much deep pride for all on board.

1981
Ambush in South Lebanon

Capt John Sheehan

At last light on 7 December 1981 Pte Edward Doyle, A Company, 50 Irishbatt, was driving with a passenger Signalman Christopher Mc-Nally along a narrow unsurfaced mountain track. On rounding a narrow bend, he was confronted by an ambush situation. A large stone had been placed on the track as an obstruction and there were armed men astride the track covering the obstruction. These men, six in number, opened automatic fire on Pte Doyle's vehicle from two sides. Pte Doyle skilfully drove his vehicle around the obstacle while under intense automatic small arms fire. In the process, he received bullet wounds in the right shoulder and left hand. Notwithstanding this severe disability, Pte Doyle drove on and brought his vehicle and passenger safely to his destination. Eleven rounds impacted within the passenger area. Pte Doyle's wounds necessitated surgery and he was subsequently repatriated to Ireland.

For displaying courage and determination of a high order when under intense automatic small arms fire from close range, he maintained control of his vehicle despite severe injuries and drove it with great skill and courage out of range of ambushers to a place of safety.

Pte Edward Doyle was awarded The Distinguished Service Medal.

LEBANON NEWS

Extracts from the UNIFIL Daily News Summary *covering the period 15 December 1980 to 15 March 1981*

1. On 17 December, at 1200 LT (Local Time), two United Nations Military Observers (one American, one French) attached to UNIFIL were stopped in the vicinity of Bidyas, near the Litani river, by seven elements of Arab Liberation Front – a Palestinian faction. The armed elements forced the unarmed observers to lie face down on the ground and fired one rifle round to within one metre of one of the observers while their vehicle was searched. The two observers were released at 1235 LT.

2. An armed element patrol was intercepted on the night of 13 December one kilometre north-west of Rachaya El-Foukhar. Norwegian patrol fired a warning shot, the armed elements fired back with rifles and three hand grenades. UNIFIL Patrol fired back. One armed element was wounded through right arm. Armed elements were then surrounded and apprehended.

3. On 19 December, between 0630 and 0640 LT, the Norwegian and Ghanaian-North battalion areas were hit by rockets from armed element positions north of the Litani. Twenty-six rockets impacted in the Norwegian sector and twenty in the Ghanaian sector. There were no UNIFIL casualties. Several prefabricated installations and vehicles were severely damaged in both battalions. This is the first time since the inception of UNFIL that a massive rocket attack has been launched from Palestinian sources into UNIFIL positions.

4. On 20 December, a Fijian soldier was wounded when a Lebanese civilian fired two rocket-propelled grenades at UNIFIL position near Glaile. The civilian was upset because UNIFIL wanted to search his car.

5. On 21 December, armed elements opened fire, including rocket-propelled grenades against two Fijian positions south of Qana. Fire was returned. During the incident, a UNIFIL vehicle with four Fijian soldiers was hijacked. Three of the soldiers managed to get away, one of them bringing an AK-47 rifle belonging to the armed elements. The fourth Fijian was later released.

6. On 21 December, a UNIFIL vehicle with two Nigerian officers from UNIFIL HQ came under fire from five armed elements on the coastal road in the vicinity of Ras El Ain. One officer sustained minor

injuries, the vehicle was damaged.

7. *On 23 December, De Facto Forces fired 40 heavy machine-gun rounds towards Irish listening posts in the vicinity of Bra'shit. Fire was returned.*

8. On 25 December, a UNIFIL helicopter flying to Tibnin to evacuate an injured civilian came under HMG fire from Palestinian positions around Rashidiye Camp. The same helicopter was also fired at on its return flight.

9. On 26 December, four armed DFF personnel attempted to hijack a Norwegian battalion vehicle, south of Marjayoun. The Norwegian officer in the vehicle prevented the attempt as well as a second attempt on the same road.

10. On 30 December, at 2000 LT, a four-man armed element patrol approaching a UNIFIL position east of Blate was challenged by Norwegian soldiers. When this warning was not heeded, the UNIFIL position first fired warning shots. When the armed elements kept on advancing, firing for effect was initiated. The armed elements then withdrew to north.

11. On 31 December, some armed elements attempted to occupy a hill feature in Wadi Jilu area. They withdrew after negotiations.

12. On 31 December, two unarmed UN military observers were ambushed by four unidentified armed elements south of Tyre and robbed of all their official and personal items, including money.

13. On 1 January, at 1700 LT, there was a tense confrontation between a Fiji patrol and an 11-man armed element patrol in the vicinity of Aytit. The armed elements eventually withdrew from the area.

14. On 5 January, a Fiji patrol was ambushed by armed elements north of Qana. Tension was defused through negotiations.

15. On 13 January, at 2345 LT, a tense situation developed at Wadi Jilu, when armed elements opened fire at the Fijian positions. Warning shots were returned by Fijian soldiers. Armed elements then intensified their fire with small arms and four RPGs, impacting directly on the house occupied by Fijian personnel, who fired back for effect. Fijian soldiers then withdrew to a high ground. Tension was defused later. No known casualties on either side.

16. On 16 January, a UNIFIL helicopter conveying the Force Commander General Erskine from Naquora to Fiji battalion headquarters in Qana was fired at from a National Movement position at Jabal Kabir. Between 10 and 15 HMG rounds were fired at the helicopter at about 1230 LT. A nearby Fiji position fired with light machine-guns to the origin of armed element firing to neutralise their fire. There were no casualties on UNIFIL side. Subsequent investigation revealed one bullet hit on the UNIFIL helicopter.

17. On 17 January, during the early hours of the morning, Fiji bat-

talion carried out an operation to occupy an armed element position previously set up in its area. The operation was carried out without any incidents and the position occupied by UNIFIL troops. At 1148 LT, one armed element approaching the position was waved away and when he did not stop, a warning shot was fired, about 10 minutes later Fiji battalion headquarters' complex in Qana was sprayed with approximately 45 machine-gun rounds. Fijian sentries returned the fire. During this indiscriminate firing directed to Fiji battalion headquarters one Fijian soldier was critically wounded. He was evacuated first to UNIFIL hospital in Naquora and then to Ramban Hospital in Haifa where he died two days later. During the incident two Fijian soldiers were briefly detained by armed elements in Qana and then released.

18. On 18 January, at about 1910 LT, one Dutch patrol intercepted three armed elements in an area north of El Mansuri. Three AK-47 rifles and four hand grenades were confiscated from the infiltrators.

19. During the period under review, in other incidents:

a. Fiji battalion denied entry to 66 armed elements and confiscated two AK-47 rifles, 11 pistols, two hand-grenades and assorted ammunition from vehicles searched at checkpoints. Fiji battalion also prevented movement of three armed element patrols of 24 men.

b. Dutch battalion prevented movement of six armed element patrols of total 36 men, six AK-47 rifles and four hand-grenades were confiscated.

c. *Irish battalion checkpoints confiscated one hand-grenade and one AK-47 rifle.*

d. Ghanaian battalion denied movement of two armed elements.

e. Nigerian battalion confiscated two pistols.

f. Armed elements fired close once to a Dutch position south of Siddiqine, once to the Dutch position north of Mansoura, twice to the Dutch position at Rishknaniyeh and twice to Dutch armoured personnel carriers.

20. On 19 January, at 1800hrs, De Facto Forces fired two artillery rounds to Tyre with one round impacting in the town. At 0230hrs on 20 January, three artillery rounds were fired from the enclave to Rashidiye area. At 1200hrs, Palestinian positions north of Litani fired two mortar rounds to an area west of Marjayoun. DFF responded with two mortar rounds at 1325hrs. At 1612hrs, Palestinian positions resumed firing with 13 mortars to west of Marjayoun. At 1653hrs, DFF opened up and fired a total of seven tank and 13 artillery rounds. Firing in this sector ceased at 1835hrs.

At 1930hrs, an Irish battalion listening post in the vicinity of Haddathah came under light machine-gun fire from three unidentified armed elements. Irish troops returned fire.

21. On 20 January, at 1540hrs, a Fiji battalion checkpoint at Ain Baal denied entry to a vehicle of Iraqi Bath transporting military uniforms. The vehicle turned back into the Tyre pocket. At 1600hrs, armed elements, reinforced by other factions, returned to the area and two Fijian positions at Ain Baal came under fire with many machine-gun rounds impacting within the positions and on Fiji quarters. Fijian troops could not return fire as the armed elements were using as cover a UNIFIL truck they had detained at their checkpoint on the road leading to Tyre. The situation was defused after 10 minutes of firing with the intervention of UN military observers and PLO liaison officers in Tyre. However, at 1730hrs, the same two Fijian positions again came under automatic rifle, machine-gun and rocket-propelled grenade fire from armed elements. Four Fijian positions in the vicinity returned fire. Firing lasted about 20 minutes. There were no UNIFIL casualties. A 15-year old girl from Ain Baal village was hit on her arm with an armed element bullet. She was treated at Fiji battalion medical centre.

22. On 21 January, a Dutch patrol apprehended three armed elements (two from PFLP and one from Fatah) at Kafra.

23. On 22 January, Israeli Defence Forces fired close to a Dutch position at Ras Al Bayyadah and a Dutch armoured vehicle in the vicinity.

24. On 23 January, eight armed elements with a jeep with mounted anti-aircraft gun tried to force their way through a Fijian checkpoint. They were denied entry.

Heavy exchange of fire in which artillery, mortars, tanks and rockets were used broke out initially in the north-east sector when PLO forces started to fire at 1107hrs to an area immediately west of Marjayoun and El Qlaiaa. In this sector, until 1705hrs, PLO forces fired approximately 129 artillery/mortar rounds mainly to Mahmoudiye and Mourbhiye areas until 1745hrs. In the western sector, at 1535hrs, DFF fired three artillery rounds into Tyre and three artillery rounds to Rashidiye. At 1732hrs, Palestinian elements fired six rockets from an area east of Tyre towards south.

25. On 24 January, IDF fired close to the Dutch position at Ras al Bayyadah.

DFF fired three artillery rounds from Tair Harfa to an area south-east of Wadi Jilu.

At about 2030hrs, five suspected armed elements fired with small arms to the DFF tank position at Bayt Yahun. This position returned fire with HMG and three mortar rounds to Haddathah. *Irish battalion immediately initiated patrols which compelled the armed elements to with-draw from the area.*

During the week of 19 to 25 January, DFF fired close, one to Dutch position at Majdal Zun, another on the coastal road and a third near Sribbin.

26. On 28 January, the Dutch position in Chihine blocked an attempt by six DFF personnel in a half-track to enter into UNIFIL area.

Exchange of fire started at 0920hrs with firing of two mortar rounds by DFF to Mourbhiye ended at 0406hrs, on 29 January. In the exchange more than 500 heavy artillery, mortar, tank rounds and rockets were fired.

First firing from the Palestinian positions to an area west of Marjayoun was at 1314hrs. In this area, DFF resumed their firing targets north of Litani river at 1500hrs. In the western sector, between 1616–1640hrs, DFF fired nine artillery rounds to the vicinity of Tyre-Rashidiye. At 1830hrs, Palestinian units fired six rockets to Tair Harfa, to the vicinity of DFF artillery piece used for shelling of Tyre and environs. Rate of firing by the sides then rapidly escalated.

In the western sector, the exchange lasted until 0100hrs with DFF firing a total of 32 artillery rounds and the Palestinians firing 20 rockets. In the north-eastern sector, approximately 215 artillery/mortar and tank rounds were fired from the enclave to a wide range of targets including Kfar Tibnite, Rihane and Mourbhiye. Palestinian forces, believed to be mainly Fatah elements, fired approximately 220 artillery/mortar rounds and rockets impacted in northern Israel. Firing in this sector ceased at 0406hrs. During the exchange, three mortar rounds fired by Palestinian units impacted close to a Norwegian position at the Khardala bridge while two rockets impacted close to a Ghanaian position at Blate.

27. On 29 January, at 1413hrs, four Israeli Air Force jet aircraft conducted airstrikes against Mashuq (about two km east of Tyre) and Hammadiyah, three km north-east of Tyre. Heavy anti-aircraft fire and at least four ground-to-air missiles (shoulder held Strella type) were observed in this area.

At 1417hrs, two Israeli jets struck Mazraat Ouazasiye, approximately three kms north-east of Jarmaq. At 1545hrs one mortar round fired from Palestinian positions impacted within 20 metres of a Norwegian position, east of Blate. No casualties.

At 1930hrs, Palestinian positions fired five mortar rounds to Marjayoun. DFF fired back two rounds at 0200hrs. During the early hours of the morning of 30 January, Palestinian positions in the vicinity of Beaufort Castle fired eight rockets into Israel. Israeli media reported impacts in Kiryat Shemona.

28. On 30 January, at 0710hrs, elements of Popular Front for Liberation of Palestine (PFLP) fired six rockets from south of Tyre pocket into Israel.

At 0905hrs, Israeli Defence Forces and De Facto Forces opened heavy artillery fire mainly towards Jarmaq, Mahmoudiye, Mourbhiye and Nabatiyah area. Until 1135hrs, an approximate total of 142 artillery /mortar rounds were fired. One round was fired from an unidentified armed element position to Marjayoun.

29. *On 01 February, DFF fired indiscriminately to an Irish foot patrol in the village of Ayta az Zutt.*

30. On 02 February, DFF fired close to the Dutch position at Al Jibbayn.

31. On 03 February, DDF fired close to a Nigerian patrol.

32. On 05 February, during the night DFF fired close twice to the Dutch position at Majdal Zun and once to a Dutch position at Jabal Basil.

33. On 06 February, DFF fired six mortar rounds to targets north of Litani while Palestinian position fired two rounds to east of El Qlaiaa.

34. On 07 February, DFF fired close to a Dutch armoured vehicle at Al Bayyadah. Between 2037 and 2333hrs, Palestinian positions fired seven mortar rounds to an area south of Khiam village. In the exchange, 27 artillery/mortar rounds were fired from the enclave to targets north of Litani.

35. *On 08 February, at 2155hrs, eight unidentified armed persons were detected immediately to the west of Bra'shit. Irish battalion patrols were sent out and the area was illuminated with mortar flares. The eight-man group then started to withdraw south towards Bayt Yahun. In the pursuit, warning shots were fired by Irish patrols. At 2230hrs, DFF position at Bayt Yahun opened up with heavy machine-gun fire towards Irish patrols. Further contact with the armed persons was not possible due to heavy driving rains and very low visibility which also made positive identification of the armed group impossible.*

36. On 09 February, at 2000hrs, a Lebanese boy of 16 years of age was kidnapped from the village of Majdal Zun, in Dutch battalion area, by four armed men. The car used for the kidnapping was stolen from the same village. The car was stopped at a Dutch checkpoint in the village of Mansoura where the kidnappers opened fire on a Dutch battalion vehicle. The Dutch soldiers of UNIFIL returned the fire. The armed men then fled leaving the boy behind. UNIFIL patrols sent out spotted three of the kidnappers in the vicinity of Buyut as Sayyid. Another clash took place in which Dutch soldiers fired warning shots and gas grenades. The three men withdrew south towards Al Bayya-

dah, in the enclave. A few moments later, a Dutch battalion check-point on the coastal road came under heavy machine-gun fire from the DFF position at Al Bayyadah.

37. On 11 February, an artillery exchange took place in the eastern sector between Israeli Defence Forces/De Facto Forces on one hand and Palestinian units on the other. Between 1630 and 2030hrs, Israeli Defence Forces/De Facto Forces batteries fired approximately 170 artillery/mortar rounds from seven positions in the enclave to targets north and west of Litani river. Palestinian units fired approximately 70 artillery/mortar rounds from four positions into the enclave. During the exchange, 12 mortar rounds impacted in the Norwegian battalion area, with six rounds hitting close to UNIFIL positions. There were no UNIFIL casualties. Subsequent investigations indicate that some of the rounds were fired from armed elements positions to the north.

38. On 16 February, early in the morning, at 0130hrs, there was an exchange of fire between unknown number of unidentified armed elements and a Fijian post near Al Hinniyah. The Dutch battalion supported the Fijians by firing flares over the area. The armed elements withdrew into Tyre pocket. This was confirmed by UNIFIL patrol sent to sweep the orange groves. There were no UNIFIL casualties.

39. On 16 February, at 1600hrs, a seven-man unidentified armed element patrol was detected moving towards the village of Kafra in Dutch battalion area. A Dutch interception patrol was sent out and blocking positions established. After visual contact was made with the infiltrators at about 1630hrs, UNIFIL troops fired warning shots which did not initially deter the infiltrators, UNIFIL troops then started to use gas grenades and the armed elements withdrew from the area.

40. On 17 February, De Facto Forces fired close to a Dutch position south of Yatar.

41. On 19 February, at 2000hrs, DFF fired six artillery rounds to north of Litani river. At 2307hrs, Palestinian positions returned six rounds to west of Marjayoun.

42. On 20 February, at 0445hrs, small arms fire broke out from Tulin and an explosion was heard. The firing was directed to a Nigerian position where the tent of Lebanese soldiers was damaged. Fire was returned. It was discovered later that a clinic used by two doctors was blown up under peculiar circumstances. The explosion which caused no casualties but destroyed medicines and equipment of the private clinic was on a second floor of a house. The owner of the house, living on the ground floor, was unhurt. Investigations are underway.

Tension rose in Bra'shit when a pro-National Movement group and a family supporting AMAL movement decided to pursue their difference with guns. Irish troops immediately intervened and deployed between feuding parties. An intervention attempt by DFF from the south was blocked. The Irish officer in charge of the area arranged for a meeting in the village mosque between the parties and the problem appears to have been solved peacefully.

At 2000hrs, a mobile Dutch checkpoint stopped a patrol of four armed elements of different factions, in an area between Siddiqine and Kafra. Four AK-47 rifles, one anti-tank mine and one blasting charge were confiscated. At 2150hrs, a Dutch patrol intercepted an 18-man Israeli Defence Forces/DFF patrol, south of Zibqin. The intruding patrol, which initially refused to negotiate, was persuaded to withdraw from the area under the control of the Dutch patrol.

43. On 22 February, many overflights of Israeli planes over south Lebanon were observed. Between 1000 and 1100hrs, two Israeli jets attracted heavy anti-aircraft fire from Tyre region. Starting at 1900hrs, Israeli helicopters started to drop illumination flares over Tyre area as well as western part of Senegalese battalion area, while helicopter and jet overflights continued on a large scale in all sectors.

At 2225hrs, gun positions in the enclave started to fire to targets north of Litani, concentrating mainly on vicinity of Nabatiyah and Beaufort Castle. Palestinian gun positions responded after midnight by firing mainly to Marjayoun and environs. In the exchange lasting until 0515hrs, 23 February, DFF positions in the enclave fired approximately 300 artillery/tank/mortar rounds and Palestinian positions north of Litani fired approximately 180 artillery/mortar rounds.

UNIFIL has no observation reports on Israeli Defence Forces operations during the night in the vicinity of Nabatiyah, as reported by the media. This operation, originating from an area not under UNIFIL control, was directed against targets well to the north of Litani river and there was no movement through UNIFIL controlled sectors.

44. On 24 February, DFF fired close to a Dutch patrol in an area west of Majdal Zun.

45. *On 25 February, DFF personnel at Bayt Yahun created tension in the area by attempting to establish a checkpoint north of Bayt Yahun. Irish battalion reserve was activated. DFF personnel then withdrew.*

A Dutch patrol intercepted a three-man armed element patrol, north of Kafra and confiscated four hand-grenades. DFF fired close to a Dutch position near Sribbin.

46. On 27 February, DFF fired close to a Dutch position near Yatar, to a Dutch position at Majdal Zun, and four mortar rounds close to a Ghanaian position south of Kaoukaba. A Norwegian position blocked four armed elements attempting to infiltrate through the Hasbani valley, south of Kaoukaba. The armed elements withdrew north, threatening reprisals to UNIFIL personnel.

Between 1336 and 1414hrs, DFF fired one artillery round to vicinity of Rashidiye and three rounds to vicinity of Tyre. Between 2234 and 0315hrs, DFF fired 43 artillery/mortar rounds to Beaufort Castle and Jarmaq areas. At 0115hrs, Palestinian position fired 13 mortar rounds to vicinity of El Qlaiaa.

During the night, Israeli Defence Forces fired illumination flares over Beaufort Castle, over the seas of Al Bayyadah and around Marwahin. Later in the night heavy firing was heard form IDF south of Naquora and DFF north of Naquora to unknown targets.

47. On 01 March, during the night, unidentified persons fired one rocket-propelled grenade into Fiji battalion headquarters in Qana, causing some damage but no casualties.

48. On 02 March, PLO elements fired close to a Dutch position north of Siddiqine. Unidentified armed elements fired close to a Fijian position south of Qana.

DFF fired close to an Irish position near Haddathah.

At 1540hrs, six Israeli Air Force jets attacked an area to the north of Kasmiya bridge, on the Litani river. At 1830hrs, 14 unidentified projectiles, some believed to be Katyushka rockets were fired from general area of Beaufort Castle, some impacting in Israel. At 1830hrs, second Israeli air strike, lasting 20 minutes was observed in the same area as the first one. In the second strike, approximately 23 explosions were noted. In the Marjayoun–Nabatiyah sector, exchange commenced at 1900hrs, and ceased at 0200hrs. While IDF and DFF fire concentrated around Beaufort Castle, Zawtar ash Sharqiyah and Shukin, Palestinian fire was directed mainly to the vicinity of Marjayoun. In the western sector, firing started at 1900hrs, and lasted until 0200hrs. After a lull of three and half hours, firing was resumed by the sides until 0700hrs. In this sector, IDF and DFF concentrated on Rashidiye, an area south of Tyre town and Burj as Shamali. There were also reports of firing from an Israeli gunboat. On the Palestinian/National Movement side, there was heavy anti-aircraft fire to overflying jets, and approximately 64 Katyushka rockets fired from Tyre pocket towards south. Some of the rockets impacted in Israel. Four rockets impacted approximately three kilometres north-east of Naquora.

49. On 03 March, at 0843hrs, DFF later joined by IDF opened up from the Marjayoun area and started to shell general area of Hasbaya, Bourrhoz, Dellafi, Yohmor, Beaufort Castle. Up until 1400hrs, IDF/DFF had fired approximately 140 artillery/mortar/tank rounds. In this sector, Palestinian positions fired five mortar rounds to Marjayoun area. In the western sector at 0855hrs, six Katyushka rockets were fired from Tyre pocket to north-west Israel. At 0902hrs, DFF started mortar fire from Al Bayyadah and fired 16 rounds to general area of Al

Qulaylah and Rashidiye until 1400hrs. Unidentified armed elements fired close to a Fijian position near Qana. At 1730hrs, DFF resumed shelling of Tyre pocket and fired 10 artillery rounds from Tair Harfa to vicinity of Rashidiye, and Tyre. At 2007hrs, unidentified armed elements fired five rockets from an area south of Hasbaya towards south. No impacts observed or reported.

50. On 04 March, two Fijian soldiers came under fire from a civilian vehicle in the vicinity of Ain Baal. Fire could not be returned because of presence of other vehicles on the road.

51. On 05 March, Between 0200 and 0300hrs, DFF fired three mortar rounds to Hasbaya area and 22 rounds to targets west of Litani. A Fijian patrol came under fire from unidentified elements in Qana.

52. On 06 March, DFF fired close to a Dutch position near Yatar.

53. On 07 March, DFF fired close to a Dutch position at Chihine, also twice to the Dutch position on the Hamra bridge at Ras el Biyada.

54. On 09 March, at 1300hrs, a Nigerian position detected five armed elements attempting to infiltrate into UNIFIL area by crossing the Litani river from a point west of Yohmor. Nigerian soldiers fired warning shots and the armed elements withdrew north. At 1700hrs, a Dutch position detected five armed elements from an unidentified faction attempting to infiltrate towards Haris. A Dutch patrol took up blocking positions and gas grenades were fired as warning. The armed elements withdrew northwards. 45 minutes later, the Dutch position involved in the operation came under heavy and light machine-gun fire, lasting 20 minutes. There were no UNIFIL casualties.

55. On 10 March, situation in Jwayya was defused during the morning through negotiations. However, during the afternoon there was some tension when two UN officers were detained by PLO elements in the area for a short period and then released after intervention by UNIFIL HQ. UNIFIL deployed reinforcements at Jwayya and the situation has stabilised. Reinforcements were withdrawn on 13 March.

56. On 13 March, at 0040hrs, four unidentified armed elements fired four rocket-propelled grenades to a DFF position in vicinity of Blate. DFF position returned heavy machine-gun fire. An intervention patrol by UNIFIL came under rifle fire by the armed elements withdrawing northwards. UNIFIL troops fired 20 mortar illumination towards the AEs during the pursuit. Following threats by DFF against the stationing of one platoon (about 30 men) of Lebanese army in Qantara, at 1215hrs one Lebanese army doctor, two army medical assistants and one driver visiting Qantara were forced at gunpoint to drive in their ambulance into the enclave held by the militia.

DFF fired close to an Irish position near At Tiri and close to a Norwegian position north of Mari.

57. On 14 March, an exchange of heavy shelling was observed in the eastern sector, with DFF firing approximately 45 artillery / mortar / tank rounds to west of Litani river while Palestinian forces fired 30 mortar rounds.

DFF fired close to an Irish armoured personnel carried at Bayt Yahun. At 1140hrs, DFF fired six tank rounds from south of Taibe to an area immediately to the east of Qantara. Two of these rounds impacted close to a Nigerian patrol. At 1515hrs, DFF fired seven further rounds to Qantara.

58. On 15 March, unidentified armed elements fired close to a Fijian position at Qana. UN personnel returned fire. No further contacts. DFF fired close to Ghanaian position in vicinity of Blate, close to two Dutch positions near Yatar. At 1910hrs, 13 heavy shells were fired by DFF into Qantara, with some of the rounds impacting close to the Nigerian position in the village. Four civilians (one child, one woman, two men) were wounded and treated by UNIFIL medical personnel. Two of the civilian casualties were from a house hit by a round which did not detonate. At 2215hrs, one more round was fired into the village.

Patrolling the countryside

INTERVIEW WITH BBC RADIO

MAJ GEN BILL CALLAGHAN (IRL)
[FORCE COMMANDER UNIFIL]

General Bill Callaghan is the outspoken new Irish commander of the United Nations Peacekeeping Force in southern Lebanon and has indicated that he is going to get tough and intends to stop PLO infiltration into Israel. He also says he is determined to restore southern Lebanon to the Lebanese government. General Callaghan also warned recently that he will use force if necessary to enforce the mandate after Israeli-backed Christian militia were responsible for killing three Nigerian UN soldiers in a shelling attack. That is tough talking to say the least from any UN commander.

The interviewer asked this top veteran of many a UN Peacekeeping Force why he was so outspoken.

Gen Callaghan: 'Well the Lord made me a certain way and I don't think I can change that, and anyway I wouldn't want to change. I am a very positive professional soldier.'

Q: What does that mean in terms of on-the-ground operations?

Gen Callaghan: 'It means professionalism, directness, honesty of purpose, objectivity, and a willingness to negotiate with anybody at any time on ongoing peacekeeping, but never, and I repeat never, in response to the threat of fire or any threats like that. Nobody can do negotiation that way, and I would clarify and say that negotiation does not [necessarily] mean coming to what are reasonable accommodation.s'

Q: What would you like to see Major Haddad do now to make your task easier?

Gen Callaghan: 'I do not isolate Major Haddad, or the armed elements, or anybody, because co-operation is the name of the game here. You know I find it very hard to explain to volunteer soldiers sent by participating nations to do a job to help Lebanon re-assert its authority why they come here and are fired at, mortared, tanked. You know I find it very hard to get my soldiers to understand that situation – but I think they do. However I also think this is so unfair, and so unjust, and so unreasonable in our circumstances.'

Q: How do you reply to Major Haddad's comment that the attack on the Nigerian soldiers was an accident?

Gen Callaghan: 'The word "accident" in the English language is very clear. It means that it was unavoidable. Certainly let me say, without any doubt the word "accident" is not in context here.'

Q: Do you accept that if you want to adopt a more positive role in southern Lebanon your forces will have to take more casualties?

Gen Callaghan: 'You know in a situation such as this, one has to accept casualties in the implementation of a mandate. But you only get casualties when somebody fires at you, and I say stop the firing at us. I think it is unfair to the soldiers, it is unreasonable, and it is wrong.'

Q: Finally you are a soldier who has seen experience on the Irish border with Northern Ireland partly stopping infiltration as you are doing here. Can you compare the two jobs in any way? Are they similar?

Gen Callaghan: 'That's a political question, but I will comment on infiltration. When you talk about infiltration I think UNIFIL should be complimented on its effectiveness in preventing infiltration. You know recently there was much made in Jerusalem about an attempt to over-fly the UNIFIL area of operations – and indeed one was successful. But surely, this is a compliment to the work of UNIFIL on the ground if one has to adopt that method to infiltrate.'

On patrol

1982
FOUR OBSERVERS KILLED

CAPT JOHN SHEEHAN

In the late afternoon of 25 September 1982, four United Nations military observers operating in the mountains east of Beirut were reported as killed when their vehicle hit a number of anti-tank mines. UNTSO's Beirut HQ tried without success to obtain details as to the exact location of the incident, or the extent of the casualties. The location was a front line area in the conflict between Syrian and Israeli forces known to be mined and subject to frequent exchanges of artillery and mortar fire.

In these circumstances Comdt Michael Lynch volunteered without hesitation to secure an ambulance from the Lebanese Armed Forces and recover the bodies of the fallen UNMOs. He went to the Lebanese Armed Forces HQ, secured an ambulance and escort of four soldiers and set out for Bzibden, behind Syrian lines, where the bodies were reported to be. Operating under an imposed radio silence he reached Bzibden, returned with the bodies, and succeeded in bringing them to the American University Hospital.

As the circumstances of the accident itself illustrate, the dangers involved in undertaking such an operation late at night in hostile territory, between the opposing armies of Syria and Israel, were considerable and would be difficult to exaggerate. One of those killed on that day was Comdt. Michael Nestor from Newbridge, Co. Kildare.

For showing exemplary loyalty to his fallen fellow UNMOs, and with disregard for his own safety, displaying the highest degree of courage and initiative in undertaking and successfully following through a difficult and dangerous mission behind Syrian lines in the mountains east of Beirut on the night of 25 September 1982, and for reflecting through his actions during the mission outstanding credit on himself and his country Comdt Michael Lynch was awarded The Military Medal for Gallantry.

1982

AMAL – THE LEBANESE RESISTANCE REGIMENTS

CAPT WALLY YOUNG

The recent Israeli invasion of Lebanon has highlighted the relatively unknown Muslim group AMAL. Immediately after the invasion, the International Press reported that the Israeli army were arming AMAL members in south Lebanon with light weapons and entrusting them with the security of an area already cleared of PLO fighters.

During a recent tour of duty in Lebanon, my attention was immediately drawn to the presence of AMAL. Their symbolic black flags were prominently displayed and posters and photographs of their leaders were visible in many villages. AMAL officials also had direct liaison with the UN. During the course of this short article, it is intended to discuss the development and doctrine of the AMAL faction.

AMAL has grown and developed from the poorer Shi'ite Muslim classes of southern Lebanon. (It is reckoned that Shi'ites form only 10% of all Muslims while the Sunnis are the majority sect with 80%.) In July 1975, the AMAL group as we know it today was established. The driving force behind its foundation was Imam Moussa Sadr who had come from Iran in the early 1950s. Sadr was politically motivated and endeavoured to organise the Shi'ite Muslim population. He tried to make them aware of their limited influence in Lebanese politics, and as a forerunner to the formation of AMAL he created the 'Movement for the Deprived' in 1973.

In 1975, after their formation, AMAL members declared that their aim was 'to protect Lebanon and maintain its dignity'. Today this aim is simply stated as 'Lebanon for the Lebanese'.

A tragic but major factor in the group's development and popularity was the unexplained disappearance of Imam Moussa Sadr while in Libya in 1978. He is still recognised as leader of the group and his untimely disappearance has never been explained, thus he holds an air of mystique for his followers.

AMAL is a national movement and at a time of overt outside influence in Lebanon, this was a factor in gaining popular support. Its leaders preached the 'Lebanon for the Lebanese' policy and voiced continued support for the official government. AMAL strongly favoured the UN presence in Lebanon and it clearly understood the UN presence was there at the request of the government. Indirectly it created some problems for the UN as its 'Lebanon for the Lebanese' policy occasionally developed into clashes on the ground between PLO and AMAL fighters.

AMAL is also a religious movement but its only condition for enlistment is a belief in God. It openly declares that people of all religious backgrounds are welcome to its fold, whether they be Muslim, Christian, or Jewish. The group also aims to assist the poor and deprived in Lebanon and helps in educating those in need, and indeed there was some initial evidence of these aims being realised. Despite AMAL's flexible outlook on membership, the accomplishment of those latter aims would certainly benefit the Shi'ite Muslims of Lebanon more than any other group.

AMAL's open-minded outlook was of course one of the reasons why the Israelis armed AMAL members after the recent invasion. From the outset, this seemed an unlikely alliance and it was not surprising to read in a back issue of the *Irish Times* that 'Last month the Israelis attempted to arm local Muslim support of Israel but after two weeks took the arms from them again'.

Despite its declaration to be 'a religious, popular and nationalist movement', which corresponds to the declaration of the Islamic revolution in Iran, AMAL claims to have no contact outside of Lebanon. In some villages, however, photo-posters of Ayatollah Khomeini hang alongside those of local leaders and it must be remembered that Imam Moussa Sadr did come from Iran in the first instance.

Despite being a relatively new political group AMAL is known to have its political/military structures. Imam Moussa Sadr is still regarded as a national leader but the leader in effect is Nabbih Berri. As far as AMAL is concerned the country is divided into three areas of influence: Beirut, which is also their headquarters, south Lebanon, and finally the Bekaa Valley which came to prominence during the recent war with Syrian forces occupying large parts of it. Each region is broken into different sectors over which there is a commander and each sector comprises villages in which there is also an appointed leader.

In the light of current events it would be difficult to assess AMAL's military strength and organisation. It fought alongside its Muslim brethren during the civil war in 1976, and since then with the PLO, and now it is reported that the Syrian forces have trained some of its members. The weapons used by AMAL are mostly small arms and from this one can reasonably assume that their military function, for the present at least, is purely defensive.

It is also difficult to assess AMAL's future in Lebanon in view of the current crisis there. Some months ago, I was chatting to an AMAL member who spoke emotionally of Lebanon and its people and seemed concerned about the future. He was not very complimentary of the PLO and stressed that they were not contributing to the welfare of the people. He was also concerned about Israeli intentions in south Lebanon especially in the area as far north as the Litani river where a large percentage of the Shi'ite populations live. His reasons for concern about Israeli intentions in the area were centred on Israel's historical claim to this region, and the fact that the Litani would provide a clearly defined and secure national boundary.

Since that conversation the PLO have left Lebanon and on several occasions since the recent crises began Israeli politicians have declared total disinterest in even 'one square inch of Lebanese territory'. If the people of Lebanon are allowed to settle their own complex political affairs, it seems certain that the AMAL group will represent the Shi'ite community in all areas.

AMAL remains a religious, popular and nationalist movement and as such is in conformity with the new trend of Muslim doctrine in the Middle East. In this context it will be interesting to see if AMAL opens up to outside influences, which, depending on the outcome of the Iran–Iraq wars, may also increase its status considerably.

In Arabic the word AMAL means 'hope' but the initials AMAL represent the first letters in an Arabic translation of 'The Lebanese Resistance Regiments'.

Observation Post – Hill 800

A scene from Operation Grapes of Wrath, 1996 [Photo: Armn John Daly]

Maj Gen Bill Callaghan – Force Commander UNIFIL [Photo: Irish Times]

The DFF in the early days – complete with half-track

*Never stuck for words – Abbas in
full flight* [Photo: Willy Barr]

The Ryan Line is open ...
[Photo: Armn John Daly]

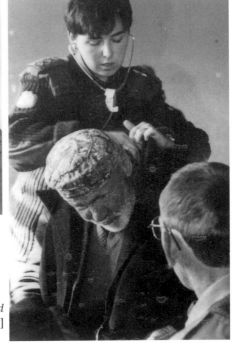

Smiling happy people
[Photo: Armn John Daly]

A helping hand
[Photo: Armn John Daly]

Patrolling in in the aftermath of the IDF withdrawal [Photo: Pádraig Higgins]

Picking up the pieces – again

Just another day in paradise ...

Check point 6–48 at Tibnin East [Photo: Armn John Daly]

Tell me now, what's a nice man like you doing in a place like this?
[Photo: Armn John Daly]

The Commander-in-Chief faces the media in Tibnin [Photo: Armn John Daly]

Early bird on the prowl

We will never forget

Painting the Blue Line at Rosh Haniqra

Walking 'The Line' at Manara

FIRST IMPRESSIONS

LT JOHN BROPHY

At one stage or another during an army career you hear the expression 'first impressions are lasting'. We all know by now that there is a lot of wisdom in that saying. Very few soldiers do *not* remember their thoughts on the army during those first 'strange' hours of training. Those are the kind of memories which stay with one forever. Likewise, anyone who has been to Lebanon and served with UNIFIL will have his own opinion of the country, its people, and the role the United Nations plays in trying to keep the peace there.

There are many wide and varied opinions however about Irishbatt and UNIFIL; possibly because every trip is so different, and the situation here is ever-changing. What forges lasting impressions as regards overseas service is a combination of many factors, but the most important thoughts and insights are provided by the people that make up each unit and formation.

For this reason the forming-up period in Ireland is very important. This provides an excellent opportunity for all ranks to get to know each other under working conditions, and gives an insight into the reaction of personnel when placed in different and difficult situations. This is a vital aspect of the training as everyone comes under pressure at some stage of the trip. There must be no doubt that all personnel are dependable in all foreseeable situations and that they thus maintain the high standards set by previous Irish battalions.

By the time training at home is complete everyone is prepared physically and mentally for a six-month tour abroad. Having put in long hours and hard work together for eight weeks, all ranks are eager to get there and settle into the job. While it can be hard to say goodbye at home, it becomes obvious as soon as the aircraft lands, that thoughts of home must temporarily be put aside and attention turned to the immediate work of taking over control from the outgoing battalion.

Upon arrival at Tel Aviv, with a full chalk standing on the tarmac, who arrives only the first chalk of the homeward bound battalion. We have not been there an hour and already the envy on some faces is obvious. Although the chalks don't mix, you can pick out the occasional greeting shouted from beyond the Aer Lingus 747, 'Hey Spike, Spike it's me. How's the form?' It takes Spike about half a minute to realise that the Indian-looking gentleman in the Khakis is none other than his old mate, Jockser. Alas, there is little time for jovial jibes or shouted replies as the convoy of white UN vehicles is readied to take us to the mountains and the battalion Area of Operations.

After a long journey, lasting four to five hours, the convoy finally arrives in Irishbatt AO. The different companies split up and make their way to the various company HQs. Here more greetings are exchanged, and almost immediately the briefings begin. The two platoon sergeants work together sorting out which posts need men immediately. This accomplished, the lads mount up again, and within the hour all the posts have a mixture of personnel from both battalions.

That night, despite the fact that everybody is very tired, few go to bed early. The new lads eagerly try to find out as much as possible about the scene in general, and the old ones want to get news of things at home first hand. Eventually a compromise is reached and information is traded. When everyone is satisfied, the groups split up and drag themselves under their 'Mossey Nets' for some well-earned sleep.

The first morning dawns, and it's straight to business. Six white men on the roof of a house in south Lebanon, listening to a well tanned and weathered lieutenant as he starts his briefing. 'North ... etc'. The white faces all turn as one, as another village is indicated within the small area that is the new company AO. Still it takes a few days to get to know the names of the different villages, and the radio call signs of the various UN posts. Over the two weeks of the handover period, the old battalion has to tell the newcomers as much as they can. By the end of the fortnight, everyone is looking forward to the arrival of the third chalk and the departure of the 'Heroes' Chalk. No disrespect to the outgoing lads, but it is not until they leave and our Chalk Three has arrived that the unit really settles in and begins to function efficiently and cohesively.

Meanwhile, our friend Spike finds himself moved to Hill 880 after the arrival of Chalk Three. He opens his locker, and is just about to unload his gear when he notices a piece of paper stuck to the inside. It is addressed to himself. Curious he picks it up and reads it: He smiles wryly and carries on. The note is now stuck on the locker door, and it reads: 'Don't worry Spike, the last five-and-a-half months are the hardest – Jockser'.

1984
54 IRISHBATT

COMDT PAT SULLIVAN

54 Irishbatt assumed operational control of the AO on 4 November 1983. The first problem encountered was the fact that just prior to our arrival the Dutch Battalion had been withdrawn from UNIFIL and was replaced by a Dutch Company. This led to a re-adjustment of all inter-battalion boundaries with a consequent increase in the size of Irishbatt's area and of course new responsibilities given that our area is now some one hundred square kilometres and includes fourteen villages the most important being Tibnin and Haris, the original home of HQ 43 Irishbatt back in 1978.

The population of the area is approximately 30,000 but this rises to about 50,000 during the summer holiday period or when there is heavy fighting in Beirut. Almost 100% Shia Muslim there are a small number of Christians in the villages of Tibnin, Bra'shit and Safad. However, the local Christians and Muslims co-habit peacefully in the area where the main means of livelihood is agriculture, with tobacco providing the main cash crop. In this regard, the closure of the main road to Beirut prevented the sale of this year's crop to the government monopoly and this in turn caused hardship for almost the entire local population.

Each village has its quota of small shops, garages, metals works, and schools. Building is also an important source of local employment with many houses and business premises in the course of construction for Lebanese who currently live abroad.

Geographically the area is characterised by numerous hills surrounded by deep wadis and this causes a communications problem both for road and radio traffic. The hills take the general form of two ridge-lines running east-west through the area. The southern ridge-line runs through Hill 880, while the northern line goes through Tibnin and Al Yahun.

The old Dutchbatt area is however more disjointed and poses greater communications difficulties with the important villages of Kafra and Yatar accessible only by one road each.

The battalion is deployed in three company areas running east –west in line with their headquarters at Bra'shit, Haddathah, and Haris (rotating every two months). Recce Company is located at Al Yahun to the rear, HQ Company is in Camp Shamrock, and battalion HQ is in Tibnin itself. Thereafter the battalion operates 38 posts including 14 checkpoints (six of which are containment positions around militia checkpoints), and 19 observation posts.

In light of the redeployment, Irishbatt's concept of operations was re-examined and it was decided that rather than focus on manning OPs the new emphasis would concentrate on controlling the road network, containing the militia CPs, and maintaining a village presence.

However, the battalion has had to contend with the fact that there are three other armed parties operating in our AO with six positions between them. First there is the DFF, the late Major Haddad's forces, who maintain three positions on the boundary between Irishbatt and the so called 'Christian Enclave' to the south – a CP at Bayt Yahun, a CP and an OP at the Cuckoo's Nest near R'shaf, and a CP on the road between Sribbin and Beit Leif. In each case, Irishbatt operates a CP on our side and in case of the Cuckoo's Nest also operates an OP.

Shia Militias known by UNIFIL as LAUIs (Locals Armed and Uniformed by the IDF) have two CPs actually in our AO at Bra'shit and Yatar, and our approach here is to contain their activities as these undisciplined illegal militias are much resented by the local population.

The third armed party is the IDF who occupy a house between Haris and Haddathah from which they mount mobile and foot patrols, occasionally setting up temporary CPs for short periods.

Another branch of the IDF also operates in civilian clothes and uses civilian vehicles in a measure to control the local population, the battalion response to these is one of observing and reporting their activities to UNIFIL HQ.

In response to all of these groups Irishbatt mans its OPs, CPs and containment positions while also conducting foot patrols, mobile patrols, armoured patrols, contributing to the Force Mobile Reserve, and maintaining a fire support plan. This ensures that Irishbatt controls entry of all armed element traffic onto the roads in our AO and enables us to deny entry to armed DFF except when they are accompanied by the IDF.

The battalion also maintains a village presence in all villages except Ayta az Zutt, Safad and Kafra. All villages are extensively patrolled by day and night and this was intensified following IDF activity in some unoccupied places.

Up to the end of March 1984 the principle incidents which occurred involved the confiscation of small arms from militiamen, denial of entry or exit to armed and/or uniformed militiamen, and a number of situations when LAUIs detained UN personnel and their vehicles at gunpoint. There were also a number of incidents in which militiamen fired small arms close to Irishbatt positions or personnel. The battalion response was to reply in kind and no more shooting took place.

The village of R'shaf, which was almost destroyed in 1978 and had remained unoccupied ever since, was re-occupied by its people shortly after 54 Irishbatt arrived. Then the DFF from the Cuckoo's Nest set up a CP on the road to Haddathah. Irishbatt responded by setting up its own CP to monitor what was now a new entry point into our AO. We also arranged a number of humanitarian measures to assist the villagers in making their homes habitable again, including the erection of a prefabricated building for use as the village school and the setting up of medical and dental clinics. All of this helped maintain and foster good relations with the local people and once again Irish soldiers proved themselves excellent in their ability to win friends, gain confidence and earn the trust of those with whom they work.

UNIFIL's AO provides a strong contrast to many other parts of Lebanon right now. Peace and stability in the area has allowed the people to go about their lives with confidence. 54 Irishbatt has seen the fruit of its labours reflected in increased population in the area, more use of arable land, new commercial activity, and a large number of building projects. This provides clear evidence, if there was any doubt, that both Irishbatt and UNIFIL remain central to the entire peace process.

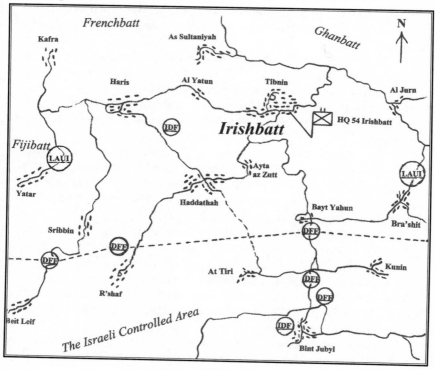

UNIFIL – AN INTERIM ANALYSIS
THE DIPLOMATIC AND POLITICAL BACKGROUND

CAPT RAY MURPHY

In 1978, the Israelis launched 'Operation Litani' and invaded south Lebanon as a reprisal for the killing in Israel of 37 civilians by the Palestinian Liberation Organisation. This massive Israeli response was predictable as retaliatory attacks had by then become established Israeli practice. The attack was an acute embarrassment to Prime Minister Begin's government as it highlighted a seemingly major weakness in Israel's security.[1]

In the debate which followed the formal request by Lebanon and Israel for the Security Council to discuss the situation, Israel sought to defend its actions while the Arab members present called for immediate action by the Security Council to ensure an Israeli withdrawal.[2] Egypt stated the consequences were not confined to Lebanon but extended to the whole Middle East area.[3] In fact the Israeli action also threatened the negotiations to conclude a formal peace treaty with Egypt.

In common with most problems of this nature brought before the Security Council, the parties to the conflict only sought a solution to the crises within the framework of the UN, when the problem otherwise proved insoluble. The UN has therefore borne much of the blame for failing to resolve an intractable international problem not of its making.

The Superpowers, in particular the US which originally sponsored the initiative to establish UNIFIL, did not give the force the support it required in the Security Council. Furthermore, neither the US nor the Soviet Union put sufficient pressure on their respective allies in the Middle East region to co-operate with UNIFIL.

The UN Secretary General, Kurt Waldheim, from the outset made it clear that the force required certain essential conditions fulfilled before it could be effective. In particular, it required the co-operation of the parties concerned. The fulfilment of these conditions was largely outside both the Secretary General's and the Force Commander's control and thus one of the primary reasons UNIFIL is unable to fully carry out its mandate.

France was the first member to publicly state that it was ready to consider a proposal for the stationing of a UN force in Lebanon, aimed at restoring peace and strengthening security in the region. Canada then made a similar proposal. It was the US however, that made the formal proposal for establishing a UN peacekeeping operation and introduced a draft resolution which, when put to the vote, was adopted as Resolution 425 (1978).[4]

This demanded strict respect for Lebanon's territorial integrity and called upon Israel immediately to cease its military activity and withdraw its troops. It also authorised the establishment of the United Nations Interim Force in Lebanon (UNIFIL) for the purpose of

- confirming the withdrawal of Israeli forces,
- restoring international peace and security,
- assisting the government of Lebanon in ensuring the return of its effective authority in the area.

The Lebanese government's strategy at this time was to internationalise and highlight the problem and thereby extricate itself from the regional conflict taking place in Lebanon between Israel, the Palestinians and Syria.[5] With this in mind it successfully obtained UN support for the establishment of a peacekeeping force in the south.

The various contributions to the debate in the Security Council clearly showed that while there was general support for the establishment of a peacekeeping force, there did not exist any general consensus on what the mandate of such a force should be, or how the force should carry it out. Furthermore, all parties involved were critical of various aspects of Resolution 425 (1978) itself. It is this writer's opinion that even at this very early stage in the creation of the force, the lack of political consensus within the Security Council, which was to hinder the effective functioning of the force over the next eight years, was already apparent.

CRITICISMS OF THE MANDATE

The Israelis condemned the lack of explicit condemnation of the Palestinian guerrilla attack that had precipitated the Israeli invasion and considered the resolution as inadequate and lacking. The Arab states were critical of the omission of any condemnation of Israel by name and considered that, in general, the resolution was couched in weak terms. Kuwait in particular stated that it considered it a dangerous precedent to allow 'aggressors ... dictate terms of withdrawal'.[6]

The fact that the whole debate and Resolution 425 (1978) ignored the central elements of the crisis in the Middle East – i.e., a resolution of the Palestinian problem and the need for a comprehensive overall settlement – caused many members to vacillate in their express support for the establishment of the force. In the event, the establishment of a UN peacekeeping force with ambiguous and unrealistic objectives and terms of reference was hastily agreed to, in order to solve the immediate crisis. In this regard, the Secretary General has stated that: 'when a peacekeeping operation is firmly based on a detailed agreement between the parties in conflict and they are prepared to abide by the agreement, it is relatively easy to maintain ... (e.g., UNEF and UNDOF) When, however, an operation is mounted in emergency with ambiguous or controversial objectives and terms of reference, and on assumptions which are not wholly realistic, it is likely to present far greater difficulties. This is undoubtedly the case with UNIFIL ...'[7] It is hardly surprising therefore, that UNIFIL has encountered major difficulties in implementing its mandate.

Around this time, the United States' primary concern in the Middle East was the Camp David Accords and concluding the Egyptian–Israeli peace treaty. In fact, President Carter was later to identify this as his most significant foreign policy achievement.[8] The Lebanese government had requested the US to sponsor the peacekeeping initiative as it realised that America was the only country likely to be able to bring about sufficient Israeli co-operation. This premise was certainly true, however, they seem to have overlooked the dilemma that the US would face in the Security Council as guardian both of Israel's and of Lebanon's interests. The Lebanese appeared to have exaggerated their own importance to the US and Lebanon's significance in American foreign policy. In fact, American policy regarding Lebanon was rooted in domestic, regional and global considerations which did not always coincide with Lebanese interests.[9]

US JEWISH INFLUENCE

The Lebanese government may also have underestimated the influence of the Jewish community in the US. Relations between Israel and the US were often turbulent.[10] In many instances it appeared as if the Israeli tail was wagging the American dog. In August 1979, the US permanent representative at the UN was forced to resign his post for holding a meeting with the PLO's UN observer, in contravention of official US policy. His resignation was strongly criticised by the substantial pro-Palestinian elements within the American Black community, which saw it as capitulation by the Carter administration to the American Jewish lobby.[11]

The following year the US was forced to do a complete turnaround in the Security Council when it criticised Israeli settlement policy in the occupied Arab territories. Within two days a White House official in Washington announced that the US vote in favour of the resolution had been a 'mistake' and a result of 'failure in communication' as its delegate had really been instructed to abstain from the voting.[12]

The influence of the American Jewish community, and the domestic importance to an American president of US policy towards Israel and the Middle East in general, was further demonstrated by the repeated congressional resistance to, or actual blocking of, certain proposed arms sales to Jordan.[13]

The early years of UNIFIL's deployment and abortive attempts to carry out its mandate also coincided with a series of crises in American foreign policy. First, the Iranian revolution took place. Then the seizure of the American hostages in Teheran occurred. This series of related events, along with the Soviet invasion of Afghanistan, pre-occupied the final fourteen months of President Carter's term in office much to the detriment of other significant foreign policy issues.[14] In particular, it meant that little attention was paid to the peacekeeping force in Lebanon except during the debates in the Security Council on the renewal of the mandate.

When the proposal to establish UNIFIL was made some senior UN officials expressed strong reservations regarding the UN assuming such a role. There was concern at some of the assumptions US policy was based upon. An Israeli withdrawal from all of south Lebanon was central to the success of UNIFIL's mission, yet it was not clear that Israel would co-operate fully.

How was a peacekeeping force to restore Lebanese government authority to an area where it was non-existent, when the Lebanese army was divided, and the government concerned probably couldn't maintain control for very long anyway?

There was no clear policy either on how the peacekeeping force would deal with the various armed elements in and around its area of operation, or what action the force would take if the Israelis did not withdraw completely. When the Dáil approved the dispatch of Irish troops for service with UNIFIL, certain deputies expressed similar reservations, especially regarding the failure to clearly state 'the precise role of the force'.[15]

In the final analysis, the urgent necessity was to do something to alleviate the immediate crisis and while there was some broad consensus in the Security Council meant that such misgivings had to put aside. A resolution establishing a peacekeeping force in a region of such conflicting American and Soviet interests had to be a delicate balance of political pressure and persuasion. A word here or a phrase there might cause either superpower to exercise its right to veto. Further prolonged discussion could therefore have jeopardised the whole initiative.[16]

In his report on the implementation of Resolution 425 (1978) the Secretary General first set out the terms of reference for UNIFIL and then outlined the three essential conditions which must be met for the force to be effective.[17] First, it must have at all times the full backing and confidence of the Security Council. Secondly, it must operate with the full co-operation of all the parties concerned. Thirdly, it must be able to function as an integrated and efficient military unit.

Did the Force Receive the Full Backing and Confidence of the Security Council?

The fact that the Secretary General felt constrained to expressly state these essential conditions in this manner indicates that he was concerned that some of the conditions might not be fulfilled. The most important of which was that the force receive the full backing of the Security Council. Once a force is established and deployed, the overall direction of the operation is the Secretary General's responsibility, acting on behalf of and being answerable to the Security Council.[18]

The importance to the Secretary General of proper support and guidance from the Security Council cannot be over-stated. This support has not always been forthcoming and is often too ambivalent in its nature. The serious problems that can arise when this is not forthcoming were evident during the UN Peacekeeping operation in the Congo.

Within three months of the establishment of ONUC the consensus among the permanent members of the Security Council had disintegrated. Throughout the operation the Secretary General frequently turned to the Security Council for clarification of the mandate and support, he received neither. At one stage, in answer to criticism of his handling of ONUC, he reminded the Security Council that it was their responsibility to 'indicate what you want to de done ... but if no advice is forthcoming ... then I have no choice but to follow my own conviction.'[19]

Fortunately, the Secretary General has not found himself placed in such an untenable position with regard to UNIFIL to date. Nonetheless he declared in early 1986 that this condition identified in 1978 as essential for the force to be effective had not been fully met.[20]

This unusual step of openly criticising the UN organ to which he himself is responsible, in such a manner, indicates the despair and frustration felt after so many years of trying to make UNIFIL more effective, particularly when the reasons for the failure to fulfil its mandate lie outside his control. Once again, he appealed to the member states to give the force full political backing and to meet their assessed share of its costs.

The Secretary General has refrained from criticising any particular member of the Security Council by name. However, the USSR abstained from voting on every resolution concerning UNIFIL from 1978 until April 1986. From the beginning, the Soviet Union stated it was not satisfied with the mandate. In particular, it disagreed with UNIFIL's function in assisting the return of effective Lebanese government authority in the area and the absence of a time limit on the force's stay in Lebanon.[21] The USSR also consistently refused to contribute to the financing of the force as it considered they 'should be defrayed by the aggressor – Israel'. However, in April 1986, the Soviet Union changed its stance in the Security Council and announced that it shared 'the opinion of the government of Lebanon about the need to retain, in present circumstances, the presence of UNIFIL in Lebanon'.[22] It considered that the force had an important role to play in confirming the Israeli withdrawal. Furthermore, the USSR declared its willingness henceforth to take part in the financing of the force.

After the last major outbreak of hostility between the Arabs and the Israelis in October 1973, the Soviet Union's influence declined in the region.[23] In fact, its influence further declined because of the 1982 Israeli invasion of Lebanon. The credibility of the Soviet Union was undermined by its failure to respond to appeals from the PLO and Syria for aid. Its warning to the US not to commit its forces had been ignored and Soviet weaponry once more proved qualitatively inferior to its American equivalent.

During this period, the Soviet Union attempted to exploit the propaganda value of resorting to the Security Council to bring pressure upon the Israelis to withdraw. In this way, they achieved the optimum result. They avoided the danger of direct involvement while at the same time drawing attention to American support for Israel and US vetoes of certain resolutions in the Security Council. They also heightened tension between the US and its European allies in NATO.[24]

In this way, the change in Soviet policy can be seen as an attempt to regain some of its lost credibility and influence in the area. In particular, the USSR sees an opportunity to play a more meaningful role since the decline in US fortunes in Lebanon and the Middle East. The US support for the 1983 Israeli–Lebanon Agreement and the debacle of its direct involvement in Lebanon has weakened the American position. A central element in the USSR's policy is the reconvening of an international conference in Geneva where the USSR can occupy a position equal to the US, and all parties to the Middle East conflict, including the PLO, can attend. The key to US influence in the area, especially since 1973, has been the American role as mediator in the Arab–Israeli peace process.

The present situation may allow the Soviet Union further erode this US role and at the same time enhance their own prestige and influence. It is my opinion that the Soviet Union's recent conversion to the cause of UNIFIL does not stem from a genuine interest in the plight of Lebanon. In this regard, its policy is similar to that of the US. Lebanon is perceived by both super-powers not as an end in itself, but as a means to gaining influence and power in the region as a whole.

The American attitude within the Security Council and its Middle East policy has been no less opportunistic than that of the USSR. Even if the political will existed in the US administration to bring pressure to bear on the Israelis to co-operate with UNIFIL, it is doubtful whether any US President could have endured the backlash from the American Jewish community for a sufficient period to allow this pressure to be effective.

Did the Parties Concerned Co-operate with UNIFIL?

Unfortunately, many of the parties did not co-operate as anticipated or as promised in some cases. In particular the Israelis and their allies in south Lebanon, known generally as the De Facto Forces and more recently referred to as the South Lebanese Army, have not only failed to co-operate, but have deliberately harassed UNIFIL and prevented it from carrying out its mandate.

Some of the problems that have arisen in this regard are directly related to other assumptions made concerning the deployment of the force. The Secretary General envisaged UNIFIL as a two-stage operation. In the first stage, the force was to confirm the withdrawal of Israeli forces from Lebanese territory to the international border. Once this was achieved, UNIFIL was to establish and maintain an area of operation defined. The Secretary General was unhappy with the ill-defined reference to an area of operation.[25]

However, it was impossible to be more specific at this stage, as discussions in the Security Council and consultations with the governments of Israel and Lebanon revealed profound disagreement on the subject. The force commander at the time was later to identify this as one of the basic and fundamental flaws in the deployment of UNIFIL.[26] It caused major problems when the force attempted to deploy in certain areas where the PLO maintained strongholds and in areas from where the Israeli Defence Force withdrew without handing over to UNIFIL.

The dangers of not defining the precise area of operations became all too evident when UN troops from the French contingent attempted to deploy around the PLO stronghold in the southern city of Tyre and in the vicinity of the Kashmiye bridge.[27] The PLO put up strong resistance to the French presence in this area. This resistance on the ground was combined with a diplomatic campaign in New York by Arab states on their behalf. The PLO objected to UNIFIL's deployment in these areas because the Israeli Defence Forces had never occupied them.

During the invasion, the Israelis bypassed this area known as the 'Tyre pocket'. The PLO therefore considered that UNIFIL should not be deployed there either. The matter was complicated by the so called 'Cairo Agreement' of 3 November 1969 between the PLO and the Lebanese government which legitimised the former's presence in Lebanon and supposedly governed its activities there.[28] In the end, the Secretary General reported to the Security Council that 'the deployment in the vicinity of the Kashmiye Bridge and the Tyre pocket was pressed'.[29]

At the time, the force commander was in favour of taking stronger action against the PLO within UNIFIL's area of operation.[30] His recommendation was not accepted in this case. It is also reported that the Lebanese government would have supported a stronger stance in the case against the PLO presence. However, as already pointed out, UNIFIL was a very precarious political creation. It is almost certain that the USSR and the pro-Palestinian lobby at the UN would have strenuously objected. The Soviet Union had the power to veto any further mandate renewals.

UNIFIL was a peacekeeping mission, not a peace enforcement mission. It relied totally upon the co-operation of the parties concerned. Any problem of this nature that arose had to be resolved by negotiation, however unsatisfactory a subsequent agreement arrived at in this manner turned out to be. By the end of 1978, the Secretary General was able to report that relations with the PLO in the area had created major problems.[31] Later the DFF used the agreement concluded between the UN and the PLO in their propaganda campaign against UNIFIL. They also used it as an excuse for refusing to allow UNIFIL to deploy in the area under their control.

It is my opinion that under these circumstances, the Secretary General had no option but to reach some negotiated settlement with the PLO. If a firm stance had been taken against them at this stage, it would have been equally important to take similar action against the DFF. It is probable that neither the US nor the USSR would have been willing to support such a policy in the Security Council. In any event, many of the contributing countries, including Ireland, would have been unwilling to continue to supply troops to a force suffering the numbers of casualties that offensive action of this nature would entail. It would also be incompatible with the respective foreign policies of certain of the troop-contributing countries as well as being clearly outside the terms of reference of the force that it would only act in self-defence.

Prior to the anticipated final withdrawal of Israel, the UN held discussions with representatives of the Lebanese government regarding the deployment of UNIFIL in the area to be evacuated. Particular attention was also paid to the status of the armed elements under the command of Major Haddad.[32] Unfortunately the Lebanese government made a major error of judgement at this stage. It was decided that pending full establishment of Lebanese authority, including military forces, in the UNIFIL area of operation, the Lebanese authorities provisionally recognised Major Haddad as De Facto commander of the Lebanese forces in his present area for the purpose of facilitating UNIFIL's mission.[33] This further added to UNIFIL's difficulties in its relationship with the DFF during the vital early days of its deployment. As events unfolded it became clear that the Israelis and Major Haddad's forces would not co-operate with UNIFIL. The Israelis strongly objected to the agreements concluded with the PLO and claimed the situation 'bodes ill for the future'. If the UN did not take full control of the PLO territory then it would not be permitted to deploy in the areas controlled by the DFF.[34]

When the Lebanese government decided to revoke the provisional recognition given to Major Haddad in September 1978, much valuable time and ground had been lost. The Lebanese government rightly complained 'that Israel was actively opposing the deployment of both the Lebanese army and UNIFIL by military, political and diplomatic action'.[35] Israel's reply was terse and to the point. As far as Israel was concerned, it had fulfilled its part in the implementation of Resolutions 425 (1978) and 426 (1978), which, it claimed, did not require control of any area to be turned over to UNIFIL.[36]

This was a narrow and erroneous interpretation of the resolutions in question, which were not supported by the US. Relations between UNIFIL and the IDF/DFF deteriorated. Over the next number of years, IDF/DFF not only harassed UNIFIL but also indiscriminately shelled and fired on its positions. They also attempted to seize UN positions and were indifferent to the safety of both UN and civilian personnel. Major Haddad and his forces also strongly resisted attempts to deploy elements of the Lebanese army in the UNIFIL area of operation.[37]

In 1987, the Secretary General is still calling upon the Israelis to withdraw from south Lebanon in accordance with Resolution 425 (1978) and other similar resolutions of the Security Council. The Israeli authorities continue to claim that it is not their intention to maintain a military presence in Lebanon. However, in their view, neither UNIFIL nor the Lebanese government can guarantee Israel's security and therefore they must make their own arrangements. Nonetheless, the longer Israel continues to deny UNIFIL the opportunity and means to implement its mandate the longer and more difficult the task of restoring Lebanese government authority in the area will be. It also makes the task of deploying the Lebanese army in the south more difficult. In this way, Israel's own policies are counter-productive and will continue to prevent it reaching a long-term solution to its security dilemma along its northern frontier.

DOES UNIFIL FUNCTION AS AN INTEGRATED AND EFFICIENT MILITARY UNIT? Many observers consider that this condition has not been met. I do not fully share that view. The Secretary General's own choice of words was unfortunate in that they may create the impression that the force established was to be a conventional military unit properly constituted for traditional military operations. This is not the case. The UNIFIL mission, even if unclear in certain respects, is a peacekeeping mission. With the exception of the UN operation in Korea, peacekeeping missions have been based on well-established principles and precedents.[38] On account of this, peacekeeping is a relatively new military concept and the mounting and conduct of such operations is very different from conventional military operations.

The UN organisation does not have a military branch.[39] While the Secretary General has a military adviser he does not have sufficient military staff employed in UN headquarters for the planning and organisation of peacekeeping operations. The conduct of these operations has been on an *ad hoc* basis to date, and due to the inability of members to agree to a comprehensive set of guidelines to govern all UN peacekeeping operations this is likely to remain the status quo.[40] The omission of military personnel from the UN secretariat stems from a deliberate policy to maintain the strictest possible control over the military. The planning and in particular the early stages of all UN peacekeeping operations to date have suffered on account of this.[41]

However, the potential political ramifications of all decisions made by the force commander or by any of his subordinates on the ground have also been a major factor in determining the UN's reluctance to relinquish any part of its overall control and responsibility for peacekeeping operations. Much more so than in conventional military operations, almost every move in peacekeeping operations is liable to have political consequences. A seemingly inconsequential initiative in the field may precipitate an international incident. This may cause frustration among the military involved in a peacekeeping force and lead a limited number to conclude that it is not functioning effectively as a military unit. The problem is often exacerbated by the political necessity of implementing a deliberately vague mandate.

When a peacekeeping force is being established the Secretary

General looks for troop contributions from many countries. In order that the force be acceptable to the Security Council, to the parties involved and to the international community, it is necessary to ensure that there is a wide geographic distribution and a political balanced among the contributing states. This can be detrimental to the smooth operation of the force as an integrated military unit. There are large differences in training, experience, culture and political background among the states that currently contribute to UNIFIL. When these disparities are taken into account it is remarkable that the force does in fact work so well and this is a reflection of the high standards and professionalism of its officers and men.[42]

The military effectiveness of UNIFIL was also hampered by the location of its headquarters in Naquora. However, the two other locations considered, Tyre and Bahrain, were found unsuitable due to the presence of the PLO in Tyre and elements of the Arab Deterrent Force in Zahrani. Naquora would have been a good location had the Israelis co-operated as planned. Similarly, lack of co-operation has prevented the force from operating effectively in an area that forms one uninterrupted unit right up to the internationally recognised boundary. In the final analysis, a peacekeeping mission must be judged primarily by how it fulfils its political purpose and not solely on its military efficiency.

In 1983 the newly retired Under-Secretary General of the UN with special responsibility for peacekeeping operations, Mr Brian Urquhart, stated 'that successful peacekeeping depends, *inter alia*, on a sound political base, a well defined mandate and objectives, and the co-operation of the parties concerned.'[43] Ironically he was drawing attention to deficiencies of this nature in the multi-national force deployed in Beirut in 1982 and 1983. These conditions have not yet been sufficiently satisfied in the case of UNIFIL. One of the reasons for this is that in recent years there has been a return to bilateral diplomacy among the superpowers and international institutions like the UN are only resorted to when it suits their purposes.

The establishment of UNIFIL was primarily sponsored by the US to facilitate a speedy withdrawal of Israel from Lebanon in 1978 and to ensure that the so-called Camp David Accords were not further jeopardised by Israeli actions. The force would also help prevent the outbreak of another major conflict between Syria and Israel, which had the potential to lead to direct super-power conflict. However, Israel and the US, despite their otherwise strong links, did not always share perceptions as to what constituted a common threat in the Middle East region. In particular, the Israelis saw Arab nationalism and the PLO as the real threat to their security, while America saw the USSR and the spread of Communism as the common enemy.

Co-operation from the Israelis was vital to the success of UNIFIL. When it became clear that it was not forthcoming, the US never brought sufficient pressure to bear on the Israelis to ensure that they would succumb. In the Security Council, the normal political divisions underlying any agreement of this nature to establish a peacekeeping force were temporarily put aside by its members due to the urgency of the crises. Nonetheless, the mandate agreed upon for UNIFIL was unrealistic and lent itself to different interpretations by opposite parties. Many elements of the overall plan for deployment of UNIFIL had obvious deficiencies. Its success as a peacekeeping mission was dependant on factors outside its control.

The Middle East has for centuries been an area of strategic importance in the world. In more recent times, the UN has played a significant role in the maintenance of international peace and security. The volatile and dangerous nature of the region was particularly evident in 1973. During renewed fighting at that time between the Arab States and Israel, a global nuclear alert was diffused thanks only to the UN.

The organisation could play an even more significant role if it was permitted to do so but the US has consistently sought to exclude the USSR from all negotiation and mediation efforts there. It is not surprising therefore that the USSR refused to agree to the renewal of the UNEF II mandate after the conclusion of the Egyptian–Israeli Peace Treaty. Similarly, the Soviet Union was excluded from US peace efforts in Lebanon in 1983. When the US and its NATO allies in the multinational force needed to be rescued from their Beirut debacle in 1983, the Soviet Union refused to agree to the stationing of a UN force to replace the MNF. This further highlights the urgent need to include all parties, especially Syria, in negotiations for a settlement of both the Middle East and Lebanese problem.[44]

In the meantime, UNIFIL should remain to represent the will and authority of the UN and the international community. The force plays a vital role in the maintenance of international peace and security in the region. A withdrawal at this stage would escalate the level of violence there. Despite UNIFIL's inherent flaws and the constraints inhibiting it in the fulfilment of its mandate, the force must not be seen to relinquish its role as international policeman in an area where scant or no regard is paid to international law or the UN charter.

CONNEMARA DRY STONE WALLING

LT MAOLIOSA Ó CULCHÁIN

All of us who have been in the west of Ireland will be familiar with the dry stone walls which decorate our countryside. They were built over millenniums and the skills developed over generations. Post-cards have been made of many a wall silhouetted against a setting sun. They lend a distinctive character to our landscape. Picture then that character transposed from the friendly scenes of Connaught to the alien aspects of southern Lebanon. It is an image that catches the attention.

The 'Céad Chath' has long drawn men from the west into its ranks. Many of these go on, in turn, to serve with the United Nations far from home. These men from the rural areas of Connaught bring with them many diverse skills. Since these skills are secondary to the skills of soldiering, they often lie dormant and untapped. Now and then, they emerge. So it was that stone walls started to crop up in strange places and this has not gone unnoticed.

All through the UNIFIL area troops are to be found living in com-pounds. These are constructed by throwing up mounds of earth around pre-fabs which serve as living accommodation. The protection provided by these mounds can be enhanced by the use of 'Gabions'. These wire cages are filled with stones. Tests have shown that they are quite effective in stopping most ammunition. If stones are piled in hap-hazardly then they will gradually subside and cause the cage to sag and come apart eventually. The trick therefore is to build up the stones so that they don't shift. Building gabions it seemed was second nature to the stonemen of Connemara.

Once they started there was no holding them back. The only limit it seemed was the quantity of suitable stones. So when the platoon transport was not busy doing essential tasks it could be seen disap-pearing down side roads and over tracks. Stranger still were the antics of the men it disgorged at remote spots for they were to be seen picking stones and throwing away stones and casting others onto the back of the truck, and not any old stone would do. There must be at least one flat face. Even then, the mason could reject it.

Soon the gabions were done. Not so our stonemen. Day by day, the walls went up. The suntans got deeper. The *craic* was good too.

For the soldiers in observation posts time can pass slowly but not when they are busy and active. Not only did the wall-building pass the time but there was a kick in improving not only the presentation of the posts but the security as well. So, visitors could trace the progress of our mason as he went from post to post. Everyone who visited the posts manned by these men remarked on the wall-building. Without exception, they were impressed by the result of many hours of work.

The beauty of it was that everyone participated by gathering and hauling the only material required. It cost nothing and was easily obtainable. The skills and time were available and the end result not only improved the security and presentation of our posts, it gave everyone involved a sense of achievement and pride. These men left their mark and created a bit of home away from home. All we were waiting for was one of our Lebanese neighbours to look in and say 'God bless the work'. And he did.

Medevac

1988

TEN YEARS LATER

COMDT DONAL BRACKEN

Since 1978, the Irish have remained in the same area of operations, the epicentre of which has been the village of Tibnin. Of late, redeployment northwards towards the old Ghanbatt positions (where Irishbatt was originally deployed) has taken place, and the villages of Majdal-Silm, Tulin and Quabrikha are back again in Irishbatt. The AO now covers approximately 140 sq. km.

No village wants the Irish to leave and At Tiri is a case in point. Irishbatt left the village briefly during the redeployment but local pressure groups managed to convince UNIFIL HQ that Irish troops were vital to the security and peace of their village. In a very short time, we were back – a singular tribute by the villagers to the Irish battalions with whom they have developed an unspoken empathy over the years.

Operationally Irishbatt AO has always been active. In fact, one only has to look at UNIFIL's yearly statistical analysis to see which areas are the most active – and they are Irishbatt, Finbatt and Norbatt. In terms of Firings Close and Denials of Entry Irishbatt heads the field. The figures for IDF/DFF compounds attacked and road-side bombs detonated show that the Irish AO is again the most active.

All of this activity has given various Irish battalions invaluable experience but this has not been without cost. Twenty-six Irish soldiers have died thus far in the cause of peace in Lebanon and sceptics now ask if it has been worth it? The answer is that all those who have served in Irishbatt know that without their continued presence the area would become a 'killing field'. Without the stability of an international force, the situation in south Lebanon would almost certainly deteriorate into civil war with all the ugly consequences that would then ensue.

Over the years, every effort has been made by successive battalions to improve its defensive positions and progress in ten years reflects how the military and political situations have evolved.

In 1978, 43 Irishbatt were billeted under canvas with little protection. By 1982, we had moved on to protected OPs manned mostly by 1 NCO and 3 privates. When the IDF withdrew in 1985 massive compounds were constructed within Irishbatt's AO and it became obvious that unless UNIFIL was prepared to do the same the security of our personnel would be at risk. Isolated OPs were quickly closed, more secure compounds were opened up at an impressive speed, and today 63 Irishbatt can report that our defensive positions have never been better.

However, an area that has become progressively more important in Irishbatt is the whole matter of Humanitarian Assistance. In the early days, the main form of assistance included medical, dental, and processing requests for needy cases. Nowadays with the poor state of Lebanon's economy much funding is urgently needed for self-help projects in which the local people are provided with the tools to help themselves. In Irishbatt's AO our humanitarian success story is the enclave village of At Tiri.

At Tiri is a village of 131 families located at the south-western tip of Irishbatt AO. While it lies within the UNIFIL AO, it is also within the Israeli Controlled Area and this means that freedom of movement is very restricted. The population is composed of old people and young children. Irishbatt are the only outsiders with free access to the village and have become relied upon over the years to bring in essential foodstuffs and other supplies.

There are also times when people need medical attention above the level which can be given by soldiers administering first aid, or medical officers conducting a clinic, and on these occasions Irishbatt will evacuate the sick person to the regional hospital in Tibnin. However, the list of items still needed in At Tiri is almost endless, and supporting this humanitarian project has become a constant drain on Irishbatt's limited resources. Nevertheless, all tasks continue to be willingly undertaken by all ranks.

UNIFIL's contribution to peace in Lebanon over ten years is incalculable, and the Irish contribution must be viewed in that context. That Irishbatt holds one of the most volatile areas in UNIFIL is a factor which should not be forgotten – a factor which makes peacekeeping more difficult.

During ten years Irish troops have witnessed many changes – reinvasion by the IDF; expulsion of the PLO; the rise of AMAL; and the steady decline of a once proud nation.

Nevertheless, our contribution has been to provide a consistent level of stability in which the population can live as normal an existence as possible in circumstances which can change by the hour – from relative peace to open conflict. Irish soldiers have become part of the life of south Lebanon. Rural village communities rely on our protection in order to harvest their crops in the fields and they rely on our doctors to provide badly needed medical attention. The list of request for help is extensive and will increase.

UNIFIL has been in existence now for ten productive years. There

117

are few who wager on UNIFIL not being here for another ten years – and that's the pity!

These vehicles delivered water, twice a week in some places, to the Irish Area of Operations

1989
NO LOVE STORY – NOT HALF!

JUSTINE McCARTHY
(The Irish Independent)

'There is a very nice young man from the Irish army down here to see you,' said a foreign female voice on the hotel phone, which had shattered my sleep. Squirming into the same stale clothes in which I had travelled from home the previous day, the sands of sleep eroded the barricades of memory and it all came flooding back.

I was billeted in a small hotel in a town called Nahariya, somewhere close to the Israeli/Lebanon border with my luggage gone missing; presumed still dizzily spinning round and round on a carousel somewhere in Heathrow airport. Without base or baggage. And this was the trip my editor had given me as a pleasurable forerunner to the freneticism of Christmas time in Grafton Street, Davy Byrne's and the Fianna Fáil end of year party.

It was hardly the embodiment of the season of goodwill who crawled downstairs to meet one Capt Declan Greenway and his plastic bag. But then, just as there is a Murphy's Law; there must be a counter law too: Mitty's Law – anything that can go right will go right. For the first time since waving goodbye to Comdt Dave Ashe and Capt Peter Burns at Dublin airport and sipping – well quaffing – British Airways Charles Heidseck over the Irish Sea, the predicted was right on schedule. The 'nice young man from the Irish army' really was a nice young (ish) man. And what he carried in his plastic bag came all the way from Mingi Street – a thoroughfare that has assumed sweeping romantic proportions in my imagination – was even better.

My travelling companions and soul mates in my plight, the bold and twinkling Treasa Davison, and the delightful young and enthusiastic Lorraine McDonald, had been shopping, with a chap called 'Mac', for a few essentials on my behalf. Earlier as they had prepared to swan effortlessly over the border – while a dogmatic, autocratic, egotistic Israeli major in Jerusalem decreed that I sit out the Sabbath on her side of the fence – I had scribbled out a list of things I needed to supplement my lost luggage.

Out of the plastic bag came one pair of blue Levis (slightly large at the waist), one pair of white flat shoes (a perfect fit when the filling eventually dislodged itself), an economy pack of the most horrendously coloured made in Lebanon underwear (how will I ever look this mystery man 'Mac' in the eye?) and one extra large lipstick pink T-shirt with the legend, emblazoned in daffodil yellow: 'DON'T LET THE BASTARDS GET YOU DOWN'. Things were starting to look up.

It was with pride (and the Levis) that I wore the T-shirt crossing the border on Sunday morning. Behind the wheel of his UN Passat, my pillar of patience and yet another very nice young man from the Irish army, Capt John Minihane, gently assured me that I was going to be a physical wreck, a shadow of my former self, a laboratory specimen of exhaustion by nightfall. Not only had I missed out on the helicopter flight with the Italian Air Force (ITALAIR) – upon which Treasa had insisted – and the mass at Camp Shamrock where Lorraine and the Fijians had activated a legion of tear ducts with their music, but I had also missed out on a day and a half of encounters with 'Our Boys'. I knew I was going to have to work twice as hard to find 2,500 words to write for the paper.

At this stage, let me say that I had absolutely no intention of being wooed by the Mills and Boon notion of 748 members of Irish manhood living a tough and dangerous life in the valleys and foothills of a strange land, strong, brave, dashing, tanned and pining, unseen, for their women back home. Such clichéd scenarios do not impress the cynical feminist hackette weaned on the gung-ho machismo of Ernest Hemingway.

It was to my horror, therefore, that I found the empathy instant. I took to the kissing and the hugging, the joking and the flattery like a child takes to Smarties and wondered vaguely at the back of my mind: 'How is a girl supposed to work?' But only vaguely. I loved the 'Dubs' in A Company (like Sgt Gerard Cunningham) for their uninhibited welcome and their honest answers. ('What do you miss most about home?' 'Tayto').

I loved the Men from the West in C Company (Flanagan, McLoughlin, Walshe, and Boyle), men of little faith who were reluctant (justifiably) to pass me the volleyball and fed me tea and currant cake when I thought I would just lie down and die from the hunger. And, of course, I loved the Corkmen in B Company, like Dave Heaphy in his red and white-striped T-shirt in the kitchen on Fraggle Rock.

Most of all, I loved Camp Shamrock – the sentries with their serious faces at the barrier breaking into broad grins, the spotless shower room reserved for female visitors, young Airman John Kennedy, who became an *Irish Independent* photographer for a day, the singing and the satire on the stage, the 'snack' that was rustled up in the kitchen and would have fed the entire battalion, the men clamouring in the mess to have their messages of love and longing printed in the paper, the officers discreetly slipping me little cards with messages to be relayed to their wives when we got back home, and the delightful pomp of dinner. And dessert.

What with the race to various OPs during the day, it had (conveniently) slipped my mind that Sunday was my birthday. That was until a piper, with lungs the size of punch bags and a gold kilt of which Coco Chanel would have been proud, led in the cook with his tall hat bearing a large chocolate cake complete with a red rose. When I found out that the confection had been flown all the way from Beirut, my heart melted faster then an ice-cream cone in a sauna.

Later, in the men's mess, Treasa, Lorraine and I mingled – or were mingled – and the delight at having visitors from home really humbled us. They wanted to put their arms around us, to kiss us, have their photographs taken with us, talk to us, sit beside us. It was both a humbling and confusing experience, leaving us feel like 'crossbreeds' of Vera Lynn, Mata Hari and Caithleen Ní Houlihan.

Lebanon itself was another surprise for me. Treasa (now a veteran of two visits to UNIFIL) had warned us about lethal roads. Yet nothing had prepared me for the desolate beauty of the countryside where women wash their clothes and their faces in the local waterhole, where dusty angelic children skip happily like new born lambs, and where men like Ali Kilkenny, defy the laws of nature as a pronounced Connemara dialect spews forth from a dark Arab face. I felt proud that, in this eerily seductive place, the men of Irishbatt had made its heart their special conquest.

And I felt ashamed too. Ashamed that the people back home with no connections to the army, could not possibly appreciate the role being played by Irishbatt in the Middle East. Ashamed of my own initial scepticism when Dave and Peter in the Defence Forces press office had briefed me on the humanitarian works being done by the Irish in Lebanon. And ashamed to think that, despite being recipients of the Nobel Peace Prize and, *ergo*, acknowledged by the whole world, the families of some of our soldiers could hardly afford to survive.

As we left Naquora – having, at last, cut the chocolate cake sent by convoy from Camp Shamrock – I was filled with three overwhelming desires. One, for obvious reasons, was to enlist on the spot. The second was that every Irishman should do a stint with the army – just long enough to put a bit of manners on them. And the third was that, some day, maybe that the cheerfulness and the friendliness of our troops would help bring peace to this beautiful and troubled land.

I will keep forever Sgt Michael Clarke's painting, 'Home Before Dark' with which each of the three of us was presented by Lt Col Pat McMahon, the blue cravat somebody wrapped around my neck in Camp Shamrock, the memories of the best birthday I have had since

I was allowed to cut Battenburg cake on my sixth, and, of course, my pink T-shirt. The underwear, far less enduring then the memories, has, by the way, long since disintegrated into a mass of frayed and tangled elastic.

Camp Shamrock

NOBEL PRIZE FOR PEACEKEEPING

PTE COLIN McGRATH

When told of the full extent of my participation at the ceremonies in Oslo, I was honoured, not only to be representing 64 Irishbatt, but also all members of the Irish army who had served with the UN.

On the morning of 8 December 1988 I arrived at the Force Commander's office and met up with my travelling colleagues, Warrant Officer A. S. Najorijani from Fijibatt and Cpl Stephane Mathiev from Frenchbatt. Lt Gen Lars Eric Wahlgren arrived and following introductions we were escorted to the border and on to Jerusalem. Larnaca, Cyprus was the next stop, at 0230hrs the next morning, we caught a shuttle flight to Vienna.

There we were introduced to more colleagues from Cyprus, UNTSO and the UN Field Service. We had a short stay in Vienna before departing for Frankfurt and eventually Oslo.

On arrival, the Chief of Staff of the Norwegian Forces welcomed us. We were met by our escort driver Major Thor Eid in the VIP lounge and escorted to Linderud Army Academy where we were to sleep for the next three nights. After a quick wash and brush-up, we departed for the 'Aula' where the ceremony was to be held the next day.

We were then introduced to the 'Nobel Prize' committee. The government press centre was the next destination to meet pressmen from the individual nations. The Secretary General of the UN, Perez De Cuellar, was also in attendance.

In the evening, we attended an official dinner at the 'Old Lodge' hosted by the Minister of Defence and the Foreign Ministry. During the dinner, I was seated at the head table beside the Norwegian Foreign Minister and the Assistant Chief of Staff of their forces.

Following breakfast the following morning, those of us lucky enough to be picked for the Guard of Honour went to the 'Aula' to get in a quick rehearsal with the television cameramen. HM King Olav V arrived for this ceremony, which lasted about one and a half hours and during which the Nobel Peace Prize for 1988 was formally awarded to United Nations Peacekeeping Operations worldwide and the UN Secretary General, Perez De Cuellar, duly accepted the award on behalf of all of us. Then it was back to 'Linderud' again to freshen up and change to attend the official Nobel Prize dinner.

On Sunday, we attended a memorial mass for all Norwegian and

United Nations fatalities on the different missions. The Norwegian Chief of Staff and other high-ranking officials attended the mass as well as His Majesty King Olav V and members of his family. This was a very moving and emotional celebration for everyone.

Following the mass, we returned to the 'Old Lodge' to meet Norwegian veterans of UN missions. The evening's entertainment included a concert by the Norwegian No. 1 Military Band, followed by several comedy acts. My only wish was that I could understand Norwegian as everybody else was having a great laugh.

Three hours later, we travelled up to a height of 350m above Oslo to the Holmenkallen Hotel for the final official dinner. When the meal was finished we all had a 'soldiers get together'.

We arrived at Fornebu airport early the next morning for the journey back. Here we were met by the Chief of Staff and wished *bon voyage* on our return flight. We boarded the flight, flew out over the 'white mass' of Norway, and arrived shortly in Copenhagen. From here, it was on to Athens and then back to Larnaca. The following morning, we departed for Jerusalem, where we parted ways and I travelled back to our mission area in south Lebanon.

It is difficult for me to get the whole occasion and ceremony into perspective. My own feelings are easier to describe: pride for my family, my comrades, and myself at home and with the United Nations at this worldwide recognition of our efforts as soldiers.

Sadness too, when I remember all the Irish soldiers who have died 'in the service of peace' with the UN down through the years. They, and their families were not forgotten in Oslo either and indeed I had not known how many had died until I saw the 'Roll of Honour' in *An Cosantóir*.

Gratitude was also in my mind, that I, a Private soldier, was there as a representative of our Defence Forces – I suppose at times I was simply in awe of the whole thing. I wore my uniform with such pride throughout and in a way, I felt that I was representing all of the people of Ireland.

10 December 1988 and 64th Irishbatt will forever be etched in my memory. It was an experience and an honour, and I will be forever grateful to those who selected me to travel – my platoon commander, company commander, and OC 64 Irishbatt. I am also grateful to force commander UNIFIL, Lt Gen Lars Eric Wahlgren, for making it all such a pleasant trip, and offering his assistance whenever it was needed.

A Wife at Home

Cpl Paula McCusker

The long discussion ended in the joint agreement that the money would come in handy, maybe a holiday, a new car, renovations to the house – his list of suggestions endless and the money well spent before his name was given.

The training period was OK, he was away all week, but at least he had all the weekends free, Lebanon all seemed so far away. Then one weekend he came home, his hair cut really short, he looked like a marine.

He began to get his stuff ready, the 'essentials' he told me, 300 tea bags, flashes and name-tag, shorts. He was travelling on the second chalk. It was becoming a reality. He was going away for six months. I was on my own.

I know each time the UNIFIL chalks are rotating many wives are left on their own, but each wife is so alone – unlike the husbands who have the companionship of 600 men, each one with similar feelings.

The first few weeks went by, no letters – had he forgotten me? Is he sick? All sorts of thoughts go though your mind. Then you get your first letter, telling you, if it's his first trip, all about his blisters from the sun, and if it's his second, all about how the place hasn't changed.

You, in your letters and wisdom, tell him all the nice things that have happened during your day. No bad things, no bills, no blues. He must feel like you are better off without him – life at home sounds so idyllic!

The Lebanon to most wives is a place that is 4' x 3', the size of a photograph. I'm sure every wife is shown the pictures of 'Old Mama' and 'Old Finta', and this one and that one, all seemingly over 90 years of age. Just once, we would like to see a 20-year-old female, or would we?

Then there are the pictures of stone buildings, distant hills, winding roads – 'that's the CO's house', 'Fraggle Rock', 'the road to 48 alpha' – although this probably means something of real significance to our husbands it is all Arabic to the wives at home.

Perhaps if the army were to make an information video showing, what the area/countryside looks like, explaining the culture, traditions, etc., wives could at least be slightly *au fait* with something of what their husbands talk about when they get back home.

Ah, home again! I suppose that has to be what makes the six months worth it. The feeling of anticipation as you wait at McKee Barracks cannot be matched. Every truck that passes makes your heart beat faster. When you finally see him he looks tanned, slim and gorgeous, you dash into his arms. And yes – the wait has been worth it!!

Battalion switchboard, Tibnin

1991

First-hand Reporting

Paul Williams
(Sunday World)

As the small convoy of vehicles climbed slowly up the rocky route between Naquora and Tibnin, the rugged, hilly terrain of south Lebanon rolled out behind us.

After spending the day travelling through Israel, coping with probably the strictest security in the world, not to mention a hangover incurred on a 'mission' with some UNTSO chaps in Jerusalem, I was finally in Lebanon.

It had been a personal ambition of mine to go to Lebanon ever since I joined the FCÁ as a fresh-faced kid eleven years ago. In canteens in Longford, Mullingar and Finner I had been regaled with tales from the 'Leb' and the exploits – some true, some not so true – of the regulars who'd put in their six months tours between the squiggly lines on a map which I first saw in the 17 Inf. Bn (FCA) HQ.

And when I joined the *Sunday World* as a journalist, four years ago, my ambition was fuelled even more. My bosses, Bill Stuart and Seán Boyne were 'Leb. vets', as journalists, and the more I was told about the place, the more I wanted to go, until it became an elusive hope and I resigned myself that I'd probably never set foot on its sun-burned soil. Anyway, I finally got to the place with Sandy Kelly and her band in December for what I can only describe as the trip of a lifetime.

You really have to see south Lebanon and experience the situation first hand to understand just what our troops are doing out there. You can read about it, talk to Lebanon veterans about it, and watch television programmes about it, but it doesn't prepare you for the actual experience.

Hearing about the Fijian soldiers shouting about being 'on the ball' is not quite the same as actually seeing a big black soldier springing smartly to attention and whooping: 'On the big Irish ball Paddy'. The first time myself and colleague Liam O'Connor heard it we almost fell apart laughing – indeed Comdt John Speirin, our 'escort' didn't know what was wrong with us.

At the time of going to print, 754 all ranks in Lebanon are officially there to oversee the withdrawal of Israeli forces from south Lebanon and the re-establishment of central government there. The Irish battalion area covers about 100 sq. km. where they have a number of company posts, platoon posts, outposts and permanent check-points.

To the south of the Irishbatt area of operations are the De Facto Forces compounds, this is the so-called South Lebanese Army which is paid, armed and equipped by the Israelis. They occupy the high ground and their compounds bristle with firepower, including tanks and tracked APCs. The SLA forms a defensive line that works as a buffer for the Israeli's northern border. In the gathering gloom of our first night in Camp Shamrock, battalion operation's officer Comdt Frank Burns pointed to the sinister-looking humps etched against the darkening skies. That was our first glimpse of a DFF position.

Less visible are the AMAL militia and the other resistance factions who regularly take pot shots at the DFF, who in turn reciprocate with heavy machine gun fire and tank and heavy mortar rounds. The Irish job is to closely scrutinise the activities of all sides in this bleak part of the world. They prevent, as often as possible, one side taking on the other. Theirs is the constant, unrelenting task of watching, listening, patrolling and checking for the slightest hint of trouble.

The 68 Inf. Bn have been having a quiet time so far in their tour, but, as Comdt Burns put it, 'peace wears thin in this part of the world', so nowhere is the term 'on the ball' more apt.

From a military point of view the UNIFIL experience has been of immeasurable benefit to the Irish army. During the week I spent there, I saw a finely tuned military machine working very well. In south Lebanon, the Irish have proved their mettle as a well-trained convent-ional army. And nowhere have I seen the 'buddy buddy' system work-ing so well.

Here, everyone from the guy driving the water truck, right up to the battalion OC has an important part to play and does his job to the best of his ability. Every man is a cog in the machine: if anyone relaxes then the whole machine might fail ... the consequences could be dire. The battalion has a heavy operational workload. Checkpoints, camp guards, mobile and foot patrols and OPs, are a constant feature of life. Then there are men resting off and of course, the huge task of servic-ing the 'machine' with food, equipment, transport, etc.

Through their twelve years with UNIFIL the Irish have adapted to the environment and smoothed out their standard operational pro-cedures so that things run efficiently. Back home, the troops rarely, if ever, have an opportunity to operate as a full unit. Recruitment em-bargoes and operational demands dictate this. With border duties, escorts, guards, etc., troops sometimes don't have the opportunity to get to know other personnel in the unit.

But in Lebanon, they live and work together at full unit strength for every day of their six-month tour. Guys have to work closely together, get to know each other through their personal bad times. On the ground, the ordinary soldier has to work on his own initiative. He has to be diplomatic, helpful and watchful but at all times remain forceful – it's no easy task. As Lt Gen Bill Callaghan, DSM (Retd), a former UNIFIL force commander, put it: 'He defuses more problems in a day than any senior officer has to deal with in a week'.

Regularly the soldiers have to call on their wily Irish instincts to talk either side down from bloody confrontation in the wadis, on the roadsides and in the hills.

But the Irish have more than proved to the rest of the world that they are the best. They have brought their own expertise to south Lebanon and the other forces have learned from them. Take for example the specialist search teams and EOD (bomb disposal) people who have been passing on their skills to the other units in UNIFIL.

Experience and training at home has been invaluable – and possibly a life-saver – in a country like Lebanon where the booby trap and mine are favoured weapons among the warring factions and where UNIFIL personnel have been victims in the past.

The week we were there morale was at its best in south Lebanon. After all Sandy Kelly was there with her band, so it was like Christmas came early for the troops. But travelling around the different locations it was obvious that morale was good anyway. There have been no fatalities so far in this tour and generally things have been running smoothly.

68 Irishbatt has a wealth of talent among its ranks and the shows they put on for their visitors were second to none. The important message for those at home is that the Gulf war situation is not worrying them. They have been extensively trained in the use of NBC suits and there are elaborate contingency plans should they have to pull out.

Since their arrival in south Lebanon, the Irish have become an integral part of the local community. An important part of the Irish mandate is to offer humanitarian assistance wherever possible to the local community. The Irishbatt has been a calming influence on the area and the locals readily admit that they have given them the chance to live normal lives.

Driving up to Tibnin from Naquora it was obvious that normality was returning to this war-torn land. Scores of new houses are being built throughout the Irishbatt AO and the local economy seems to have prospered from the 'Irish Dollar'. Even 'mingy' men are speaking with Cork and Dublin drawls!

One of the more touching stories is the one about the school in Quabrika which was shelled by a DFF tank some years ago. The school was badly damaged and the teacher was forced to close it down. The Irish placed a sentry on the roof, in an OP, they placed gabions in the path of the DFF tank's line of fire, supplied money, and helped rebuild the damaged school and the children were able to return, safe in the knowledge that they were being protected. In other times, the children's education would have suffered and the school would not have re-opened.

In Tibnin, the Irish have assisted in building the local orphanage and supplied money to run the place. Nowadays they are teaching the local people the skills necessary to help themselves. It is very easy to see just how much the Lebanese need their Paddy friends!

One of the regrets I had about my visit to Lebanon was that I didn't get to spend more time with Lt Col Maurice Walsh's FMR in Grottle Camp. I found the concept of the FMR most impressive and especially the fact that it is under the command of an Irish officer. The idea of an FMR was mooted in 1986 when things came to a head in the UNIFIL sector and it was officially formed early in the spring of 1987.

It was decided to set up a multinational force drawing platoons from all the contributory countries to UNIFIL. The purpose of the FMR is to send a visible armoured force into any battalion area should they be required at short notice ... a sort of fire brigade unit.

According to the avid hurler from Cork, his boys can be on any spot in the UNIFIL AO within 40 minutes. The FMR has had four commanding officers since its inception and these have all been Irish officers of Lt Col rank, The OCs tour lasts twelve months and Lt Col Walshe is due to be replaced this month by Lt Col Pierce Redmond.

The FMR's senior NCOs are also Irish and the current strength is 178 all ranks. In its three-and-a-half years of existence it has been honed into a highly efficient and well organised unit. From a leadership point of view, it is a formidable task to command a unit of so many ethnical and cultural differences, not to mention such varying culinary tastes! The fact that the Irish have been given the job of running the FMR is a reflection of their impressive record in Lebanon and the esteem with which they are held by other forces.

Because UNFIL's role in Lebanon is purely non-aggressive and peacekeeping, it is, therefore armed accordingly. The force's weaponry is intended solely for defensive purposes. The Irishbatt equipment consists of the standard issued Steyr Rifle. The .5 HMG and the 7.62 GPMG are deployed at practically all Irishbatt locations. Mortars include the 60mm, 81mm and 120mm weapons.

In the anti-tank role are the 84mm and 90mm recoilless guns and the UN has issued the FMR with the disposable LAW M72. Irishbatt also employ the reliable Panhard AML90. The best addition has been the Finnish-built SISUs which have replaced the Panhard APCs. The SISU is a formidable looking vehicle and is armed with a Russian built .5 HMG and 7.62mm GPMG. It has already proved its worth in absorbing impact from landmine explosions, saving the lives of the men inside.

The benefit to the army from UNIFIL involvement has been immense and the Defence Forces as a whole have gleaned much experience and expertise during the twelve years they have been in Lebanon. It is real soldiering for all ranks and the chance to practice skills they may need to employ back home.

Like our colleagues, Seán Boyne and Bill Stuart, Liam O'Connor and myself felt very proud of our lads over there – they're doing a damn good job and showing the rest of the world professionalism at its best. And they've done great things for Ireland's reputation internationally. When UN peacekeepers won the Nobel Peace Prize in 1989, it was recognition of Ireland's important role in this crucial peacekeeping mission. The Irish temperament has made many friends on all sides and earned them much respect, and, even more importantly prevented much bloodshed in this complex land.

Military police on patrol

Lebanon and the Lebanese

Abbas Awala
(Irishbatt Interpreter)

After the Israeli invasion of Lebanon in 1978, the Lebanese government requested the presence of UN soldiers, to confirm the Israeli withdrawal and to assist the government in the restoration of its authority over all its territory. The UN at this stage passed Resolution 425, which required an Israeli withdrawal from Lebanon and the reinstatement of Lebanese government control right up to the Lebanon–Israel border. UNIFIL came into effect, with a further task of extending protection and humanitarian assistance to the population.

Over the past thirteen years the Lebanese government was unable to take control of the country due in a large part to the factional control of the local militias whose policy was not to allow the government to assert itself. Also, outside forces exerted pressure over the militias who in turn acted on their behalf. At no time did Israel show any seriousness to co-operate with the UN or to implement Resolution 425. These are the two main factors that did not facilitate UNIFIL in its peace mission. Over the years, UNIFIL has helped by its presence in the lives of the local people in many ways, e.g., security, medical, economical, educational and humanitarian.

From the security point of view, the people were suffering bombing and shelling and what would be described as the internal problems of Lebanon, with interference by Israel from time to time. Meanwhile the UN AO became a haven to many Lebanese people who, because of troubles in Beirut and other parts, were forced to flee to the south where UNIFIL had set up its presence. As I am living in the Irishbatt area, I can see a lot of improvements and confidence in the local population. People who emigrated and returned were encouraged to stay and build their homes because of the presence of UNIFIL and to establish businesses and other industries. In all UNIFIL posts, medical assistance is available to the locals. This advice in turn has brought a lot of comfort to those who avail of it.

From an economic point of view, UNIFIL has helped local business by encouraging the building of shops and factories, thereby helping with local employment. The estimated amount of money spent in the AO by UNIFIL troops is in the region of 50 million US dollars. This is significant when compared to the income from the tobacco crop in the region which brings in approximately 12 million US dollars annually. As a result of this trade some of the towns have now set up permanent local markets, such as Tibnin, Shibia and Haddathah, to mention but a few. Because of the security imposed by UNIFIL, many of the local farmers are able to attend to and harvest their crops, especially those opposite the Security Zone.

Arising from the Irish battalion's presence many of the local people, especially the younger generation, are able to speak the English language without having to study it in schools. This, in turn, allows the young people to stop and talk with the Irish soldiers which helps to cement and build a relationship and to bring all concerned closer together. In some of the villages, teaching in schools, especially those opposite the security zone (e.g., Qabrika, Madjel Silm, Haddathah) would not be possible but for the presence of Irish troops during teaching hours.

The Irish battalion continues to provide humanitarian assistance every six months in money terms to help the poor families. This money also helps the agricultural co-operatives in the Irish battalion AO. The Irish contingent recently provided escorts to water company workers to repair the main water line that had been broken down in Wadi Saluki below the Israeli security zone. This pipe supplies more than ten villages, Tulin, Majdel, Silm, Qabrika, etc., and is one of the main water supplies in the area.

I should like to express my thanks to the Irish personnel who have served and continue to serve with UNIFIL and have come to know us on a personal basis; especially those who have returned here from time to time (some now on their fifth and sixth trips). I would also like to express our sadness and sympathy to the relatives, friends and comrades of those who gave their lives in the service of peace in Lebanon. But most of all I would like to thank the families of all Irish soldiers and the Irish government for allowing troops to come here and bring stability and security.

Today, Lebanon is enjoying relative peace and calm and the government is exerting control over a greater part of the country. Because of the disbandment of the militias, the Lebanese army is being rebuilt and has already shown hopeful signs of effective control of the situation in the south. The Lebanese people would like to see the full implementation of Resolution 425, which received a new impetus through the Taif Agreement. All parties to the resolution must press for its implementation, which is the only real prospect for long-term peace and stability in Lebanon.

1992

A VISIT TO THE 72 IRISHBATT

TREASA DAVISON (RTÉ)

MONDAY

Leave Dublin 070hrs. Arrive Tel Aviv 1900hrs. Comforting to see army presence waiting, with UN land cruiser. My first 'Minder' is Capt Brendan McWilliams.

TUESDAY

Early start. It's a three-hour drive to Lebanon. Cross the border at Rosh Hanigra. Brendan was great with all the paperwork. It's best to have patience and facilitate.

Once over the border it is necessary to have an armed escort. Necessary also to wear flak jacket and helmet. Arrive at Naquora in time for lunch. Spent afternoon with my next minder, Capt Marie Flynn. Record that evening with the BBC – the Blue Beret Club. There's a dart competition between the officers and other ranks. Lots of singing from musicians Derek Delaney, Brian Fitzpatrick from Crumlin, Timmy Donovan from Kilkenny, Jimmy Smith from Co. Monaghan. Also, there was Noel Keogh from Co. Wicklow playing Scrabble with his mates. Billeted in the VIP quarters. Room next door has a Maj Gen, and on the other side is a Lt Col. Forget the VIP bit. Queued for the bathroom with soldiers. It is now extremely cold. Winter arrived overnight. All have been instructed to don their winter garb. Wish I had the thermals.

WEDNESDAY

Did some Naquora High Street shopping with Capt Marie Flynn. Another minder. That's a joke – it was Mingy Mingy all the way. Arrive Camp Shamrock 0930hrs meet OC Rory Campion. My host for stay here in Tibnin. Later I visit A Company, and BMR. Escort is Mark Prendergast. A Company consists of fellows from Dublin, Drogheda, Dundalk and the border areas. Arrive Al Yahun. High up in the mountains. Grey skies, rain and cold. After lunch, visited the outlaying posts. Like post 6–42 with 14 men, Shaqra post with 17. Here you must get on with each other – there is nowhere to go, not even down the road for a walk! Just work – 8 hours on, 8 hours off. Met Ray Reynolds from Drogheda, Noel Murphy, Nick Cox and Mick Gormely.

Ray Reynolds decided to read out a load of requests until the generator went off, a frequent occurrence in the hills. Tony O'Riordan is going to take his wife on holiday to Kenya and is saving the few bob to do that. Edward Murray from Cavan has no complaints. Here too I met Pat Graham who thought of the delightful idea of reading a book for his son. He has recorded it on tape in short extracts, and his son doesn't miss his dad's bedtime story. Day continues with visits to all the A Company posts.

After dark, travel has to be in a SISU, an APC. Best too for the bad roads. No one has ever experienced a pot hole if they haven't been to Lebanon. Travel in Jeeps or Landcruisers – speed must not be more than 5 to 10 mph. Some stops at checkpoints. Men wrapped up against the now bitter cold. Fortunately, their mouths were freed for the mike.

This evening, its time for Bingo with the boys in Camp Shamrock. All evening there are dollar fines. Swear, give a wrong number and a hundred men yell ... 'Dollar dollar dollar'. I was caught. These dollars are collected in a gaily-painted ammunition box, and later that week 300 dollars were presented to the local orphanage. It's a lot of money when you can buy a car for 5,000 dollars, and I mean a Merc!

At checkpoint in Atya as Zutt met Paul Murray, who has just bought a house in Cavan. He is saving up for the furniture. Had a steep climb at this checkpoint. Up a very slippery iron ladder. Sergeant Cleary offered to carry me down. Here too, I met some of the local girls who run a small shop, and who remembered the very first battalion to go there, and even remembered the OC: Lt Col Guerin.

The RAP post at Camp Shamrock where I stayed has a small ward with four beds. There are three patients. One football injury, one sore throat and one case of dehydration! (The weather had been very warm). Medic Richie Barry took the fourth bed in the ward because he willingly gave his room to me. I sleep amongst his army paraphernalia.

THURSDAY

Early breakfast. Move to B Company in Haddathah. After recordings – on to At Tiri and a medical clinic manned by Dr Bobbie Hume from Galway. Part of the humanitarian work done by Irish battalion clinic is in part of dilapidated mosque. On the move again to visit Bra'shit. Here I met Capt Pat Lyons and some Donegal lads. Amongst them – John O'Connor from Cork; Ciaran Crawford from Galway; Peter Coppinger, Whacko Mahon from Ballinasloe; James Geoghegan, Gerard Gately, Stephen Beirne and Martin Foley, all from C Company. Rosie, more western Ireland than the lads themselves, is also present, and she's Lebanese.

I am driven back to B Company by one of the chaplains, Fr O'Keeffe. Commandant Goulding takes me on a tour of the school which is in good condition, but totally deserted. At another school, our boys have designed a playground, and instructed local folk how to make a swing, slide and roundabout. Another humanitarian project. Lt Adrian Jacobs, who has learnt Arabic from cassettes, is giving English instruction at the school in his spare time.

Around about this time, I am introduced to the Damascus heater. A contraption that, as yet, none of the soldiers seem to have conquered. Sat in on the intricate lighting of one. One of the main complaints at the clinics run by our doctors, are burns from these stoves. They give out clouds of sooty smoke and stink of diesel and paraffin. After much cursing, swearing and discussion around them, they do eventually light, and they do give heat.

FRIDAY

Tour of Camp Shamrock. Visited the PX. Here I was presented with my medals. One for the UN duty and the medal that was issued to the UNIFIL troops when they were awarded the Nobel Peace Prize. I shall wear them with pride. Later visited the orphanage, founded by the Irish and Norwegians. Again, extremely primitive conditions. All the children line the walls sitting on pieces of foam covered by army blankets. The walls are bare, so is the floor, yet they all smile and sing songs for me.

Also, visited a Christian church, where we gave a new door, and then just opposite the mosque, where we have repaired the roof. Record more greetings, including one from Lt Col Rory Campion on behalf of all the 700 men there, and of course Cpl Cecilia Carberry, Pte Karina Hayes, Capt Marie Flynn, and Capt Clare O'Flynn. As recently as last autumn Clare was a civilian. On 8 October she was commissioned, and two weeks later she was in Lebanon with the 72nd.

SATURDAY

Record in Shamrock. Pipers Jim Fitzpatrick and Johnny Butler play a Christmas song for me and see me off. Bless 'em ... Oh Bless them all. Drive to the border, cross to Israel, leave the armed escort, leave the flak jacket and helmet and off to Tel Aviv. Border closing times can vary, so it is important to be there on time. On to Tel Aviv, and a hot bath. The most delicious prospect in the world, and a warm room.

SUNDAY

Rise at 0430hrs to catch a plane ... to Zurich, to London and to Dublin. What an exciting life!

1995

A Helping Hand

Comdt Liam McNamee

One of the primary tasks of the Irish battalions peacekeeping operations in Lebanon is to provide humanitarian assistance to the local community. This includes medical assistance, help with the purchase of farm machinery, and the provision of catering and school equipment. In addition, part of the battalion's role is to build confidence within the community by its presence and patrols are carried out in areas where locals are fearful of working. Our troops' presence in the fields overlooked by DFF compounds enables the local farmers to tend their animals and carry out the sowing and harvesting of crops.

The morale of the troops is heightened by their involvement in humanitarian work. Many novel and enjoyable events are organised by the soldiers through which they raise funds to provide for local needs. Our very presence is vital to enhance stability in south Lebanon.

An annual £20,000 fund, provided to the battalion through the Department of Foreign Affairs, for the provision of humanitarian assistance, is also a major asset. Among the projects undertaken is the provision of medical assistance and this is provided through clinics run by the battalion medical staff in a number of villages such as At Tiri and R'shaf. Medicines are also purchased, through the fund, for the local community, with about 7,000 patients seen by the medical staff on an annual basis.

There are continuous projects, such as Tibnin Orphanage, which are handed over from battalion to battalion, and there are also one-off items, for example the purchase of machinery and equipment, and of course other needs that arise because of damage caused by conflict in the area.

In recent years, following a period of heavy shelling, the home of a local family was destroyed. Local leaders made a request and following discussions, funding was provided by the battalion for the building of a new house. Happily, the family has now been rehoused largely because of Irish funds and materials, and no small measure of Irish skill and labour.

On another occasion the Tibnin fire tender was fitted with a new set of tyres. The following day there was a fire adjacent to, and endangering, an Irish position. The newly shod fire engine came immediately to our assistance and of course saved the day!

Peacekeeping and humanitarian assistance are intermeshed. Through the combination of willingness, enthusiasm and the availability of funds, a good measure of assistance can be provided. This is very necessary if the battalion is to continue making a confidence-building contribution to the community, and thereby help to make our area of operations a happier place in which to live.

Funeral honours at UNIFIL HQ, Naquora

PLACENAMES IN SOUTH LEBANON

LT COL DES TRAVERS

Placenames in south Lebanon, like many other names in the Arab world, are usually very descriptive, and often have a lyrical ring to them. Two examples in the area policed by Irishbatt personnel illustrate this point. Hill 880 is called 'Shqif an Nahl' ('The Hill of the Honey Bee'), and the ridgeline running north-east/south-west between R'shaf and At Tiri is referred to as 'Birkat Al Hajar' ('The Water Pool of the Stonemason').

Incidentally, Birkat Al Hajar is the site of a considerably sophisticated village settlement, having among its ruins some 15 major cisterns, tiled pathways, terraces and irrigation systems, two tiered tombs and a prominent fortified habitation at the extreme south-western slope of the ridge. It is estimated that the cisterns' capacity alone could have sustained a population of 150–200 persons and their livestock.[1]

This area of Irishbatt comprises 14 such towns and villages, scattered over an area of 125 sq. km. With an average altitude above sea level of 400m, this area is midway between the north/south rift of the Bekaa valley, Lake Tiberias, the Dead Sea and the Mediterranean. It is also approximately midway between the east/west flow of the River Litani to the north and the Armistice Demarcation Line of 1949 in the south between Israel and Lebanon.

However, some placenames cannot be translated, and presumably describe places of great antiquity. Such placenames may have come from one or other of the many dialects, usually Canaanite or Phoenician in origin, such as Syriac or Aramaic.[2] The name of the village R'shaf, for example, may have derived from the name of the Canaanite God, Reshef. If so, it is an irony of circumstance, given the village's recent troubled history – Reshef is the God of Pestilence. Two kilometres north-east of R'shaf, on the Al Hima ridge, is the prehistoric village settlement of Al Junjulat. Unfortunately, the name cannot be translated.

Some placenames describe the form of existence the people practiced there in early times. For example, the prefix, Khirbat, in a place name is derived from the word 'Khirbe' or 'Khirba', now generally understood to mean a ruin or the site of a ruin.

Many examples exist – Khirbat Silm, Khirbat Immiyah (ancient habitation south-west of Birkat Al Hajar) – and are found in great

abundance in northern Galilee, south of the ADL. This modern interpretation, however, is misleading. In fact, it meant 'temporary' or 'sea-
sonal' residence, usually occupied by farming communities during
the summer months when they had to cultivate their uphill lands,
which were too far from their original habitations. War and population shifts, and changes in farming methods, may have resulted in a
misinterpretation or change of meaning.

Other place names are Franco–Arab in origin and date back to
Crusader times. The town of Jwayya gets its name from the corruption of the French word 'Joyeaux' ('A Happy Place'). The name
'Burj', as in Burj Rahal, Burj A Semali and Burj Quallawiya is derived
from the French word 'Bourg' ('town'). All Crusader towns had a cita-
del or tower constructed within them to provide security in the event
of attack, so the term 'bourg' has come to mean 'tower' in Arabic today.
It is sometimes mistranslated to mean 'elevation' also, and this can be
seen in some of the glossaries on the margins of US Defence Mapping
Agency maps widely in use with UNIFIL.

Another Crusader word frequently found in both surnames and
placenames is 'Marun' ('Maronite'). Some examples are the Crusader
castle north of Dayr Kifa (in the area policed by Finbatt troops) –
Qualet Marun – and the hill due east of there, Jabal Marun (now the
location of Finbatt HQ).

Toron was a Crusader regional administrative area with its headquarters at Tibnin. The Crusader administrative region immediately
south of it and straddling the present ADL, had its headquarters at
Marun A Ras – 'Jabal' and 'Ras' are Arabic terms for 'Mountain' and
'Mountain Peak/Rock', respectively.

'Khans', or 'inns', dotted the Middle East from the Euphrates to
the Levant, and were sited within one day's journey of each other, at
distances usually of between 12 and 20 miles. Old maps and placenames helped me to determine a resting place near Tibnin. The valley
immediately south of, and overlooked by, the castle is called Sahl Al
Khan – 'The valley of the Khan'. In that valley is to be found also a
well, called 'Bir Al Khan' ('bir' means 'well'). Unfortunately, no evidence of the Khan exists today. Travellers may have journeyed south
from here to the Crusader castle at Marun A Ras.

A number of placenames have emerged quite recently. The original name for the village of As Sultaniyah was 'Yahoudaria' ('The
Jewish Woman') and may have been changed sometime after the
emergence of the state of Israel (the name 'Yahoudaria' remained on
British War Office maps up to the Second World War).

The name 'Tayr (originally "Deir", meaning "monastery") Zibna'
had been mispronounced to mean an impolite term, and was changed

on the urgings of the village Sheikh, to 'Shihabiya', after General Shihab, President of Lebanon from 1958 to 1964. The name was introduced in 1981, but seems to have been gradually shortened to Shabiya over the years.

The people of the village of Ayta Az Zutt are now attempting to change its name to 'Ayt Al Jabal', some claiming that this was its original name. Maps going back to 1878, however, suggest otherwise.

Some placenames reveal the site of a building no longer to be found, or removed by cartographers from more modern maps. The name 'Qualat' for 'castle' usually reveals the presence of a Crusader stronghold. Two such outpost strongholds existed to protect and control the important north/south Caravan Route along the Wadi Saluki. On the western side of the wadi and south of the village of Majdal Silm was Qualat Al Kott, no trace of which is to be found today. Down in the wadi proper, and clearly visible on a hillock, is Qualat or Khallat Al Dubbe which can be seen as one travels along the Shaqra–Houle road.

If the cartographers of the last century have been assiduous in their work,[3] we may also assume that some placenames and the area they describe have emerged only in this century. Bir As Sanasil and Al Jurn are two such examples. Both names describe water points ('Bir' –'Well': 'Jurn'–'Cistern') attesting to the importance of water as a place for the establishment of communities. 'Ain' ('source' or 'spring') has also given its name to many Arab places, the most significant in south Lebanon being Ras Al Ain, south of Tyre.

At the time of writing, settlements as yet not named are beginning to emerge. For example, the community building up around Tibnin bridge may eventually be given a name. If so, it is likely to be Al Ain, after the springs to be found there.

Irish troops have, over the years, also ascribed names to various places, such as 'Fish Junction', and 'Flangan's Cross', as well as 'Fraggle Rock' (Qualat Al Kott), 'Gallows Green' (Irishbatt MP centre), and 'Cuckoo's Nest' (DFF compound, R'shaf), to name a few.

The Irish also brought a word home from another mission and another language, adopted it into the army patois and then introduced it to Lebanon, where it was adopted as a term and as a place. The word, of course, is the Swahili 'Minghi', which may have meant 'baksheesh' or 'plenty'. Transposed to Lebanon, it was used mainly to describe the trade of goods, oftentimes in little shops, which sprouted up around UN posts throughout the area.

At home, it gave us the 'Mingy Prayer Book' (the Irish soldiers first such prayer book). Abroad, it gave us 'Minghi Shop', 'Minghi Man' and the ubiquitous 'Minghis' which, in context, could mean 'gifts for

141

homecoming', 'spare food or drink', or a shoddy, cheap or reproduction article. It has also given us the name of one of the busiest thoroughfares in south Lebanon (Al Junub)[4] – namely 'Minghi Street' in Naquora, home to UNIFIL HQ. Today local Lebanese have also begun to use these names too.[5] Perhaps maps of the future will reflect the absorption of these placenames into the language of the area too.

Platoon HQ, R'shaf

1996

THE MELKITE COMMUNITY IN IRISHBATT

COMDT CATHAL LOFTUS

Limestone rock gives a special shape and geographers use the Yugo-slav word *karst* to refer to such landscapes. Features of karst include the limestone pavement exposed at Dún Aengus on the Aran Islands – identical to that on Hill 880 in Irishbatt; the *polje* (Yugoslav for 'hole' or 'depression') such as the one near Cartron, Co. Clare – also west of Bra'shit; and the temporary lake or pond for which geographers use the Irish term *turlough* is to be found at Irishbatt's post 6–28 and at Turlough Hill in Co. Wicklow.

Turloughs point to the fact that only rarely do we find water rest-ing above ground in karst. Usually it lies, and flows, under ground and to get at the underground water, deep holes are made. The name for such a hole is neither Irish nor Yugoslav, but the Arabic *Qana*, as in the name of the town recently shelled in which 106 Lebanese perished.

Happier by far is another coincidence of karstic placenames. 'An Boireann' (Co. Clare's world-famous karst) and 'Al Dabsh' (the town-land around Irishbatt's post 6–6) are identical! Both the Irish and the Arabic names translate into English as 'The Stony Place'. Furthermore, I am happy to report that in both stony places little spring gentians and other typical Burren flora are to be found in abundance.

Humanity acts upon the natural landscape. In the earth's marginal-to-barren places, humanity's mark is especially inspiring, for here, usually, is evidence not of opulence but of endurance: not of super-ficial materialism but of deep spiritual values. Our Boireann is rich in such evidence. So too is Al Dabsh.

On the west-facing slope of Al Dabsh, high above post 6–6, we find a cluster of windowless cube–shaped buildings. Each measures three metres cubed approx, is whitewashed, and has an iron door approximately two metres high by a metre wide. On each door is the same motif – an arc surmounted by a cross. All very mysterious!

Among these cubes there are inscribed slabs laid flat on the ground for all the world like the stones we use to mark the burial places of our parish priests in Ireland. The Arabic inscriptions on these stones confirm our suspicions: here indeed lie the remains of deceased parish priests, and their wives and children. And on each slab is a logo similar to the one on the cubes' doors, but different: the cross surmounts an oblong shape. What does all this mean?

The cubes are the family tombs of the Melkite community of Bra'shit. While Shi'ite neighbours and even their own pastors find rest below ground level, for the Melkite laity it's got to be in a cube – it's 'tradition'! A very ancient, honourable, and enduring, Greek tradition. But how ancient, how honourable, how enduring, and how Greek?

When Ptolemy III was King of Egypt, in the third century BC, he received a letter from the famous geographer, Eratosthenes, who had measured the size of the earth by using geometric methods. That letter concerned cubes. Eratosthenes quoted an old tragic poet who told of King Minos erecting a tomb for his son, Glaucos. The tomb, Minos thought, was not grand enough, so he ordered the workers to 'double it, but preserve the cubical form'.

Forms, numbers, and related matters had a certain sacredness for the ancient Greeks. We must remember that Pythagoras had actually headed up a maths-based religion in Calabria. For the Pythagoreans, and for the classical Greeks, forms, numbers and the like not only denote something; they very often connote something else.

For the Greeks each of the four Platonic Solids connotes one of the four elements: the Tetrahedron-Fire; the Octahedron-Air; the Icosahedron-Water; and the Cube-Earth, heavy solid immovable Earth. Moreover, old Pythagoras always regarded the cube as 'the culminating perfection', for it was impossible in the geometry of ancient Greece to proceed further than the three dimensions of length, width, and height. So the cube is indeed very ancient, very honourable, very enduring, and very Greek. But what of the logos?

The classical geometry of Ancient Greece is based on two tools – the straight edge, and the compass. Lines must therefore be either straight or circular. A straight line can go on forever (like Eternity), while a circular line returns (like Time). The motif on the door of the Melkite cube tombs accordingly must be more than the abstract 'Cross on Calvary' that I first assumed it to be.

In fact it denotes the concept 'Here, Time meets Eternity' and the cross on the priests' stones denotes 'Here, Eternity meets the Church'. However the cubes, the slabs, and the logos also connote something additional – Greekness! But Al Dabsh is not in Greece: there are no Greeks in Tibnin. So why are Greek shapes appearing in Lebanon? The answer is neither pure nor simple because places like Al Dabsh are also to be found in Greece, Egypt, and Rome!

Our story begins in 333 BC. Alexander the Great had defeated the Persians and was hailed as the liberator of Egypt, which had been

Persia's most western outposts. Egypt was the part of Alexander's vast empire which he subsequently left to his descendants, the last of whom, Cleopatra, lost it to the Romans in 31 BC.

However the Romans retained the Greek-speaking soldiers, administrators, and artisans who were the descendants of Alexander's original entourage and these were called 'Melkites' because they were 'the king's people' (*Melek* being the Semitic word for 'king'). They were adaptable people and when Alexander had become Pharaoh and adopted the Egyptian religion the Melkites adopted it too.

However, they also retained their Greek culture in various ways. The language was one survivor – the cube was another. Egyptians preferred pyramids for tombs but the Melkites stuck with their cubes and they were able to reconcile the culture clash by pointing to the 'dynamic equilibrium' existing between the faces of a pyramid and the cube. After all Plato himself had demonstrated the relationship between pyramid and cube.

But some Egyptian traditions did cross over with the Melkites. For instance, the Egyptians customarily buried their dead west of the Nile, while living east of it and the Melkites adopted this tradition (the burial ground at Al Dabsh is west of Bra'shit). Later when the Emperor Constantine became a Christian he gave Imperial sanction to the Church's doctrines as defined by a series of Ecumenical councils (such as the Council of Nicea in 325 AD). At this point the Melkites became Christians, and doctrinaire Christians at that, and there developed certain tensions between them and the 'Aegyptos' (also known as Copts or Coptics) who had embraced Christianity long before their Melkite overlords.

Later again the Melkites not only followed the Emperor into the Church of Rome but also when the Great Schism occurred in 1054 they, like the eastern Emperor, stayed in communion with Rome and are sometimes called 'Greek-Catholics' as distinct from 'Greek-Orthodox' (although there is great similarity between both traditions). By this time Melkite communities were to be found in Alexandria, Babylon (old Cairo), and Syene (Aswan). The Romans employed them in their administration and in the army where they were used to secure the trade routes but in 642 AD Egypt was invaded by Arab armies and it became time for the Melkites to leave taking some traditions with them.

They fled to Malta, to Calabria and to Tyre in Lebanon, where to this day their distinctively patterned boats are still built and can be seen with their ancient Greek shape and Egyptian decoration. Tyre was also the bishopric of Origen, a father of the Christian Church in Egypt and spreading out from there the Melkites built communities throughout Lebanon including one in the area we now know as 'Irishbatt'.

Today, the Irishbatt Area of Operations is a Melkite parish dedicated to Our Lady and St George – just as their old parishes in Babylon were almost fourteen centuries ago. The parishioners of both places still share some common traditions. The Melkites of Irishbatt and the Copts of Babylon still celebrate a 'Pattern Day' or 'Moulid' for St George on his feast day and the ceremonies are conducted with exemplary panache. In both cases their Muslim neighbours join in the festivities!

There are now 10,000 Melkites left in Egypt (a Melkite newspaper, Al Ahram, is the top daily there), but most live elsewhere. There are an estimated 350,000 in Syria; 300,000 in Lebanon; 50,000 in Palestine; and 25,000 throughout the remainder of the Middle East. Further afield there are some 350,000 in Brazil; 175,000 in Spanish America; 120,000 in the USA; while Canada, Australia, and Europe are home to approximately 40,000 each. There are probably no more than 4,000 in the Archdiocese of Tyre and these are scattered over an area of 1,500 sq. km. in six parishes: Tyre itself, Qana, Yaroun, Alma Shabb, Ain Ebel, Rashidiye, and 'Irishbatt'. I use the name Irishbatt for the last parish because which of us would prefer to use its correct title, 'the parish of Derdghaya, Safad El Batfiq, Bra'shit and Tibnin'? I do not intend to write about all four centres in the the parish. Instead, I shall confine myself to the centres of Tibnin and Bra'shit because they are well known to everyone who has soldiered in Irishbatt and they still have more than a trace of old Egypt about them.

These remain exciting places because they each have a special blend of ancient and modern – of Greece, Egypt, and Rome – of what went before, and of what came after. These centres contrast in many ways but they also compare, for they have a family resemblance that I term 'The Irishbatt Melkite Shape'. Just like the individual body has its DNA, it is also possible that a community has its own DNA, determining its shape and influencing its destiny.

The Ancient Greek philosopher, Plato, posited the notion that there are 'Forms' to which various classes of things conform. Evidence for this idea can be seen in many guises: our UNIFIL battalions 'form up' taking a distinctive, laid-down shape before departing for Lebanon; every hurling of football team has a 'shape' which fans and coaches implore it not to lose; and each Melkite community in Irishbatt's AO has a distinctive shape. Get the idea?

When we talk of a 'right-corner forward' or when I get an order like *'Dearcaigh fo dheis'* ('Eyes Right') there can be problems unless all concerned understand 'right' to mean the same thing. We must all be similarly oriented if we are to have any cohesion as a group.

Before map and compass appeared, our ancestors merely faced towards sunrise to become oriented. Using this form of orientation: behind is *west* (iar, as Gaeilge); in front is east (*oir*); south is to the right (*deas*); to the left (*tuathal*) is north. Hence, there is a Gaelic expression to describe the act of taking somebody by surprise: *ag teacht aniar aduaidh,* which may be translated as 'coming from the north-west'. However, what it literally means is 'coming from behind the left-hand side'.

Orientation is obviously important in many ways but it is especially so in establishing harmony between Man and the Cosmos or Universe. Most Melkite houses in Irishbatt are on the eastern slopes of Al Dabsh and they generally face east. Here there is social cohesion and, especially, cosmic harmony (not to mention mortal danger, of which more anon).

The front entrance to a Melkite home is on the east side. As one enters its reception room one may look to the north-west corner of the room and one will invariably find the icon(s) most cherished by the family, and, in some homes, statues of Maryam (Our Lady).

That north-west corner is the place of honour, and it is also where the most honoured guest would be seated – that is to the left-hand side of the host or hostess. In Christian convention, and in ancient Palestinian conventions, the guest of honour sits to the right-hand side of the host. Melkites handle this matter differently: they do it the old Egyptian way. Only a guest who may be trusted not to come *aniar aduaidh* gets to sit to the left of the host.

As one leaves the reception room one may see by the door an icon of St George (the dragon-slayer). St George is the patron saint of the Irishbatt parish. His feast day, 23 April, is celebrated in great style. Most people put on new clothes, emigrants return to have their new babies baptised in the old parish church, and relatives from Beirut return for family reunions. Back in Babylon (old Cairo) it is Egypt's 'party of the year'!

St George died a martyr early in the third century at Lod (where Israel's Ben Gurion airport is today) and by the sixth century he was universally revered. The icon image of lancing a dragon is a metaphor for 'nailing a lie, 'spiking a rumour', and 'impaling' anxiety, doubt, fear, suspicion, phobia, panic or negativity in general. As a Melkite goes outdoors he touches the St George icon, much as a Catholic might use the Holy Water font, or a devout Jew would touch the phylactery, affixed nearby their respective front doors. Each can then proceed with a calm and resolute spirit into the outside world.

The imagery, or iconography, of George and the Dragon derives from the Egyptian depiction of the Falcon-god Horus slaying the Crocodile-god Seth. Several saints have been depicted this way. Most of what we have covered so far deals with metaphor, not actuality but the mortal danger alluded to earlier is also very real.

The eastern slopes of Irishbatt are what might be described as 'forward slopes' in that they face 'Gate 12' (Echo 219), the home of an Israeli Defence Forces 155mm artillery battery whose guns fire into Irishbatt and where it is the eastern slopes that inevitably receive the most impacts.

During the July 1993 IDF bombardment called Operation Account-ability more that half the houses destroyed in Tibnin were Melkite. The church (not for the first time) had to be re-roofed. For Tibnin, such bombardment was a Low-Frequency, High-Magnitude event. For Bra'shit in contrast the bombardment was, a High-Frequency, Low-Magnitude event, with most of the incoming shells being fired by the DFF soldiers in the nearby Bra'shit compound (Whiskey 144).

The Melkite burial place, or necropolis, in Bra'shit overlooks the polje but cannot be fired upon directly by the DFF compound. Access to this necropolis is by a long, descending, chicane path: 'We pray all the way down and we curse all the way back', said one weary, experi-enced mourner. So the Bra'shit Melkites have taken to building their burial cubes in what military analysts call 'dead ground' (rather apt in these circumstances!).

One old man showed me the cube he built in his back garden in order to spare his family the danger of visiting the necropolis when he dies. He would not otherwise lie easy. However, there is an important difference in Bra'shit. Here, the cube is only a transitory burial place and an even deeper-seated burial tradition is honoured!

Bra'shit is a very special name. The first two books of the bible, Genesis and Exodus, were written in the Aramaic language. The first words in our bible today, 'In the beginning', are a translation of the Aramaic compound word *Bereshit*. Aramaic developed into what is now called 'PC Aramaic' (not 'politically correct' but Palestinian Chris-tian!) by way of the Phoenician vowel shift, whereby 'eh' sounds be-came 'ah' sounds. When the Melkite refugees came to what is now the Irishbatt area in the seventh century, they found devastated PC com-munities to which they gave a Melkite shape. The placename Bra'shit would later chime with the Arabised word for the Holy Spirit, *Baraclit* (from the Greek word *paracletos*). The placename therefore has an af-finity with three successive cultures and may derive from the com-munity's adherence to a primal tradition of communal burial in a natural cave.

There is a cave in the Bra'shit necropolis, the entrance to which has been damaged by DFF mortars. In that cave lie the bones of countless generations awaiting the Resurrection. Bar'shit's dead lie in cubes only until the flesh decomposes. The bones are then taken to this cave, the communal ossuarium. That is how the ancients did the business 'bereshit' – 'In the beginning'. And in the caves of Mount Carmel near Haifa, Israel, and, more recently, near Nazareth, archaeologists have now found burial arrangements, of similar antiquity.

However in Irishbatt there is another cave below Bra'shit in which the living must often shelter and sit out yet another High-Frequency, Low-Magnitude event. Here Melkite is host to beloved Shi'ite neighbour, whose houses are nearer to the DFF compound and therefore more vulnerable to shooting and shelling. Here too some of Bra' shit's old folks are more or less in permanent residence. When Bra'shit takes cover from IDF/DFF shelling the citizens all pray together to the one God and feel His Holy Presence, while living in the hope of Peace and Justice in a world gone mad. Violence, they know, cannot endure. Love never dies. 'Ya Rub', they pray – 'Be with us, God'.

Nevertheless miracles happen all the time in Irishbatt but one particular miracle is recurrent, and celebrated, in Tibnin and Bra'shit - the survival of the family icon when the family home is wrecked and Melkites show off such icons with a special delight. Is this survival due to the location of the icon in the north-west corner, most remote from the IDF to the east, and the DFF to the south? One is assured by the Melkites that the icons are simply *marhoom* ('blessed').

Indeed, in literal terms, there is no doubt that they are blessed. The Arabic word we translate as 'blessed' derives from the passive of the verb 'to be merciful'. Accordingly, 'blessed' should be construed as 'the recipient of mercy'.

Equally the word *Abrashiyya* is a special word for, and only for, a Melkite church. The word's meaning is a bit like 'headquarters' (*rash* means 'head') but the really unique and distinctive thing about each Abrashiyya in Irishbatt is the iconostasis – the partition, between the altar and the mainly public area (colonnade), upon which stand the icons. Outside of Irishbatt, every iconostasis seems to have the twelve apostles' across the top with Our Lord's icon (or a Last Supper icon) in the middle. In Irishbatt however, there are fourteen icons across the top – the twelve apostles and, nearest Our Lord, Maryam and Iussef. This is deliciously Melkite – the (Holy) Family elbows out the (Apostolic) Clergy!

It is also anciently Egyptian. Fourteen is the number of pieces into which the body of the god Osiris was chopped by his enemy, the Crocodile-god, Seth, and widely scattered. However, the Falcon-god, Horus, son of Osiris, overcame Seth, located the body parts and brought them home to his mother, the goddess Isis, spouse of Osiris. She put all the parts together and Osiris came back to life. Osiris is therefore the god who came back from the dead and in whom Many (parts) became One. (The political metaphor: ancient Egypt had fourteen constituent provinces.)

Osiris would have been lost were it not for the family – the dutiful, hardworking son, and the loving spouse. There is much that is inspirational in the Ancient Egyptian myths, and even more so in the Melkite iconostasis – especially those seen in Irishbatt.

The role of the laity and especially of the family is emphasised in the Melkite and Coptic traditions. Some other eastern Churches privilege the clergy and call their churches *Kabbooshiyya* – Priest quarters (*Kabboosh* equally meaning saint, priest, or holyman). Melkites are also expected to serve the general community in which they live through social work and the orphanages near Tibnin are examples of where such service is rendered.

Politically the Melkites also make their own statement. In reaching out to all political factions in Irishbatt for support for the orphanage, the Melkites not only foster social solidarity, but they also do the orphans proud. In coping with the taunts of fundamentalist,s and with the 'slings and arrows' of outrageous IDF/DFF actions, the Melkites explain that they 'fight back the Good Way'. That is, they respect what moralists call the principium inculpate tutelae ('the principle of non-culpable defence') and they carry the fight in a way that causes least damage and, if possible, saves the life of the aggressor.

The courage necessary to follow this path has never been lacking and people in Irishbatt recall with justifiable civic pride the time in 1993 when 100 men – Melkite and Shi'ite – walked together unarmed, right up to the IDF/DFF positions to demand an end to harassment – fighting back the 'Good Way'.

At a time when many people in Ireland blame religion for dividing them it is nice to see that in Irishbatt it actually unites them. The moral system of Islam has four principles: faith must be true and sincere; adherents must be prepared to show it in deeds of charity to their fellow men; all must be good citizens; and the individual soul must be firm and unshaken in all circumstances. For the Melkites of Irishbatt it is exactly the same – they just call the principles Faith, Hope, and Charity.

When we think of the Melkites walking unarmed with their Shi'ite neighbours through the Irishbatt *karst*, past Total's *turloughs*, and onwards to protest the behaviour of the IDF/DFF, or of Bar'shit's Melkites sheltering with their Shi'ite neighbours in a brightly painted cave each praying to their own God we search for words to describe what is manifest. Perhaps the poet W. H. Auden anticipated our search when he said '... I know nothing of either, but when I try to imagine a faultless love, or the life to come, what I hear is the murmur of underground streams, what I see is a limestone landscape'.

Tibnin Castle

Even The Cedars are Bleeding

Comdt Liam Clancy

Lebanon's most famous and once magnificent cedar forest has been seriously neglected over the past 20 years and may soon become a victim of the country's troubled times. The Forest of the Cedars of God, in the mountains near the village of Bcharre in the north of the country, is now falling victim to a variety of diseases and many of the 2,000 year old *Cedras Libani* are dying.

The nineteenth-century French poet, Alphonse de Lamartine, once described the cedars of Lebanon as the 'most famous natural monument in the world'. *Cedras Libani* are mentioned 76 times in the bible, often as a metaphor for majesty and strength. Solomon built his Temple in Jerusalem from cedar trees supplied by King Hiram of Tyre. Today, the cedar tree is the symbol of Lebanon, with cedars appearing on the currency, the flag, and on the tail of the national carrier – Middle East Airways.

The cedar forests at one time covered vast areas of Lebanon's mountains and extended all the way north into Turkey. The forests were so large that they were thought to be inexhaustible, and for many centuries the cedar became the basis of numerous historically significant economies. The ancient Egyptians had virtually no other source of wood. Their temples were roofed with cedars that had been formed into huge rafts and floated down the Mediterranean from the ports of Tyre, Sidon and Byblos. This exportation of timber in turn was an important factor in the growth of Phoenician prosperity and provided the capital for the launch of ambitious enterprises in international trading for which the people of the region are still famous.

The Romans realised the implications of massive deforestation and posted warnings to discourage exploitation, but to little effect.

Generation after generation continued to exploit the trees but Lebanon's most magnificent natural resource stubbornly endured until the modern era and the arrival of the locomotive. During the First World War most of what was left of the cedar forests was ruthlessly used for railroad fuel leaving only twelve small stands of trees in the entire country. Now, even these remnants may soon disappear.

The Forest of the Cedars of God, located north of Bcharre, is the most famous remaining stand of cedars in Lebanon. Perched some 6,200 feet above sea-level in the magnificent north Lebanon mountains, it is a truly awesome place to visit. Try, as I did, to make it there during your next UNIFIL tour of duty and see a face of Lebanon that has remained hidden to most of us for many years.

From Beirut or Jounieh it is possible to make the return journey comfortably in a full day, provided you depart early to beat Beirut's chaotic rush-hour traffic. You motor north on a good quality dual-carriageway, enjoying superb coastal views. Within an hour, you should reach the well-preserved and historic port of Byblos, the ancient departure point for ships laden with the cedar wood that was used to build Solomon's Temple.

After Byblos, you continue north on the coast road as far as Tripoli. Now you turn into the mountains taking the most direct route via Ehden and Bcharre. This is a spectacular 56km ascent with a surprisingly good road surface. With an experienced steady driver, the hairpin bends will not present an insurmountable challenge and you should not be overly worried that the price of error is measurable in terms of thousands of feet of free fall.

If it is still mid-morning, you have plenty of time to enjoy numerous photo stops and 'chai' in the many welcoming Maronite Christian villages that dot the mountains. You will pass numerous villas, churches, tranquil green pastures and splashing streams – the contrast with the volatile south could not be greater.

Approaching Bcharre there are marvellous views of the Qadisha river with precipitous slopes falling into the deep gorge. Finally, 7 km above Bcharre you reach your destination.

The Forest of the Cedars of God, as it was named by the local Maronites, is now reduced to only seventeen acres but contains the oldest, largest and probably the most magnificently formed species of *Cedras Libani* in the world. Some are over 100ft tall and are believed to predate the time of Christ.

The Maronite patriarch celebrates mass among the trees on 6 August every year and many consider the area to be of profound religious importance. It is not difficult to understand why the Maronites are inspired by the majesty of the forest and its surroundings. When you switch off your vehicle engine and dismount you immediately become aware of the cool, clean, high-altitude air and the 'deafening' silence.

Walking through this spectacular forest is unforgettable because of the age and size of the trees. The locals will tell you, however, that the forest is seen at its best only when the surrounding mountains are carpeted in snow.

No matter when you visit, you will quickly notice that the cedars are under significant stress. Uncontrolled access to the forest meant that for many years the trees were left unguarded. Now, carvings penetrate the bark of numerous trees and many large branches are missing, having been cut for fires. Some trees are rotting and others are being attacked by tunnelling and boring insects.

You don't need to be an expert to see that the entire forest is displaying symptoms of weakness and malnutrition. Soil erosion around the base of the oldest trees is obvious but younger trees are also under stress, appearing to have been significantly damaged by grazing goats.

Locals have formed a Friends of the Cedars Committee with a view to protecting Lebanon's most important natural monument. The committee plans to plant a new forest adjacent to the existing stand and to transform the old forest into an eco-museum. Paths are under construction to prevent further soil erosion by visitors and access is now more closely controlled.

On the road outside the forest a large gathering of souvenir stalls openly sell cedarwood carvings. None of the sellers will be keen to discuss the source of the wood but before purchasing you should satisfy yourself that you are not unwittingly contributing to the final demise of the Forest of the Cedars of God.

Before your departure, pay a visit to the small Cedars ski resort a short distance up the road, where winter visitors can take in some downhill skiing or attempt the 25km cross-country track. Equipment is available for hire, but beware – Cedars is considered suitable only for experienced enthusiasts. Accommodation and *après ski* activities are catered for at two reasonable standard hotels and, if you happen to stay overnight in the high winter season, you may even be lucky enough to find the local disco open.

Hopefully, the rather belated local action to save The Forest of the Cedars of God will not turn out to be 'too little, too late'. The future of Lebanon's national emblem appears to be as uncertain as that of the country itself. Mount Lebanon's baldness is a sad testimony to man's destruction of his environment for short-term material gain.

Current efforts to reverse centuries of neglect appear unstructured, and continued instability in the region may yet again divert attention away from reforestation and the preservation of the cedars. What has been done is commendable, but it is sad to note that the cedar saplings being planted will take forty years to mature and hundreds of years to reach the size of some of the trees that are now dying.

ENTERTAINING THE TROOPS

KEITH WATTERSON

Back in June the Cork based band *The Soulmasters* were selected to entertain the troops of 79 Irishbatt.

There have been some high profile, well established acts in the past – Dickie Rock, Brendan Grace, Joanna and *Tequila Sunrise* – but the band who embarked on the flight from Cork airport on 4 September 1996, had only been active on the Irish circuit for a mere two years.

Fronted by a trio of female vocalists – Michelle McCarthy (who also plays saxophone), Sinéad Bulman and Lisa Whitley – the band included Ron Penny (drums), Pat Power (bass), Mick Finnegan (guitar), Eoghan Horgan (keyboards) and Tony Healy (trumpet).

For the troops, they were a rocking, energetic god-send from the opening Haddathah concert, through Bra'shit, Naquora and Al Yahun, and concluding at headquarter company before the battalion OC, Lt Col Gerry McNamara.

However, the visit of a band to the UNIFIL area of operations is about more than entertaining the troops; it also offers the band the opportunity to see a world they have never experienced before. MIO 79 Irishbatt, Comdt Declan Lawlor, had organised a programme for when they were not on stage they were given an insight into the work being done in Lebanon by the Defence Forces.

The band visited various outposts in the C Company AO, including Shaqra 6–28A, where the commander of the neighbouring DFF compound appeared to formally welcome them all to Lebanon.

The programme also included a visit to the Force Mobile Reserve, and Lt Col Brian O'Connor took the band to neighbouring Qana, the location of Fijibatt HQ that was so severely bombarded during the Israeli Grapes of Wrath offensive. Their viewing of the shrine erected by local Lebanese over the graves of those killed during the bombardment (which must be one of the only Christian/Muslim graves in the Middle East) was one of the most sombre moments of the trip, as was their discovery of the fact that thirty-seven Irishmen have died in service with UNIFIL – stark reminders that the atmosphere, no matter how peaceful, can shatter in a heartbeat.

The band also encountered locals who spoke with Irish accents, a consequence of the time-honoured close relationship between Irish peacekeepers and the Lebanese population and during a full Lebanese breakfast at the Tulin residence of an Irishbatt interpreter, Abbas Awala, the musicians met Abbas' brother, Yussef, who at one point asked Tony (who had some difficulty hearing what Yussef was saying), 'Are ya deaf or wha?'

'Thank you' seems an inadequate expression to those who demonstrated such generosity and hospitality to the visiting party during *The Soulmasters*' tour. As well as playing host to the visitors for the week, the troops were arising at 0600hrs to discharge their daily duties, to take their positions in this UN 'buffer zone'. It's worth reflecting that as Defence Forces personnel go to work in Lebanon, people at home are still asleep. But after this visit, there are at least nine Irish people who have had their eyes opened to what our soldiers are doing in Lebanon, and it's probably true to say that they will never think of the United Nations in quite the same way again.

Observation Duty

BRAVERY UNDER FIRE

PTE DECLAN POWER

At a ceremony in O'Neill Barracks, Cavan, on 24 January the Minister for Defence, Mr Seán Barrett, presented Pte Paul Coventry with *An Bonn Mileata Calmachta*, or Military Medal for Gallantry. It is only the eighth time in the history of the state that this medal has been awarded.

The presentation marked the final page in a chapter of heroism and tragedy that was played out in south Lebanon in the small hours of the morning of 29 September 1992, when armed elements attempted to break through the Irish battalions checkpoint 6–10 in the village of Al Jurn.

Due to its location at a crossroads leading from the frontline villages of Bra'shit and Shaqra to the villages of Tibnin, Az Sultaniyah, and Majdal Silm, CP6–10 has long been a hotspot and has been a focal point for confrontation in the past.

Earlier on that fateful day AEs had launched a co-ordinated attack on DFF compounds close to the Irishbatt and Nepbatt positions. The DFF and the Israeli Defence Forces returned heavy fire. The AEs withdrew and a substantial number tried to escape the area by breaking through the checkpoint in Al Jurn.

Due to their refusal to hand up weapons or allow their vehicles to be searched the AEs were denied passage through the checkpoint by the troops from A Company under the command of Lt John Martin who ordered a SISU armoured car to block the road. Because of this refusal the AEs radioed for reinforcements which, when they arrived increased the number of AEs to approximately 30.

Having failed to gain their objective with threats, the AEs then opened fire on the Irish positions with small arms and RPG rocket launchers. Most of their fire was directed at the checkpoint's machine gun post manned by Pte Niall Coleman, because it dominated the crossroads.

As a result of this heavy fire, Pte Coleman received a gunshot wound to the stomach. His comrades made a number of attempts to go to his assistance but were forced to retire each time due to the severity of the AE fire (it later emerged that in the region of 2,000 rounds were fired into the Irish positions including 74 hits on the machine gun post, 21 of which impacted on the inside of the post).

In a final attempt Pte Coventry, ignoring the intense fire, and without regard for his own safety, broke cover, ran 15 yards under heavy fire to the perimeter of the machine gun post and scaled the eight-foot wall. He rendered first aid to Pte Coleman, radioed for a medevac and comforted his wounded comrade while the firing continued unabated.

It was during this incident that Cpl Peter Ward from Athlone tragically lost his life when his SISU came under fire as he and other troops from C Company rushed to reinforce their fellow soldiers.

Pte Coventry (29), a native of Poppintree in Ballymun, Dublin, was originally recommended for the Distinguished Service Medal, itself an extremely high honour. However, in light of the life threatening circumstances attested to by witnesses this recommendation was upgraded to the Military Medal for Gallantry, with merit.

That was Pte Coventry's second tour overseas and he subsequently served a further tour, eighteen months later with 74 Irishbatt. He is on his ninth year of service with the Defence Forces and serves with 29th Inf. Bn in Cavan town.

Post 610 – Al Jurn

158

Perspectives

Pte Declan Power

For most Irish people Lebanon means one thing – someone's father, brother, sister, son, daughter, cousin, friend or neighbour has probably served there as a UN peace-keeper. We tend to see it as either an important role in keeping peace in a war-torn land, or a waste of our soldier's lives and time in a land where there can never be peace. So what is the situation there today and who are the main players?

The Lebanese population mainly consists of two Muslim sects (Shia and Sunni) and the Maronite Christians. After many years as a French colony, Lebanon gained its independence in 1943 with the Christian community holding the dominant positions in society. By the 1970s, the demographics had changed with the Muslim population growing much faster than the Christians. In these changing circumstances a bitter, bloody civil war erupted around Beirut that lasted until 1976.

Also, around this time, there was an influx of Palestinians into Lebanon; Palestinian guerrillas, mainly PLO, established bases in south Lebanon from where they launched raids into northern Israel. In 1978, Israeli forces invaded Lebanon to root out the Palestinians, eventually annexing the south and south-east of Lebanon, a territory which became known as the enclave, which was secured with the use of a pro-Israeli Christian Militia.

Four years later, Israel launched Operation Peace for Galilee, another invasion, which they claimed was necessary to secure their northern territory. On the subsequent partial withdrawal by the IDF, the territory of the enclave was enlarged, and the UN renamed it the Israel Controlled Area. Meanwhile, Irish troops entered the Lebanese equation in 1978 as part of the United Nations Interim Force in Lebanon and over time the main protagonists evolved to include: The Israeli Defence Forces who as well as securing Israel's northern border also operate in the ICA; the De Facto Forces, also known as the South Lebanon Army, are financed, trained and equipped by the Israelis. The DFF, assisted by the IDF, secure the ICA. At one time, the DFF's membership was predominantly Lebanese Christians, but manpower requirements have occasioned a significant increase in the amount of Muslims who serve it.

Amal (meaning 'Hope'), a Shia Muslim political movement, is a major political force in south Lebanon. Amal generally welcomes UN involvement in the region. The movement's military wing at one time engaged in actions against IDF and DFF elements. Since the April Agreement of 1996, they have reduced their armed activities against the ICA.

Hizbullah (meaning 'Party of God') is a fundamentalist Shia Muslim movement which came into being after the Iranian revolution, and which still relies heavily on Iran for backing. They first came to world prominence when they bombed the US marine barracks at Beirut in 1983. In recent times, they have been the primary protagonists in attacking Israeli and DFF troops in the ICA. The Israelis fear the Hizbullah most of all because of the movement's fundamentalist character, which makes compromise unlikely. They are very much a part of the community of south Lebanon, which makes it difficult for the Israelis to react to their rocket attacks. Like many guerrilla armies, they strike and move like fish back into the sea of their community.

In recent years, Israeli frustration at Hizbullah led to two particularly severe retaliations – Operation Accountability (1993) and Operation Grapes of Wrath (1996) devastated the infrastructure and civilian population of south Lebanon. The constant shelling achieved little apart from stiffening the resolve of Hizbullah. In April 1996, an agreement (known as the April Understanding) was reached between the different warring parties in Lebanon, which essentially aimed to take the civilian population out of the conflict. This meant not firing rockets into northern Israel, and not launching attacks from, nor retaliating on, civilian population centres. But have things changed tangibly for the local population?

Haj Mohammed Rachid is the muktar (head man) of the village of Ayta Az Zutt in the Irish sector. It's a typical south Lebanese village – most of its inhabitants are farmers whose livelihood is harvesting tobacco or (for the luckier ones) olives. As muktar, he is constantly in demand by his people. To his fellow villagers he is the face of authority in their lives.

He is the man who arbitrates disputes, signs and certifies official documents, and speaks for his community at meetings with the UN and with the higher echelons of the Lebanese administration. As I talked to the muktar there was a steady stream of visitors to receive his signature or official stamp. Now and again, he would interrupt our conversation to dispense some whispered wisdom to a visitor.

The muktar is never off duty and he believes that the UN presence makes it possible for his villagers to plough their fields and to go about their lives in some degree of peace. He is adamant that he doesn't want the UN to go until the Israelis leave Lebanon. The vil-

160

lagers of Ayta Az Zutt are particularly pleased to be in the Irish sector, as they find the Irish troops integrate well with the local population and understand their needs.

Since the April Understanding, there has been much less firing into the village from DFF positions. In that respect, life has improved in Ayta Az Zutt, but there is much to improve on.

Many of the muktar's friends moved to Beirut because of the shelling and are afraid to move back. 'It will not be until the Israelis leave that these men, and many like them, will feel safe to bring their families back to their home region,' the muktar told me. It is generally agreed by the villagers that if the Israelis do go, Hizbullah attacks will stop.

The muktar is hopeful that the US Secretary of State's visit will lessen the tension that has gripped the area since twelve Israeli commandoes were killed in an incident in Sidon. This tension has manifested itself in an increase in incidents around the Irish battalion's area of operations. Houses damaged by shellfire in recent incidents could be viewed from the top of the Irish battalion's post in the village, 6–46A. This position has been at the centre of several close-firing incidents over the last number of months, the evidence of which can be seen on the binocular stand and the perimeter wall. It would seem that the muktar's wishes for peace have some ground to cover yet.

IDF Merkava Main Battle Tank

THE MORE THINGS CHANGE

COMDT MICK O'BRIEN

Although fighting continued afterwards, the Israeli shelling of Qana virtually ended Operation Grapes of Wrath. Following the announcement of a cease-fire on 26 April, the outlines of an agreement to redefine military relations between Israel and the resistance in south Lebanon were made public.

The agreement, which became known as 'The April Understanding' differed from previous agreements in two main ways. Firstly, both sides agreed not to launch attacks against, at or from, civilian areas. Secondly, a monitoring group was to be established. This group started its work on 15 August and undoubtedly has made life less dangerous for civilians. Hizbullah and the Israeli Defence Forces have, mostly, respected The April Understanding. There are violations, but the regular attacks on and from, civilian areas have mostly stopped.

The military conflict in the Israeli controlled area has, however, intensified. Hardly a day has passed without either a roadside bomb being detonated or an attack on an IDF/DFF position.

The Hizbullah arsenal appears to have been replenished and updated. Reports claim that Iran has made about thirty special arms shipments to Hizbullah since last Aril. These are reputed to include Katyushka rockets with an extended range of 40km which Iran is believed to have developed with the help of Chinese and Russian experts. If this were true, it would bring the port of Haifa within range of Katyushka rockets.

In November, Hizbullah started using a new anti-tank missile, identified by eye-witnesses as the AT 4 'Spigot', a weapon with a high hit-rate of approximately 80 per cent. Within 48 hours, fighters had destroyed two Israeli M60 tanks, killing one crew member and severely wounding the other five. In response, the Israelis withdrew all their M60 tanks, replacing them with better-armoured vehicles. Nonetheless, on 28 February last Hizbullah hit an IDF Merkava tank with a missile, killing a soldier and seriously wounding an Israeli officer.

Hizbullah has also improved its intelligence-gathering in south Lebanon – one Israeli general came under mortar fire on two separate visits to the ICA within weeks of each other – and dissent continues to grow within the De Facto Forces, recruited and controlled by Israel. There have been a number of desertions and in December the IDF was reported to have arrested a number of dissident DFF members who were trying to negotiate a deal with the government in Beirut on what would happen to them, when, and if, peace is reached between Lebanon and Israel.

One of the main stated objectives of Grapes of Wrath was to end Hizbullah attacks in the Israeli controlled area. This has clearly failed and Hizbullah seem better equipped than ever to carry out operations against the IDF and DFF.

Israeli casualties in Lebanon in 1996 were the heaviest since 1985. Casualties have continued to mount this year, but these losses were greatly increased by the mid-air collision of two helicopters bound for south Lebanon which claimed the lives of all seventy-three Israeli soldiers on board.

Another stated IDF objective was to prevent Katyushka rockets being fired into Israel. While Hizbullah have so far abided by this condition, if the reports of their arsenal being restocked are accurate, possibly with Katyushkas possessing a greater range, then northern Israel is still at risk. This was made very clear by the firing of at least one Katyushka into Israel from Lebanon in January last, reputedly by a Palestinian group, although nobody has claimed responsibility for the rocket which landed in a remote region of Galilee.

Overall, then, the aim of ending attacks on Israeli soil seems, at least for the moment, to have been achieved, but the loss of Israeli troops and their surrogates in south Lebanon continues. That so little has changed since Grapes of Wrath, with the appalling destruction and loss of civilian life that it caused, surely indicates the futility of attempting a military solution to the problems of south Lebanon.

1997
ISRAEL'S VIETNAM

COMDT BRENDAN O'SHEA

For twenty-two years the Israeli Defence Forces and their proxies the South Lebanon Army (in UNIFIL parlance the DFF), remained hopelessly bogged down in a military quagmire which was played out daily in the hills and valleys of south Lebanon. As each week passed more Israeli and DFF soldiers fell victim to the Islamic Resistance's most effective weapon, the road-side bomb, and no amount of 'preventive patrolling' or retaliatory action was able to effect any reduction in the frequency with which these attacks took place. Neither did the huge Israeli military presence in southern Lebanon manage to confine the planting of these devices to the perimeter of Israel's security zone.¹ It was hardly surprising then that Nabbih Berri, Leader of Lebanon's Shi'ite Amal Movement and speaker of the Lebanese parliament, consistently claimed that the blood spattered hills of south Lebanon had long become 'Israel's Vietnam'.²

Early on the morning of Monday 4 August 1997 Israeli radio offered congratulatory first reports on a successful IDF incursion into Hizbullah strongholds in southern Lebanon. Later it emerged that the previous evening a patrol from the IDF's Golani brigade had been dropped covertly by helicopter into the area of Nabatiyah and had made their way undetected to the almost deserted village of Kfour.

Locating the house where Hizbullah regional commanders Hussein Zein Kassir and Sheikh Taisir Badran were staying the Israelis planted a series of high explosives and were in the process of withdrawing from the area when they stumbled upon a local Hizbullah patrol that immediately opened fire. In the ensuing gun-battle both Kassir and Badran ran from the building only to be obliterated when one of them stood on a huge mine which had been concealed in the pathway just outside the front door.³ Soon thereafter three IDF Yasur helicopters were called-in and having miraculously withstood sustained Lebanese army anti-aircraft fire on their approach successfully extricated the Israelis without loss.⁴

Using actual video footage from the operation, and interviewing some of the officers involved, Alon Ben-David later reported for Israel television that 'it was IDF Northern Command's policy to initiate and surprise. It does not matter whether you hit them in the bathroom at home, or outside in the backyard, or on the road. The aim is to hit them on their home ground. Hizbullah sustained a tough blow last night. For a small organisation, which is made up of only several hundred fighters, it is a harsh blow'.[5]

Taken at face value reports of this nature might have suggested that in 1997 Israel was winning the war against her enemies in south Lebanon. But this was not the case and there were several other less well-reported stories which painted a different picture altogether.

Take for example the events of Thursday 28 August when another 'ambush patrol' from the IDF's Golani brigade deployed in the Wadi Hujuar. Again Israel's declared policy was to 'take the fight' to Hizbullah and Amal, rather than wait for either to strike first by mortaring IDF/DFF compounds or launching rocket attacks against towns in northern Israel.

In an area of dense vegetation to the west of Qantara village on the edge of the security zone (which also over-lapped the forward edge of UNIFIL's Finnish battalion's area of operations), an Israeli patrol encountered a group of Amal resistance fighters and a frantic gun-battle erupted in which four members of the Amal unit were killed. Within a short period, local Hizbullah fighters joined the fray and succeeded in forcing the Israelis to begin withdrawing from the area.

'We were on one slope, the rest on the other slope', recalls Cpl Ronen Laloush (20), one of the IDF survivors. 'The four terrorists we killed were in a crevice. We fought them for about four hours.' Opting then to disengage completely, covering fire was requested from the nearby 155mm artillery battery at position 'Echo 219' (formerly known as Gate 12) but the 57 high explosive rounds which were fired merely succeeded in setting the entire undergrowth alight. Ditching all their equipment, both elements of the IDF patrol then attempted to climb out of the wadi as their abandoned explosives and ammunition ignited below them creating a fireball.

'The flames were as high as eight metres,' remembers Laloush. 'I put my hands up to cover my face and they got burned, I lost all feeling. I climbed up on my hands and knees. When the flames had passed, we went back down 20 or 30 metres to help our comrades. It was terrible. They were all burned.'[6] Sgts Oshri Schwartz (19), Oren Zarif (21), and Shimon Yadag (21), burned to death that afternoon and thus became further casualties in Israel's war of attrition with the many strands of Lebanon's Islamic resistance.

Accepting responsibility for what had in fact proved to be a complete debacle, and admitting that his own artillery had indeed created the inferno in which his troops had perished, Israel's GOC Northern Command Maj Gen Amiram Levine was acutely aware that these latest casualties would provide even further ammunition for the growing number of pressure groups in Israel incessantly calling for a unilateral military withdrawal from Lebanon.[7] Similar thoughts raced through the mind of Israel's Defence Minister, Yitzhak Mordechai, when he was made aware of the news while attending a graduation ceremony at the IDF's command and staff college.

Referring to this latest disaster as well as the continuing problem with roadside bombs and the deaths of 73 IDF personnel when two Israeli Air Force helicopters inexplicably collided while on their way to Lebanon on 4 February, the minister was surprisingly frank. 'We have been commanded [tasked] to protect those under our command,' he said, 'and to my regret we [have] found ourselves failing this year'.[8]

Nevertheless, and in spite of these and other admissions, Israel remained entrenched in south Lebanon, and the *Jerusalem Post* together with several other Israeli newspapers continued to tout the lie that Hizbullah was actually being defeated there by the IDF.[9] Independent observers however knew very well that this was simply not true as several other incidents provided ample evidence of the huge chasm between Israeli 'perception' of the conflict on the one hand, and the Lebanese 'reality' of it on the other. The events of Monday, 18 August, were a case in point.

It was almost lunch-time that day in the town of Kfar Houne, a god-forsaken place which lies within the area controlled by the IDF/DFF on the northern edge of the security zone. All was quiet and peaceful until a passing car triggered-off yet another roadside bomb. A shaped claymore mine concealed in an artificial garden rock, of the type that can be bought openly in any of Beirut's better garden centres, exploded with lethal effect and seriously injured both occupants of the car.

When the dust settled it emerged that two children, who just happened to be standing nearby, had also been caught in the blast. Jean Nasr (16) and his sister Rima (14) became Hizbullah's latest victims. Because the detonation of RSBs had by now become commonplace and virtually a daily occurrence, an immediate response from the IDF/DFF was not anticipated, but on this occasion the dead children turned out to have been the orphans of Major Assad Nasr, a DFF battalion commander who had himself been killed in action two years previously.[10]

Upon hearing the news at his DFF headquarters in Marjayoun, General Antoine Lahd ordered an immediate reprisal and at 1420hrs four heavy mortars smashed into the centre of the coastal town of Sidon over 20 km away to the north-west. A number of 155mm artillery shells armed with proximity fuses were also fired and this significantly contributed to an eventual casualty tally of nine dead and thirty-five seriously wounded.[11] The victims were all civilians. A three-month-old baby, and three boys aged six, twelve, and thirteen, were amongst the fatalities. Sidon was not a military target. There was no justification whatever in International Humanitarian Law for the attack.[12]

Within minutes Hizbullah Katyusha rockets[13] were on their way back towards positions occupied by the DFF's 20 Battalion near Jezzine from where the initial fire had originated. Local units of the Lebanese army, probably for the very first time, also became embroiled in the conflict and fired over 100 artillery rounds in retaliation. In the hail of high explosives that rained down on the northern part of the security zone that afternoon a 60-year-old man was killed and two women were seriously injured. Later again another ten Hizbullah Katyushas impacted in the town of Marjayoun close to where the DFF and IDF occupy a joint operational headquarters,[14] but this time without further injury. Later the IDF also decided to shell the village of Kfar Milki but fortunately only succeeded in demolishing ten houses which were already in bad repair from previous attacks.

And then the disclaimers began. 'Israel did not, I repeat did not, fire on Sidon today,' claimed Brig Gen Oded Ben-Ami, the IDF's chief military spokesperson. 'We are co-ordinated absolutely with the DFF inside the Security Zone [but] the Jezzine area is outside of this area.[15] General Lahd has his forces in Jezzine [but] they are out of our responsibility, out of our control.'[16]

Defence Minister Mordechai said he regretted the targeting of civilians and would use all his influence to halt these attacks. 'The DFF fire was without the knowledge of the IDF,' he said, claiming that he had 'no interest in exacerbating the situation and would urge Lahd not to violate the April 1996 Understanding'.

GOC Northern Command Levine insisted he was doing his best not to hit civilians but then made the fatal mis-calculation of threatening Hizbullah not to make what he called a 'mistake' by attempting to strike back at Israeli civilians in response. The following morning at 0700hrs dozens of Katyushas poured across the international border and ploughed into northern Israel.

As Irish staff from UNIFIL's headquarters in Naquora were crossing the border at Rosh Haniqra the tranquillity of another glorious summer morning was shattered by the distinctive drone of 63 Katyushas which flew into Israel.[17] Many landed harmlessly in the sea off Nahariya, while others exploded in open space, but other places along the border were not so lucky and received direct hits.[18] Once again Kiryat Shmona became a target and fourteen rockets fired from a position near Bra'shit village in Irishbatt's area of operations impacted in the town causing extensive structural damage, but miraculously no casualties.[19]

Justifying the attacks Hizbullah leader Sheikh Hassan Nasrallah was not in compromising mood. 'Antoine Lahd is a tool of Israel,' he said. 'What Lahd does Israel is completely responsible for. We call on the enemy to read with extreme care our morning message.'[20]

However, Prime Minister Netanyahu was not in compromising mood either. 'Israel will respond severely to attacks on civilian lives and Israel hopes this message will be absorbed on the other side in all its meaning' and true to form at first light on Wednesday morning four Israeli fighter aircraft took off from Ben Gurion airport near Tel Aviv and began a day exacting retribution.

Firstly, they launched a number of raids against Hizbullah bases in the Bekaa valley. This was followed up with an attack on a civilian car near the village of Touffahta just south of Sidon. Then turning north again the water and electricity station at Barja, 25 km south of Beirut, was attacked and severely damaged.

On their way back the Lebanese army artillery battery that had fired at Jezzine on Monday became their next target and the sortie was finally concluded when a number of high-tension electricity pylons near Sidon were systematically demolished. Israel had spoken, and vengeance had been exacted.[21]

The next day a new RSB was detonated near Jezzine and another civilian died in the blast, while early on Friday morning near the village of Ein Ibl, not far from the Irish UN post in At Tiri, a DFF truck triggered-off yet another RSB and the driver was killed. Later that evening a co-ordinated Hizbullah operation got under way with ground and rocket attacks mounted simultaneously against DFF compounds at Shihine (Whiskey 123) and Jabal Balata (Whiskey 125), and several infiltration attempts were made against three other DFF/IDF positions. Involving katyushas, mortars, heavy machine guns, and several ground elements, the attacks went on relentlessly for over three hours with IDF ground troops, helicopters, fighter aircraft and artillery, all becoming embroiled in the battle as darkness fell.

At first light on Saturday morning, both sides resumed where they had left off the previous evening with Hizbullah firing numerous mortars in an attempt to extricate one of their patrols which had been trapped in the area overnight. Almost immediately Echo 219's 155mm artillery battery commenced a saturation bombardment, firing hundreds of shells in a co-ordinated fire plan with 4 IDF fighter aircraft strafing those Hizbullah positions which the artillery missed or could not adjust onto.[22] As the fighting raged for several hours, Irish UN peace-keepers two kilometres away at post 6–40, in Al Yahun, could smell the odour of exploding shells and watched in disbelief as the sky became black with dust and dirt in the systematic demolition which unfolded before them. At times the noise of battle became so loud it was audible both at UNIFIL HQ in Naquora and in the busy market streets of the coastal town of Tyre, both 15 km distant.

Obtaining an altogether different impression of these events were members of the UN's Nepalese battalion in whose area the entire battle was fought but thankfully, despite several close calls, all of them eventually emerged from their positions that evening shaken but unscathed. Hizbullah were not so fortunate sustaining at least two fatalities and several wounded – but from their perspective, the attacks had served their purpose. Nasrallah's message to Israel had been clear. The IDF/DFF might well continue their operations in Lebanon but they would not do so without paying a significant price.

And then as if to confirm this position two days later an entire DFF foot patrol became victims of yet another RSB while attempting to conduct a routine reconnaissance operation close to the joint IDF/DFF HQ at Bint Jubayl.[23]

In grudging admiration for Hizbullah's capabilities, officers in the IDF's Northern Command were quoted in several Israeli daily newspapers as admitting that they were 'impressed' with what they had seen in action over the weekend and that it was clear Hizbullah 'was learning the modus operandi of the IDF and were improving from incident to incident'.[24] Brig Gen Yomtov Samie, commander of IDF's Galilee brigade said that as far as he was concerned, by applying the correct dose of infantry, armour and artillery he had succeeded in routing the terrorists, but the reality was it had still taken him three days to achieve this and he remained completely unable to prevent the further detonation of RSBs throughout the security zone. Thus was the pattern of activity that emerged in southern Lebanon throughout the summer of 1997 and less than a fortnight later came another IDF fiasco – the 'Ansariyeh Debacle'.

At half-past midnight on the morning of 6 September sixteen men from Israel's naval commando unit 'Shayetet 13'[25] waded ashore in Lebanon at a point equidistant from the cities of Tyre and Sidon. Crossing the busy coastal highway, they advanced inland for almost five miles towards the village of Ansariyeh, apparently moving with ease through the olive, orange and banana groves which abound in this densely vegetated area, and, no doubt, quietly confident of success given that one month previously the Golani brigade had managed to carry out a similar raid on the nearby village of Kfour.[26]

This time however the attack would not achieve the same result and when the commander, a lieutenant colonel, reached the gate of the last banana grove before the village an RSB exploded triggering-off several other devices which apparently had been hanging from the branches of the tress. Almost immediately one Israeli died when the explosives he was carrying ignited and in attempting to withdraw from the area the leading elements of the patrol were cut down by Hizbullah fighters who had been lying in wait nearby. A prolonged battle then ensued as the Israelis attempted to evacuate their dead and wounded and a combined force of Hizbullah, Amal and nearby Lebanese army units, conspired to prevent them.

In the midst of this intense fire fight, which was again visible to Irish UNIFIL peace-keepers on Hill 880, ten members of the Israeli patrol were killed, one was later declared missing presumed dead given that he was carrying the explosives which ignited, and a medical officer who had come to evacuate the patrol also perished. All of the remainder were very seriously injured and an operation which had begun so confidently ended up as Israel's worst military humiliation in Lebanon since 1985.

In the aftermath, it remained quite unclear why this attack was necessary in the first place, what Israel hoped to achieve by it, and why exactly it all went wrong. Certainly, this operation had been planned and approved at the highest political levels in Israel with both Prime Minister Netanyahu and Defence Minister Mordechai accepting responsibility for dispatching the force in the first instance. It is generally accepted that the objective was to assassinate either Khalil Harb, a leading Hizbullah strategist, or Abu Ahmed Soufaw, the Amal leader who had escaped the fireball in the Wadi Hujuar on 28 August, or most probably both.

It all went wrong either because an Israeli collaborator had been 'turned' by Hizbullah and was 'encouraged' to divulge the relevant information,[27] or because the naval commandos were spotted earlier that night when they landed on the shore and again when attempting to cross the highway. Either explanation will suffice because the truth of the matter probably contains elements of both.

However, for the purposes of this examination the essence of what took place on the morning of 6 September was that in 'taking the fight' to Hizbullah Israel was implementing a policy which no longer confined the battle-field in Lebanon to the security zone and its environs, an approach to 'security' which was perfectly consistent with other operations against Hamas typified by events less than three weeks later when Mossad agents attempted to assassinate Khaled Mashaal in Amman, Jordan.[28]

But while these setbacks were certainly worrying for Netanyahu it was the growth of Israeli public opinion adamantly opposed to continued IDF deployment in Lebanon which began to shake the political establishment in Jerusalem. In the aftermath of the helicopter crash in

February when 73 Israeli soldiers died while on their way to operations in Lebanon a group of Knesset members and former members of the Israeli Defence Community met at the house of Gideon Ezra[29] to discuss the possibility of an IDF unilateral military withdrawal from Lebanon.[30]

They were severely criticised at the time by the Labour party leader Ehud Barak, who claimed that 'the proposal for withdrawal sounds great as a headline but it is hardly what one would expect from people with a responsible attitude to security'. However, seven months later Barak had changed his mind, and he was not alone.

Economic Minister Ariel Sharon, the man who masterminded the 1982 Operation 'Peace for Galilee' which took the IDF to the outskirts of Beirut, had also proclaimed publicly that he was disposed to support a unilateral withdrawal which need not be linked to any regional settlement with Syria.[31] Sharon, like Ezra and others, now fully accepted that the entire Israeli political system was stuck in the middle of a Lebanese military quagmire, with episodes like Ansariyeh serving only to confirm all of their worst suspicions.

And when the speaker of the Lebanese parliament, Nabbih Berri, sat down to dinner in Tehran with Iranian Foreign Minister Kharrazi, and Parliamentary Leader Ali Akbar Nateq–Nouri, on the evening of 15 September, he too began by saying that southern Lebanon had become Israel's Vietnam and the only solution to the problem was a unilateral IDF withdrawal.[32] After 20 years of bitter, bloody, brutal conflict, it must surely have ranked as more than ironic that as 1997 drew to a close the vast majority of independent observers, a huge cross-section of political opinion in Israel, the speaker of the Lebanese parliament were all singing from the same hymn sheet. So too no doubt was Hassan Nasrallah, the 38-year-old Secretary General of the organisation Israel had thus far failed to conquer – Hizbullah.

By January 1998, Hizbullah, the Iranian-backed 'Party of God', was operating in Lebanon at a number of official levels. In the first instance, it was a political movement represented in the Lebanese parliament and accepted as legitimate by all other political groupings in the country. On an alternate level it remained a military organisation, sometimes referred to as Islamic Resistance, steadfastly committed to the removal of Israel from the security zone, and while operating independently in pursuit of this objective it also enjoyed the *de facto* permission of the Lebanese authorities to wage a war of resistance on their behalf.[33] It was in this context that units of the rival Amal organisation, and indeed the Lebanese army as well, had all now come to combine with Hizbullah in response to Israeli military activity.

Tracing its roots to the 1983 suicide bombings of the Multinational

Force in Beirut in which 241 Americans and 58 French were killed, by the late 1990s Hizbullah had moved its operations onto an altogether different plane where sacrificing fighters in resistance operations was tolerated only as a last resort. Moving through the countryside virtually unopposed, enjoying support from the vast majority of the population, and even party to the 'April Understanding', well armed, professionally trained, and vastly experienced fighters have progressively managed to turn the hills of south Lebanon into a military graveyard for both the IDF and DFF alike.

In a September 1997 interview with Beirut's *Monday Morning* magazine Sheikh Nasrallah was forthright on all these matters:

> Every occupier must eventually pull out of the territory it has despoiled. There can be no doubt that the cohesion of the Lebanese people and the effectiveness of the resistance will wear down the Israelis and speed their withdrawal. There is a positive relationship between the resistance and the state's security services that enables us to play our role without hindrance. South Lebanon poses a real problem for the Israelis who speak of it as their Vietnam, their quagmire, and it's natural that there should be differences of opinion since most of their cabinet ministers are former army officers. If we want to fuel these divergences, we must inflict more heavy losses on them so that they will realise that their logical option is withdrawal.[34]

But there were risks associated with this strategy and on the evening of Friday 12 September an IDF special forces 'Egoz' unit on routine ambush duty in the security zone encountered a four-man Hizbullah patrol near the village of Jabal Raifa and a vicious fight erupted. After several hours of gunfire two Hizbullah fighters lay dead in the wadi while a third died later from his wounds. The fourth, though badly wounded, managed to escape and shortly afterwards it emerged that one of the dead was Hadi Nasrallah, the 18-year-old son of Sheikh Nasrallah himself.

Appearing live on Hizbullah television the following day Nasrallah dismissed any suggestion that the body of his son would be used in any exchange deal for the remains of the IDF soldier blown to pieces at Ansariyeh. Instead he was uncompromising in his rhetoric and adamant that his son 'had chosen this road by his own will. We will make peace in this region with our pistols and pieces of our bodies,' he said. 'There will be no peace with occupiers. I thank God for choosing a martyr from my family.'[35]

Then, as Hadi Nasrallah's body was being removed to cold storage in the morgue at Marjayoun's hospital, the IDF decided to attack two Lebanese army positions near Nabatiyah in retaliation for what was deemed to be 'interference' in another Egoz operation in the area. Using attack helicopters, two armoured vehicles were targeted and resulted in the deaths of six Lebanese army soldiers and a local woman who had been attempting to warn them of the impending strike.

By way of explanation an IDF spokesman said that 'every time the Lebanese army interferes during battle it becomes a target', while Beirut's *Daily Star* newspaper preferred the claim that all IDF Northern Command senior officers were off-duty for the Sabbath and had left operational decision-making to junior officers who had failed to cope with the pressure.

Either way Israel had once again chosen to broaden the scope of her operations in Lebanon at the very time a firm reaction to the death of Hadi Nasrallah could almost certainly have been expected and independent observers were once again left to wonder whether the IDF really had a strategy in their on-going struggle with Hizbullah – especially since the first nine months of 1997 had already claimed thirty-seven Israeli lives.

Two days later, it certainly looked as if no such strategy existed when early on Sunday morning, a fifteen-man Golani brigade patrol on their way to an ambush site in the Wadi Saluki was struck by an RSB again made from a claymore mine packed with additional shrapnel and concealed in a fibreglass rock. Claiming two lives immediately and a third later on, the entire area was then subjected to sustained Hizbullah mortar fire making life extremely difficult for the helicopter crews who eventually managed to medevac the casualties.

By any yardstick one cared to employ, it did not appear that Israel's tactic of 'taking the fight to Hizbullah' was working. Indeed it was perfectly fair comment to suggest that when all of these casualty figures were combined with a litany of botched or failed IDF operations in the field, the resulting picture served only to indicate that Israel was barely achieving containment of the overall situation let alone actually winning anything. In fact, as the year came to an end it was hardly surprising, albeit severely embarrassing for the government, that reports began to surface indicating that a number of senior IDF officers were expressing substantial reservation about the scope and scale of Israel's operations in Lebanon.

Without any doubt, this change of heart had been brought about by a well organised mortar attack on an IDF convoy in which Brig Gen Levine was travelling, and also by the fact that Hizbullah had twice managed to target General Eli Amitay and succeeded in wounding him with an RSB.[36] But it also had much to do with a number of Hizbullah missile attacks in October 1997 which succeeded in penetrating the hulls of both the Mark 2 and Mark 3 Merkava main battle

173

tanks, the latter supposedly the best main battle tank in the world.[37] Equally, the apparent unrestricted capability of Hizbullah to detonate RSBs in the security zone, some of them a mere 100m from Israel's border fence, also bore heavily on the minds of senior IDF officers when they set about escorting Defence Minister Mordechai and Israel's co-ordinator of Lebanese Affairs, Uri Lubrani, on a tour of the area on 19 November.

Then on the morning of 25 November the *Haaretz* daily newspaper ran a banner headline claiming that a senior IDF commander had now called for a unilateral military withdrawal while addressing a high level meeting of senior infantry officers, with the commander in question apparently declaring that his opinions were shared by several others directly involved in the conflict in Lebanon.[38]

Two days later Channel 2 television identified the officer involved as none other than the GOC of Northern Command himself, Brig Gen Amiram Levine, former commanding officer and friend of the prime minister, and who up to that point in time was being tipped to succeed Danny Yatom as the next head of the Mossad. This was sensational news but Levine's remarks now placed him clearly at odds with Netanyahu who in a live broadcast two weeks previously had clearly spelled out his own position:

> We shall never leave our allies in the security zone whether they be SLA elements or civilians. We shall never abandon them because they are our true allies, true friends of Israel. I, as the decision-maker in Israel am not willing to withdraw unless our two conditions can be guaranteed, name-ly that the terrorist organisations are dismantled, and that the future of our allies plus their rights are guaranteed. When this happens we won't hesitate for one second to pull out. Till then we shall maintain our presence in the security zone until God says otherwise.[39]

Not surprisingly then Levine went quickly before a press conference to retract everything attributed to him, and while a witch-hunt began to discover the source of the leak,[40] the damage essentially was done. The head of military intelligence, Brig Gen Moshe Yaalon immediately labelled Levine a 'charlatan'[41] while in the Knesset Defence Minister Mordechai came under attack from all sides as debate on options for withdrawal intensified with the 'Movement for Peace' block even managing to produce a nine point blueprint to achieve it. In the midst of all this rancour, a concentrated newspaper campaign got underway in an attempt to discover exactly what constituted Israel's policy on Lebanon. Finding himself in an impossible position, Levine again attempted to explain his philosophy:

The present situation, in which Hizbullah is causing us to bleed and we are soaking it up, cannot continue. If you give me the means and the freedom to initiate and implement a large number of offensive activities I would be able to put Amal and Hizbullah on the defensive.

If we decide to withdraw then I would suggest that it be done in stages in order that it would not be seen as a retreat. Before starting the process of a pullback we would have to hit them a blow that they would not forget for a long time (something like Grapes of Wrath, but more painful) otherwise Hizbullah, Amal and the Palestinians would chase us to the border fence.[42]

But by the end of November 1997 a simple truth prevailed – Israel was well and truly 'bogged down' in Lebanon's military quagmire with not the remotest prospect in sight of either a political solution or immediate military disengagement. On 1 December the war of attrition continued with the detonation of another RSB which immobilised another Merkava MBT just 300m from the Irish UN post at At Tiri, and later that evening a Hizbullah rocket attack demolished part of the schoolhouse in the village of Ein Ibi.[43]

A few days later, an Amal operation went horribly wrong when a number of 120mm mortars were fired into the security zone but fell short of target and landed in the village of Beit Leif killing eight innocent civilians. With Lebanese Prime Minister Rafik Hariri refusing to guarantee security along the border with Israel even if the IDF withdrew claiming that 'only God can guarantee security'[44] and President Hrawi declaring at the Conference of Islamic States in Tehran that 're-sisting occupation is not terrorism but surrendering to occupation is treason',[45] it was hardly surprising that Israeli spokesman Uri Lubrani continued to adopt a hard-line approach even if at the back of his mind he knew that Israel could not sustain it:

I will say it clearly. Unilateral withdrawal is a recipe for even greater trouble and our aim is to prevent such a colossal mistake which if made would afterwards lead us to re-enter Lebanon with divisions and brigades and policies of burned earth.[46]

The human cost of occupying southern Lebanon has been very high for Israel with 219 IDF fatalities and 694 IDF wounded in the period 1985–1997 alone.[47] How much longer the Knesset, the IDF leadership, and Israeli public opinion, would be prepared to continue tolerating the payment of such a price remained unclear as Christmas 1997 approached. But the choice was stark. Israel would be damned if she left south Lebanon and equally damned if she stayed.

This was the ultimate 'Catch 22' dilemma – and for as long as the overall regional political situation remained unresolved the only certainty one could count on was that many more Israelis and Lebanese would continue to spill their blood on battlefields already soaked in it.

Not surprisingly then the new year began where the old had finished although throughout the spring several commentators began reporting that Israel was finally on the verge of implementing UN Resolution 425, twenty years after it had been first passed by the Security Council. If true this would have signalled the beginning of a troop withdrawal by the IDF and marked the demise of the DFF, but not for the first time rhetoric was cheap and events on the ground told a different story. Sadly, as spring turned into summer the war dragged on relentlessly – and then intensified!

On 25 June, a French military aircraft took off from Tel Aviv having filed a flight plan for Beirut. On board were the remains of several Lebanese citizens who in the course of recent years had died while participating in guerrilla operations against the IDF and the DFF. One of the caskets on board the flight contained the remains of Hadi Nasrallah.[48]

In Beirut, Prime Minister Hariri waited patiently on the airport tarmac in blistering temperatures, as hundreds of Hizbullah supporters gathered chanting the usual repertoire of anti-Israeli hate. Then with several television stations carrying the event live the French plane touched down and forty coffins were unloaded – 28 Hizbullah, 9 Amal, and 3 belonging to Lebanon's Communist Party. Two hours later, the same plane returned to Tel Aviv with the remains of Itamar Ilya on board.[49] Ilya had been the soldier decimated in the failed Israeli commando raid at Ansariyeh when the explosives he was carrying on his back detonated in the ambush.[50]

The following day a further 50 prisoners were also released from incarceration in the DFF's Khiam prison in the security zone, and other centres in Israel, prompting Sheikh Nasrallah to claim that the whole episode had been 'a great victory for Lebanon'. He went on to praise the involvement of Prime Minister Hariri in the return of the bodies but remained adamant that the struggle would continue and again acclaimed the ambush at Ansariyeh as the event which in Hizbullah's opinion marked the unification of all Lebanese in their struggle with Israel.

Jerusalem for its part attempted to down-play the entire event and Yaacov Perry, the former chief of the 'Shin Bet' security agency who had responsibility for the swap process, was dismissive of any suggested concession to Hizbullah. 'The majority of the prisoners released were not dangerous anyway', he said, 'if one can talk about terrorists in that way.'[51] Within hours, however, two more DFF soldiers were obliterated in a road side bomb at Toumet Niha near Jezzine and any suggestion of peaceful negotiation had been torpedoed.

Then on 2 July, in a measure clearly designed to confirm that Hizbullah's war was far from over, 16 IDF/DFF posts were attacked simultaneously with over 160 mortar rounds, 100 anti-aircraft shells, 80 anti-tank guided missiles, 20 recoilless rifle rockets, and thousands of heavy machine gun rounds being fired. For good measure, just after 0500hrs seven Hizbullah guerrillas succeeded in gaining entry to the DFF compound Whiskey 134, which overlooks Haddathah village, and successfully hoisted Hizbullah flags on the ramparts. Ten minutes later, all seven escaped and vanished into the wadi as Israeli shelling crept up behind them. One of the guerrillas had in fact to be carried off and later died from his wounds but video footage of the entire attack was shown that night on all Lebanese television channels and hailed by Nasrallah as a great victory.

In the programme a Hizbullah fighter could be clearly seen advancing towards the position, opening fire, throwing grenades, placing flags on the earth walls, giving the Hizbullah salute, and pledging allegiance to Nasrallah. The leader of the raid, Abu Hussein, was also interviewed and claimed the attack had taken 45 days to plan and 28 minutes to carry out. Further east, along the skyline, Bra'shit compound (Whiskey 144) was also bombarded by Hizbullah that morning and three DFF soldiers on duty there were seriously injured.

In response the IDF's retiring Chief of General Staff, Lt Gen Shahak, grudgingly admitted to the *Maariv* newspaper that 'Hizbullah is an enemy which constantly tries to learn and improve. The fact that the son of Nasrallah was killed shows that the sons of the hierarchy are in the firing line.' He went on to say that 'Hizbullah does not appear to have any recruiting problems notwithstanding that they were taking significant loses on the battlefields, and it has become very necessary for the IDF to be cautious because of the hundreds of Hizbullah operations which are now continually mounted against us.'[52]

In spite of a comparative lull in the conflict in June 1998 110 resistance operations were mounted and produced casualty figures as follows – 2 IDF dead, 7 IDF wounded, 2 DFF dead, 2 DFF wounded, and 4 Hizbullah dead.[53]

July began with more rumblings about the possible implementation of Resolution 425 with US Assistant Secretary of State Martin Indyk claiming that Israel was 'serious and flexible in its desire to get out of Lebanon and the natural consequence of implementing 425 would be a larger role for UNIFIL'.[54] But on the ground where it mattered none of this was having any impact and while the Lebanese army was busy in Beirut smashing up a sabotage ring from the outlawed Christian Militia and arresting seventeen people on charges of spying for Israel, in the south the war went on as usual. Hizbullah mortar attacks continued unrelentingly, roadside bombs exploded with lethal effect in the security zone, and Israel responded with a combination of routine shelling and combat air strikes. The summer of 1998 was proving no different from any which had recently preceded it.

Nevertheless, and in spite of the best efforts of the belligerents, by August Resolution 425 was apparently back on the table again and refusing to go away. This time it was the turn of the UN General Assembly President, Hennadiy Udovenko, who upon arrival in Beirut immediately threw his weight behind it. 'Resolution 425 should be unconditionally implemented and Israel should unconditionally pull out its forces' he told Lebanese Foreign Minister Bouez,[55] but for the moment there were two prospects of that happening – slim and none. Aside from security considerations it had also begun to emerge that southern Lebanon had become an invaluable testing ground for a new generation of Israeli guided missiles.

On 25 February, for example, a projectile was launched from the village of Taibe in the security zone and travelling at between 150 and 200 metres per second it impacted alongside a car which was parked 7.5 km. away on the outskirts of Majdal Silm village. Then on the night of 19 May two similar missiles were fired with one of them successfully locating and targeting an Amal unit on an infiltration raid, again near Majdal Silm. Twelve days later, a missile fired from a helicopter was seen skirting through the wadis until it eventually smashed into a cliff-face adjacent to where Hussein Mouqalled and his brother Mohammed were walking. Mohammed died instantly while the skin on Hussein's back became a mass of purple jelly.

This mini cruise missile, now known to have been the 'Long Spike', has been under development by the Haifa based Rafael Armaments Company for some time and a family of these weapons now exists.[56] Not for the first time southern Lebanon provided Israel with a very convenient live-firing target range[57] and will continue to do so for as long as this war of attrition drags on.

Meanwhile on 5 August a white Mercedes travelling between the villages of Zibqine and Jabal al Boutom, 25 km. south-east of Tyre and outside the security zone, was hit by a projectile and destroyed when Israeli artillery saturated the area. Hassan Ahmad Hamoudi, a senior Hizbullah activist, died instantly and his passenger was seriously wounded. Later, retaliatory attacks were launched against numerous IDF positions and several further tons of high explosives were hurled through the Lebanese air demolishing numerous houses and igniting much needed food crops in the fields. In Lebanon the olives don't bleed – they burn.

Then on the night of 20 August, two Israeli soldiers were killed in the north-eastern part of the security zone when a series of claymore mines exploded near Sujud and obliterated them. A short time earlier Hizbullah had attacked an IDF convoy near Beaufort Castle and several helicopters had to be used to evacuate the casualties.

Within hours, Yossi Beilin, the Member of the Knesset heading up the Movement Seeking Total IDF Withdrawal from Lebanon, was screaming that there was no justification whatever for these latest deaths and this was echoed immediately by fellow Knesset member Ran Cohen claiming that the IDF could defend Israel's northern territory from a much narrow strip of land in Lebanon and thereby cause far less friction and fewer casualties. Prime Minster Netanyahu replied that pulling the IDF out of Lebanon was his top priority but unsurprisingly did not elaborate on how he intended to achieve this.[58] Five days later a bad situation got worse.

Late on the evening of Tuesday 25 August, Israel sanctioned an Apache helicopter attack in which a laser guided missile atomised Amal's senior explosives expert, Hussam Al Amine. Israeli media immediately claimed the decision to eliminate Al Amine had been approved at the highest levels of government:

> It looked good on paper. The execution was surgically meticulous, thanks to good intelligence. But taking out top Amal military commander Al Amine would expose the residents of the north-west to a retaliation. However, the IDF was determined to send a message that no one behind attacks on Israeli troops is immune. Al Amine was said to be directly responsible for the increase in attacks against Israeli targets in Lebanon this year. The IDF insists the attack was strictly within the confines of the Grapes of Wrath agreements, which do not bar attacks on military personnel.[59]

Two hours later 40 Katyusha rockets slammed into the centre of Kiryat Shmona in north-western Israel destroying buildings and cars and knocking out power lines. Rockets also landed elsewhere in Galilee including the vicinity of Nahariya town. The IDF immediately claimed the Katyushas were a violation of the April Understandings although by some obscure logic they were adamant that the killing of the Amal guerrilla had been perfectly legitimate. Hizbullah then issued a statement saying it had not fired the rockets in response to the killing of the Amal fighter but in retaliation for the earlier shelling of Mashghara village during which six civilians and three Syrian soldiers were wounded. This in itself was a retaliation by the IDF for the earlier death of a DFF soldier blown to pieces by a roadside bomb.

The IDF then issued a statement attempting to absolve them of responsibility by claiming that it was in fact the DFF who had fired into Mashghara although they did admit to launching an air strike after the RSB blast. Hizbullah retorted that it would never stand idly-by while civilians were targeted and the firing of rockets was the only language Israel understood.

Establishing the truth in this convoluted self-perpetuating downward spiral of violence had now become virtually impossible. Suffice to say that this particular sequence of events illustrated dramatically the quagmire into which all belligerents in the Lebanese conflict had now lost their footing and sunk. And as if to prove this point beyond doubt the very next day began with Amal mortar attacks against several DFF and IDF compounds.

Thus, it continued throughout the summer of 1998 where the statistics for August alone read as follows: 130 Resistance operations mounted against the IDF/DFF (83 Hizbullah, 34 Amal, 12 Lebanese Squads, 1 Communist Party), 3 IDF killed, 22 IDF wounded, 2 DFF killed, 2 DFF wounded, 3 Hizbullah killed. Israel in turn launched 122 airstrikes. The 27 August editorial in *Haaretz* summed up the situation rather well: 'A war of attrition is being fought on Israel's northern front and the underlying causes of this war can only be eliminated in the form of a settlement with Damascus (Syria). Until such a settlement is achieved the fighting will continue and the IDF cannot make do with defensive measures alone.'

Into the New Year the overall military situation deteriorated further with Hizbullah intensifying its campaign on a daily basis. In this regard the killing of 38 year-old General Erez Gerstein on 28 February, when his armoured-plated Mercedes was ripped apart by a huge roadside bomb just four miles from the border, near Ebel Ea Saqi, sent shock waves through the Israeli military establishment. Coming on the heels of another Hizbullah success the previous week when three IDF officers leading a commando raid were obliterated in an ambush, Israel struck again by launching several punitive air-raids into the heart of Lebanon. The effect was minimal and the daily slaughter continued *ad nausea* until the beginning of May when an IAF cobra helicopter was shot down killing one officer and injuring four others. The response this time was a prolonged long-range artillery barrage against several suspected Hizbullah positions which again achieved nothing, and a few days later two DFF soldiers were decimated by yet another a radio-controlled directional RSB.

And then as if to prove that punitive strikes were having completely the opposite effect on 15 May Hizbullah attacked eight IDF/SLA positions simultaneously using Katyushas, 122mm artillery, a whole range of mortars, Sagger missiles, several anti-aircraft guns, and Strela ground-to-air missiles.[60]

At one DFF compound (W139) near the Irish UN position at Bayt Yahun the attackers breached the ramparts, hoisted the Hizbullah flag, killed one soldier, wounded five others, and drove away in an M–113 APC. Thereafter the DFF apparently decided that UNIFIL was not doing enough to prevent these attacks and shelled several UN positions resulting in the needless death of Pte Billy Kiedan in what was clearly a revenge attack.[61]

Meanwhile in Israel sections of the popular press began to hail the election of former IDF Chief of Staff, Ehud Barak, as Israel's next prime minister given that his election manifesto committed him to an IDF withdrawal from Lebanon within one year of taking office on 9 July. Unfortunately that task would be easier said than done and the commencement of the entire process has not been advanced one inch by Hizbullah's deliberate escalation of the conflict which included the triumphal parading in Sidon and Beirut of the captured M–113 APC, the non-stop daily detonation of RSBs, and the relentless firing of Katyusha rockets across the border. This again served only to spark-off predictable retaliation which resulted spectacularly at the end of June in Israel's toughest strikes against Lebanon for over three years killing nine people, wounding fifty-seven, knocking out two power sub-stations in Beirut, destroying three bridges on the coastal highway, and damaging a number of buildings in the eastern city of Baalbek.[62]

'Israel will not allow residents in the north to be harmed, and will react in the harshest manner,' screamed out-going Prime Minister Netanyahu, while departing Defence Minister, Moshe Arens, told Israel army radio that 'nothing happens [in Lebanon] without the Syrians wanting it to'. In the summer of 1999 Israel still enjoys a strategic advantage over Syria by virtue of its continued occupation of the Golan Heights and also exercises some moderate indirect leverage on Damascus via the 1996 Israeli–Turkish Agreement.

For Syrian president, Hafez al Assad, the return of the Golan Heights (and access to water supplies from the Jordan river) remains his top priority and keeping the IDF bogged down in Lebanon is crucial to this strategy.[63] Consequently Syria's support of Hizbullah will continue until there is some movement on the Golan and for as long as Israel is not prepared to concede it, or relinquish control of the water, then the war in Lebanon looks set to continue. In that scenario Ehud Barak may not be able to extract himself from Lebanon by any agreement no matter what timetable he cares to set himself and that does not auger well for the future.

Israel's most decorated soldier, and now her latest prime minister, may honestly believe himself to be a man of peace but the attainment of a durable settlement throughout the region may prove to be beyond even his undoubted capabilities. At the end of the day Ehud Barak may well have only one option left in Lebanon – a unilateral IDF withdrawal – and only time will tell whether he actually has the courage to take it.

A compilation from articles published in 1997, 1998 and 1999

On duty

FIRST TIMERS' DIARY

A/Cpl Paul O'Donovan, Airwoman Anne Hardy, Cpl Darina Brennan, and Signalwoman Louise Holden

'Welcome to Lebanon'. This is it, we're here. No turning back now. As soon as we reached Beirut, we were marched off for processing in the hangar where we were greeted by a chorus of 'Jingle Bells' from the members of the 81 Battalion who were waiting to leave for home. I must compliment them on their sense of humour! Then it was off to the AO, picking up our SISU escort at the Litani river. On reaching Al Yahun, it was off the buses and straight into the CQMS' stores for issuing of rifles, helmets, flak jackets and blue berets. The next morning I awoke early and was taken aback by my first sight of the Irish AO with all its villages, wadis and hills. On the tops of many of the hills, I could see the UN, IDF and DFF compounds – see how quickly I'm learning the terminology! ... which are a constant reminder of why we are here. Over the next few days, we were bombarded ... with information. It wasn't long before we were assigned to our posts. I was sent to 6–10A in Al Jurn. Then it was all go, learning all the names of the villages, posts and compounds that we would have to observe and report on. In addition, we had to rehearse all our drills, fire drill, groundhog, and scheme of defence. Shortly after arriving, I was on my first duty in Lebanon. We then had two weeks of 81 Battalion 'locals' who were in high spirits. In the end, I was glad to see them gone as they were a constant reminder of home. Now that they have gone, we're the kings of the castle; we're running the show now.

Pte Paul O'Donovan

The second chalk of 82 Inf. Bn departed Dublin Airport at 0930hrs on 28 October; destination, Beirut International Airport. We had a very pleasant flight with the Aer Lingus crew, with lots of entertainment, and five hours later, the landing gear came down and we landed in Beirut. As we taxied into the ramp area, I could see the UN vehicles and baggage party of 81 Inf. Bn waiting for us. The aircraft came to a halt, and as the cabin doors opened, I awaited the sounds of jeering (i.e. 'Happy Christmas', 'Jingle Bells', etc.) but surprisingly, none were to be heard. After an uneventful flight, we landed in Beirut, formed into our companies, and marched to the hangars to sign our UN ID cards. At that stage, I felt like a recruit again, not knowing what was really going on and depending on the 'old sweats' to steer me in the right direction. With this out of the way we set off for Camp Shamrock. On the journey, I got a chance to see some of the landscape and villages. Although it was dark, I could see that the villages were remote and that most of the buildings were very run down compared to Irish standards. We passed through many Lebanese army checkpoints before we eventually came to the UN posts. My first impressions of the Camp Shamrock were those of any barracks at home. We start work at 0800hrs and finish at approximately 1600hrs. Life is normal inside the camp with the exception of some of the sounds such as occasional shelling and gun fire. Once I step outside the camp it feels like I have gone back in time. Everything appears old and run down and the culture is very different to ours. The first big difference I noticed, being a female, is the total lack of status of the local women. Although I must respect their culture, I thank God that this lack of recognition of women no longer prevails at home. For the next six months, I will be working in the company office and here I get a very good idea of what goes on around the AO. I also get time to do 'shot-gun' which is a great way to get out of camp and see the area. At this stage into my trip, I am more than happy to be here. Every day is a new learning process and a great experience. I still have a long way to go, but I look forward to the next few months ahead.

Airwoman Anne Hardy

The pilot was trying his best to boost our morale by providing us with an excellent weather forecast for Beirut, however when we landed we were instead greeted by a torrential rainstorm unlike anything we would be likely to see in Ireland. Even stranger was the stifling heat, which accompanied the rain. My first impressions of Lebanon were of widespread chaotic building and equally chaotic drivers! The journey to Camp Shamrock took over three hours and I found myself reflecting on home, friends and family and wondering what they would be doing. After the first week in Shamrock, I was getting the hang of my new way of life; names and places on maps now began to become more familiar. My appointment as battalion pay clerk is a busy and demanding one but is also very rewarding as it will entail several visits to Israel during my term. I volunteered for the entertainments' committee that organises sporting and social events in the camp. Back home, I always took a night's entertainment for granted but out here, you have to be very adaptable due to limited resources. So far we have had successful Karaoke and Bingo nights and are due to hold an Irish night within the next week or two. The last few weeks have been extraordinary and if they're anything to go by I can look forward to the remainder or the tour.

Cpl Darina Brennan

The night before we flew out with Chalk One, I said goodbye to my family and friends in the mess with mixed emotions, apprehension but also excitement at facing into the unknown. The flight was relaxing and comfortable with a general buzz in the air. The Aer Lingus staff were great, taking good care of their cargo – approximately 200 peacekeepers. After landing in Beirut and travelling through Lebanon, it was well after dark when we finally reached our destination, A Company HQ in Al Yahun. When we had found our room Pte Olga Short, the only other female in A Company, and I made our way to the canteen where, although it was only October, we were met with Christmas decorations and songs – the traditional welcome for winter trips, I believe! Orientation day began at 1000hrs the next morning when our orders were read out and explained and we were given a tour of the camp and a talk on the surrounding posts and compounds. I spent the following week in the Comcen 'learning the ropes'. I thought I'd never get the hang of it, what with all the different radios, phones and pro-formas, never mind the call signs and extension numbers. But soon I was settled in and my confidence in the job grew day by day. One thing I've found is that the mosquitoes love me! I'm covered with bites and am trying hard to resist the urge to scratch.

Signalwoman Louise Holden

THREE MONTHS LATER

When I arrived in Lebanon six months seemed such a long time, but now that we have reached the half-way mark it feels like no time at all. My platoon has finished its term in the OPs and we are now moved into company HQ in Al Yahun. We are operating the checkpoint at 6–40 and conducting mobile and foot patrols throughout the area. We are also responsible for the upkeep of the camp so as you can imagine we are kept busy. Although I am no stranger to checkpoint duty having served on the border at home with 29 Inf. Bn, this is quite different. We conduct random vehicle searches and warn UN and civilian traffic of shelling alerts. Occasionally we also have to give directions that I find quite amusing: an Irishman in Lebanon giving directions to the Lebanese! Ah well! It's all part of the job.

A/Cpl Paul O'Donovan

We are well into our tour now and the time is flying in. Before Christmas, the place was alive with preparations for the visit of President McAleese. Unfortunately, I was not in the AO for the actual visit as I was working with the military police on Bravo-One Gate at the border with Israel at Rosh Haniqra. However, I was in Camp Shamrock during the run up to the president's visit and the old saying was certainly true: 'If you stood still long enough you could find yourself painted, cleaned or moved to another position!' My stint on the border gave me a good insight into the military police personnel's duties. It also afforded me a first opportunity to work with soldiers from other contingents. January saw our first fall of snow and it affected us in many ways: most traffic was grounded, there was very little movement throughout the AO, and there was a lot of ducking and diving to avoid snowballs! A special thanks must be given to the engineer platoon for their artistic creativity in building the first ever snow-woman in Camp Shamrock.

Airwoman Anne Hardy

Quite a lot has happened since the last time I got to send home a report. As already mentioned we had a visit from the president which really had everybody buzzing and was a great morale booster. The interest in the visit was amazing with reporters and camera crews from many countries arriving to join us on this proud occasion. Because there are so many first-timers on this trip the demand for places on the Holy Land tour is being organised. I was lucky enough to make it on the first one. It was a brilliant few days and the 54 of us who travelled got on famously. I really feel that the Holy Land tour is a must for anyone who has the opportunity to go on it.

Cpl Darina Brennan

It's into February as I write this and the trip is almost half over. The last couple of months have been relatively quiet in the AO which has left us with a bit more time on our hands than usual. I went on the Holy Land tour that was a really memorable event. On a hectic schedule, we visited places like Bethlehem, Nazareth, the Holocaust Museum, the Dead Sea and Masada. On a more secular note, we also managed to visit the renowned Underground bar in Jerusalem. On the job front, all is going well. I'm giving radio-checks in my sleep now: '6–40 You're OK, over.' We have had some rough weather including some snow. It played havoc with our aerials and wiring but everything is back on track now. We had good *craic* at our New Year's Eve party which was fancy dress. Nearly everyone who wasn't on duty turned up and I became chief make-up to the stars turning out Elvis, Michael Jackson, a drag queen and Clint Eastwood. The battalion commander even turned up dressed as Lawrence of Arabia.

Signalwoman Louise Holden

1998
2FM LIVE IN LEBANON

SGT TERRY MCLAUGHLIN

The men and women of 82 Irishbatt serving in south Lebanon found themselves at the centre of an important event when 2FM's Gerry Ryan and Larry Gogan became the station's first presenters to broadcast live from Lebanon. The two shows are among the most popular on the airwaves at home with over 400,000 tuning in to Gerry Ryan every day and a further 300,000 listening to The Larry Gogan Show.

Along with the two stars the 2 FM party included head of 2FM, Bill O'Donovan; senior producers Lucia Proctor, Paul Russell and Seán McKenna; outside broadcasts engineer Donie Strich; as well as *The Gerry Ryan Show*'s Brenda Donoghue and researcher Siobhán Hough. Covering the event for the print media were reporter Stephen Rae and photographer Colin O'Riordan from the *Evening Herald*, and Renagh Holohan who writes the Quidnunc column in Saturday's *Irish Times*.

While most of the visitors were first-timers the group did include a number of 'old sweats' – producer Seán McKenna had overseen the installation of the 2FM Lebanon studio in 1993, the *Evening Herald*'s Stephen Rae had been to Irishbatt before, and Brenda Donoghue had accompanied the president on her recent visit. Renagh Holohan had been to Lebanon before, although no one knew if that counted as it had been in the pre-civil war days.

The visitors received a very warm welcome from the troops but unfortunately not from the weather. On the day of their arrival, the 'khamsin' wind was blowing across the Middle East leading to sandstorms which shrouded Lebanon and the rest of the region. The locals say that the 'khamsin' is followed by four days of bad weather ... they were spot on!

Over the next few days, torrents of rain and hailstones lashed the country accompanied by regular bouts of thunder and lightning, and even freezing fog at one stage. Such were the conditions that the giant Ferris Wheel on the sea front in Beirut which had withstood years of civil war and numerous bombardments, finally gave up the ghost and yielded to the fury of the elements.

Luckily, the visitors toured the Irish Area of Operations on the first day before the weather closed in. Travelling by SISU they visited many of the Irish positions where they met the troops and received briefings in Al Yahun, Hill 880, the new Black Hole position, and Shaqra. It had been planned to visit C Company's post 6–28A (Alpha) deep in the Israeli controlled area across the Wadi Saluki but unfortunately due to failing light the visitors had to be satisfied with viewing the Irish position and its nearby DFF neighbours from the roof of post 6–28.

On the way back to Camp Shamrock the party stopped off in the wadi close to the old Shamrock where they received a demonstration of an 'Earlybird', the regular minesweeps carried out by Irish troops on certain designated roads before they can be travelled by UN vehicles. Personnel from each of the companies are trained by the specialist search team to carry out preliminary road sweeps and if they locate anything suspicious the SST are called out to investigate. The guests were very interested in the operation and received an extremely comprehensive and in-depth brief by the battalion's ESST (Engineer Special Search Team) officer Capt Dave Connolly.

The next two days saw over ten hours of live programming broadcast from the 2FM Lebanon studio which had been donated to Irishbatt by 2FM and installed by them during the take-over period of 73 Irishbatt in 1993. Gerry Ryan talked about Lebanon in his own inimitable fashion, pulling no punches and letting his audience know the reality of the situation and conditions in which our troops are operating. He lost no time in destroying the myth that a trip to the Lebanon is some sort of holiday or 'cushy' time for those involved; a myth which he says we are responsible for sustaining ourselves through fear of telling people at home 'how it really is' in case they might worry; always playing things down for the sake of those left behind.

Brenda Donoghue was out and about the camp with her 'radio mike' talking to the troops while Gerry played host in the studio to a large number of guests including Minister of Defence, Mr Michael Smith, TD, who had arrived for the Irishbatt medal parade; Chief of Staff, Lt Gen Gerry McMahon; and eminent journalist and writer Bob Fisk.

On the Larry Gogan Show which followed, Larry met the troops, played requests, and in some cases set up live links to loved ones back home. And of course there was Larry's hugely popular 60–Second Quiz in which one member of A Company excelled by scoring a record-equalling 20 points.

The programmes were a great success with the troops and spirits were raised even higher when news began to filter through of how well they had been received by 2FM's audience at home. Although this was a 'first' everybody involved certainly felt it wouldn't be the last such event.

When asked what he thought of it all Larry Gogan had this to say:

I have been fascinated by the trip. I had no idea that the troops worked under those kinds of conditions. I found the outposts quite an eye-opener, and I don't think anyone at home realises what it is like, how lonely it must be living in these remote posts in all kinds of weather in a difficult and tense situation. I would love to do this again because it was great for us to get so much positive reaction from the troops. I knew that 2FM broadcast to Lebanon but I didn't realise how many listened and how much it meant to them.

Gerry Ryan of course was more direct:

The Leb has been the biggest eye-opener of all. I had my suspicions that things were not quite as we were led to believe at home: that idea it was a picnic out here, some sort of Club Med experience with an extra few pounds, was erroneous. I can safely say that I have been proved right. What you see here is an operational force operating under very taxing, stressful circumstances, doing a very efficient job. They are not on holiday! But I must say, I didn't expect the Irish military to be as in control of the area as they are. And I didn't expect their operational methods to be as sophisticated because you have an image at home that the military are maybe 25 years behind the rest of the world.

Then you come out here and all the technology and the systems are here, and the *modus operandi* is something that anybody who has watched a contemporary military documentary anywhere in the world will be familiar with. It is great source of pride to see our soldiers operation at the coal-face under stress in extremely dangerous situations and dealing in such a sophisticated way with a tense, complex military situation.

I'm also very impressed to see so many really young people here, many no more than 18 or 19 years old. Another thing people at home didn't realise is that everywhere you go there are bunkers which are used on a regular basis, because of the ever-present threat of shelling. And then you go to an outpost and you see guys there in scenes like *Apocalypse Now* where there are groups on either side of them shelling each other and they're stuck there in the middle trying to evaluate the situation.

Since 2FM's broadcasts this week from Camp Shamrock the troops can stop asking the question 'Do people at home know what we're doing here?' We now know that it's a serious job, and that all the men and women of Irishbatt have every right to be proud of their work in Lebanon.

MINISTERING TO THE FLOCK

FR BRENDAN MADDEN AND FR DICK MARNELL

In the Irish Defence Forces, a chaplain is neither an officer nor an other-rank; our role is neutral, impartial and confidential. Our *modus operandi* is that we are the same rank as the person who is talking to us. Our concern is for the welfare of each member of the Defence Forces. We respect the military system and work within it to better the lot of all our personnel and their families, regardless of religious denomination or affiliation.

Traditionally, each Irish battalion serving in Lebanon has had the benefit of not one but two chaplains (also called Padres, 'Sky Pilots', 'Devil Chasers' – take your pick!) for each six-month tour. The chaplains begin their association with the troops they will be accompanying as early as possible. This usually begins during the forming-up process when the chaplains visit the troops in an effort to get to know names and family backgrounds in as relaxed a manner as possible.

Although based with the battalion we are chaplains to the whole Irish contingent and as such we are also responsible for the spiritual, moral and emotional care of the component in Naquora and our personnel serving with the force mobile reserve.

One of the chaplains is based in Camp Shamrock while the other is based in B Company HQ in Haddathah. Each morning the chaplain in Camp Shamrock attends the battalion morning brief which helps him to keep up to date with the operational situation in the Irish area. The daily routine for both chaplains consists of visiting the positions and outposts in all company areas. On his journey, each chaplain is accompanied by a 'shotgun' – a soldier who provides protection, as chaplains do not carry weapons.

As Roman Catholic chaplains, we celebrate mass in each company HQ and outpost every week to facilitate the Sunday obligation that our faith decrees. However, observance of the Sunday obligation is a purely personal matter and no pressure is put on anyone to attend these services – they are only for those who are interested, and free. Often troops who don't wish to attend mass will kindly volunteer to cover temporarily for a colleague so that he, or she, may attend to their religious duties.

Much of our work takes place following the mass during what one former chaplain to UNIFIL describes as 'the pastoral work of drinking tea'. This is when people simply gather around drinking tea, and swapping stories and anecdotes full of humour and pathos. We are there to be approached if anyone wishes. Another apt description of our methods is that given by another colleague to the work of a university chaplain (which is not dissimilar), who described it as 'loitering with intent'. Then it's on to the next post or back to our home base.

At one level, our work never ends, as mealtimes and 'the canner' or mess provide other moments of encounter with personnel who may pull you to one side to talk about something personal. Conversations such as these are not always bad news stories. Often a soldier will simply want to share some news about home, perhaps how well a child has done in exams, the birth of a new child or grandchild or some other significant family event.

On many occasions, however, there will be stories of tragedy and pain, sickness and bereavement. In such cases, we listen and help as best we can; all the time applying our Christian faith to the situation, in an effort to alleviate the worries of the person involved. From time to time, we may be asked to impart some bad news from home to a member of the battalion. This we try to do as sensitively as possible in order to soften the inevitable blow.

Sometimes 'conflict management' comes into play as we try to help out with any disputes between personnel; offering a neutral, and hopefully Christian, interpretation of events so that reconciliation and forgiveness may win out over bitterness and anger. Over the six-month period, we also have numerous religious commemorations for our fallen comrades. Once again, as Roman Catholics, we believe that our prayers can help those who have gone before us marked with the sign of our faith, and so masses are offered for our departed loved ones and colleagues.

Of course, all the major religious festivals are celebrated such as Christmas and Easter, St Patrick's Day and so on. As well as fulfilling our religious duties, these occasions also provide 'a semblance of normality from back home', as one first-timer said to me recently.

As followers of Christ the sick are always important to us and we regularly visit sick personnel in our own regimental aid post or alternatively in the Polish Medical Company Hospital in Naquora.

In all that we do we try to be cheerful and positive to help with the moral of the contingent. We also try to get involved in all other areas of Irish UNIFIL life, both sporting and recreational. In addition to our own personnel, other contingents occasionally look to us to supply Catholic services for their personnel if they do not have a Roman Catholic chaplain at the time.

We are proud to serve our God and our country as chaplains

191

overseas and over the six months we make many great and lasting friendships. Although we see our role here as purely to help others, we also gain a lot from our trip. One of the main ways is that the Christianity displayed by many of our professional soldiers is an inspiration to us as well.

Saying Sunday mass

1999

LIFE IN BEIT LEIF

COMDT BRENDAN O'SHEA

Beit Leif is a tiny Muslim village which hangs precariously on the northern slope of a deep wadi on the forward edge of the ICA, fully exposed to anyone who might decide to shell it. In a secluded court-yard just off the narrow rutted winding main street I found a woman who lost her husband on a fateful evening two years previously when stray Amal shells ploughed into the village killing eight of its citizens.

Aged well beyond her years the futility of the conflict was written clearly in the deep lines which creased her weather-beaten face. Rear-ing her young family was always a struggle in this part of the world. Now, dependent on the modest contributions her older children send from Beirut and abroad, survival has become her only priority. And as I left her sitting on the ground outside her spartan but spotless home, and harvesting a meagre pile of olives which during the winter would be sold for a few inflated Lebanese pounds, I marvelled at her resili-ence in the face of chronic adversity.

Life is difficult in Beit Leif. The water runs intermittently, elec-tricity is unpredictable, unemployment is almost universal, and the nearby presence of several IDF and DFF positions ensures this sleepy village will remain a target for as long as the conflict here continues.

Later when we went to meet the village muktar a noisy crowd gathered round to witness what was happening. They ranged in age from eight to eighty and though they bore the UNMO team no ill, their eyes revealed the full spectrum of emotion in the ICA today – anger, apathy, excitement, resentment, even commitment to their cause – but overwhelmingly they revealed an existential acceptance of their current lot and the fact that this is very likely to remain their only lot for a considerable time to come.

Beit Leif is a village on the front line, a village trapped in a war its people did not seek but from which they have no escape. There is no respite for any of them because tomorrow may bring another hail of death hurtling from the sky or the detonation of another roadside bomb along the village's pock-marked broken roads. The only con-solation – if one could call it so – is that several other places in the ICA also suffer the same fate on a daily basis, and in some instances the level of violence is appreciably worse.

A case in point is the village of Bayt Yahun where further chapters of atrocity were written on 27 September when Fawzi al-Zaghire, the 51-year-old senior DFF figure who commanded the crossing point into 'Free Lebanon', was firstly wounded by a bomb which detonated beside his car, and then killed in the ensuing ambush.

Also taking the life of his bodyguard, and wounding two others, the attack signalled a major triumph for Hizbullah because Al-Zaghire had previously been badly wounded on several occasions but always managed to survive. His demise signalled the commencement of a sustained co-ordinated Hizbullah attack on several IDF/DFF positions right across the ICA and resulted at Bayt Yahun in several firings close to the nearby Irish UN position, affectionately known to peacekeepers down the years as 'the black hole'.

Beit Leif was on the receiving end as well, with the DFF mortar position (cynically and illegally located right in the middle of the village square) taking several direct hits.

Life is cheap in this dogfight. It is only those families, both Israeli and Lebanese, who having suffered, endured and survived, can make any attempt to quantify the real indelible cost of it all.

Unsung hero – the water-truck driver

2000

A Civil Servant's View

Martin Kirwan

The engine of the SISU APC rumbled as it navigated the winding hill that led from battalion HQ in Camp Shamrock to A Company HQ in Al Yahun. As a civilian, it was a strange feeling travelling in a white armoured car along the roads of south Lebanon, wearing the blue flak jacket and helmet of the United Nations. Yet, it brought home to me the danger which our soldiers face on a daily basis.

We had arrived in Lebanon the previous day and were met at Beirut airport by Colonel James Saunderson, Capt Tom Freyne (our liaison officer for the visit), and our driver, Private John Stone. Before setting off for the UNIFIL AO, we were briefed on the current political and military situation in Lebanon and particularly on the role of the Irish peacekeepers who first arrived at the very outset of the mission 22 years ago.

Following a very warm welcome in Camp Shamrock the next day, we received another briefing, this one concerning the precise problems in our immediate area and this prepared us for the visits that we would be making to the troops on the ground, and to the various company HQs.

Seeing the soldiers at work and speaking to them individually gave us a good idea of life in the various posts. Each soldier generally spends about two months at a particular location with his platoon after which they are rotated to another area. The quality of life for the troops can change from day to day and may depend on the level of military activity locally.

To the visitor the most striking feature in the Irish AO is the up-beat mood and good humour shown by all ranks as they go about their duties. The enthusiasm that was evident in the briefings and during conversations with individual soldiers conveyed a universal sense of pride in a job well done.

The reality of life on the ground for our troops comes as quite a shock, however, and is different from the impression we get at home in Ireland. For each of the four nights we were in south Lebanon there was shelling and gunfire in or around the Irish AO. On one occasion, this went on for most of the night.

I was surprised by the level of activity that goes on, and that so much of it goes unreported in the media. Yet, this is day-to-day reality for those who serve as peacekeepers in this troubled land. Thankfully, incidents which cause loss of life are rare, but the death last year of Private Billy Kedian *(ar dheis Dé go raibh a anam)* is a constant reminder that vigilance is of paramount importance. Every day, from the sweeping of the road for mines in the morning to the last watch of the night, our soldiers must keep alert to possible dangers which may suddenly threaten them or their comrades.

The contrast in the second part of our visit could not have been starker. The ancient Sun City of Baaleck, with its ruins and vivid scenes of ancient history, lies in the Bekaa valley north-east of Beirut. We visited Baaleck on a warm, sunny, peaceful day in October, but as we walked the massive ruins, the words of Lord Byron, with their evocation of the warlike history of the region came to mind:

> *The Assyrian army came down like a wolf on the fold,*
> *And his cohorts were gleaming in purple and gold:*
> *And the sheen of their spears was like stars on the sea,*
> *When the blue wave rolls nightly on deep Galilee*
> *Amid the stately ruins how vivid were the words:*
> *And the windows of Ashur are loud in their wail,*
> *And the idols are broke in the Temple of Baal.*

Even here, in the north-east of Lebanon the gun is ever present, and there are innumerable checkpoints – a constant reminder of the fragile peace. To the south, the little town of Qana (said by many to be the biblical Cana where Jesus performed the miracle of the water and the wine) rests on a barren hillside listening daily to the gunfire, relying on soldiers from far away Fiji to keep the peace intact.

Further to the east in villages that have become household names to army families in Ireland, such as Tibnin, Haddathah, Bra'shit, and Al Yahun, other Lebanese look to the Irish to provide them with the security to carry on their lives.

Tá na saighdiúirí Éireanach ag obair go dian ar son na siochána i bhfad óna n-áit dúchais. Tá siad ag tabhairt glóire do mhuinitr na hÉireann, dóibh féin agus dona gclanna uilig. Ba chóir dúinn a bheith brodúil astu.

Ba mhaith liomsa mo bhuíochas a chur in iúil do saighdiúirí an 85ú Cathalan, do Captean Freyne agus do S/S Stone a rinne a dhícheall an fíor-sceál a chuir os ar gcomhair i gconaí. Gabhaim mo bhuíochas don Roinn Cosanta freisin as ucht an chuireadh a thabhairt dom bheith pairtech sa turas. Tá eolas agam anois ar gné eile den roimh nach raibh agam cheanna. Tá meas nua agam ar pharasanra an airm.

Home at Last

COMDT JOE McDONAGH

On Sunday 21 May, a large crowd of civilians unexpectedly gathered in Finbatt before moving out of the UNIFIL area of operations heading into the villages of Et Taibe, Qantara, Adshit and Deir Siriane. The next morning another large crowd had gathered at Irishbatt position 6–28 with the intention of crossing into Houle, which is located inside the Israeli controlled area.

The road from Shaqra to Houle had been closed to civilian traffic since 1985 and was overlooked by two DFF compounds. Many of the people who had gathered were former residents of Houle who fled during the occupation. Others were curious sightseers and supporters of Hizbullah who had travelled from all over Lebanon to be involved in the events.

It was clear that Hizbullah were controlling events and the people were determined to cross into Houle that day. They also stated that relatives living in Houle had informed them that the DFF compounds of E212 and E208A had been abandoned.

There was heavy fog that morning and personnel at Irishbatt posts 6–28 and 6–28A could not confirm that the DFF positions had been abandoned. When the mist lifted it was clear the compounds were still manned as both started firing heavy machine-guns and mortars to within 500m of 6–28, where the civilian crowd had gathered.

There was also heavy IDF artillery fire and aerial activity in the area. One aerial bomb cratered the road 900m east of 6–28A on the road to Houle in an attempt to prevent the people from reaching the village. This only made the crowd more determined and at 0915hrs they began to move forward along the road in the direction of Houle.

At this point, there were sustained bursts of HMG and mortar fire but the crowd continued to move forward. This was a tense and frightening couple of minutes because the people were determined to move forward, and if the DFF were as determined to stop them there would have been serious casualties. Given the DFF's *modus operandi* for many years and their attitude towards the civilian population it was feared that the civilians would suffer serious casualties.

However, when the firing failed to deter the people from moving forward it suddenly stopped and armoured vehicles were observed moving out of the compounds. It appeared that the compounds were indeed being abandoned.

Shortly afterwards, a group of people emerged from Houle and moved west to meet the groups advancing from Irishbatt at the point where the road was cratered by the IDF. The people moving toward Houle had brought earth-moving equipment with them and in a matter of minutes they repaired the road.

Soon, Hizbullah and Amal flags were seen flying over both compounds, as hundreds of people from as far away as Beirut, continued to stream across into Houle all in a jubilant mood. At this point, it was clear that the position of the DFF in other compounds within Irishbatt had become untenable. Before noon approximately 100 DFF soldiers were observed moving north towards Irishbatt post 6–21 on the road between Bayt Yahun and Tibnin. Some had abandoned the compounds in the Irishbatt AO and others had come from the Saff al Hawa direction. They surrendered to the Lebanese army and after processing, they were taken away to Sidon. Others were taken, by Amal and Hizbullah, to be handed over to the Lebanese army at a later stage.

As happened earlier at Irishbatt post 6–28 a crowd of approximately 200 civilians moved from the Lebanese army checkpoint at Total and proceeded towards Bayt Yahun. They now occupied the village and shortly afterwards all compounds in the Irishbatt AO were reported abandoned by the DFF. It should be noted that the people who initially made the move forward at Shaqra and Bayt Yahun were unarmed and it was after they had re-occupied the villages that the armed elements moved into the area.

Before dark on 22 May most compounds in the Irishbatt AO were flying Hizbullah and Amal flags. That night saw some of the heaviest shelling in Irishbatt for sometime, a total of 112 shootreps (reports of shooting) being recorded by Irish operations. This fire was mainly Israeli Defence Forces artillery giving cover to the IDF compounds of W141 and the remaining DFF compounds of W133, W136 and W142 in the Saff al Hawa and At Tiri areas which had not been abandoned as darkness fell. Skirmishes occurred during the night between AEs and these remaining compounds. At dawn, it was observed that Hizbullah and Amal flags were also flying over W141 and W142. It was now clear that the IDF/DFF were no longer in the area.

In an effort to ascertain how the situation was developing in the south of Irishbatt probing patrols were sent into At Tiri, the Christian village of Ayn Ibil, and Saff al Hawa, which was the main centre of AE activity after the withdrawal. These patrols confirmed that Hizbullah and Amal were in total control of the area, that families who had fled during the occupation had already returned to At Tiri and that the Christians in Ayn Ibil were unharmed. It was significant that no Hizbullah

198

and Amal flags were flying in Ayn Ibil and that there was no AE presence.

In the following days, it was confirmed that a considerable number of DFF soldiers, in some cases accompanied by their families, had fled to Israel and that many other inhabitants of Christian villages had also fled. Hizbullah and Amal had visited all the Christian villages and gave assurances that the people would not be harmed. There was no large-scale intimidation of Christians and only minor incidents of criminal activity were reported up to the end of May.

Soon some of the reported 6,500 Christians who had fled to Israel started to return to Lebanon and returning DFF soldiers surrendered themselves to the Lebanese authorities. This was mainly organised through the Red Cross, although some crossed independently. Their main reason for returning was that they would prefer to surrender to Lebanese justice rather than spend the rest of their lives in Israel where the welcome was not exactly overwhelming. They were also reassured by the fact that there was no widespread intimidation or victimisation of the Christian population.

There were considerable casualties during the disintegration of the DFF. In Irishbatt's area alone 22 civilians, including three women, were injured by the IDF shelling on 22 May. On the same day five locals were killed in R'shaf – three by DFF shelling into the abandoned R'shaf compound after the locals had gone in to salvage weapons and equipment, and two when a captured DFF T55 tank they were driving out of the compound was attacked by IDF helicopter gunships. Three other people (including the driver of BBC correspondent Jeremy Bowen) were killed by IDF tank fire in the area south of Houle.

For a number of days after the withdrawal of the IDF the area was flooded with sightseers and people returning to check out houses and property they had vacated during the occupation. This led to a situation where a large number of civilians were wandering around near the abandoned DFF compounds, all of which were mined. There were two incidents of youths losing limbs after stepping on landmines and one casualty caused by a booby-trapped camera left near one of the compounds. As a result the Lebanese authorities quickly moved to prevent outsiders from moving into the area and an effective mine awareness programme was initiated.

The situation in the former Israeli controlled area has stabilised and at the time of writing can be described as calm. The Lebanese gendarmes are now deployed in most villages, roads are being repaired, water supplies are being restored and on 31 May the Lebanese parliament sat in Bint Jubayl. Hizbullah and Amal are now concentrating on maintaining peace and on the forthcoming general election.

A lot of work remains to be done to ensure a lasting peace and all sides are cautiously optimistic. In Irishbatt AO now there is peace, after 22 years the guns are finally silent, and for thousands of ordinary Lebanese people they have returned home at last.

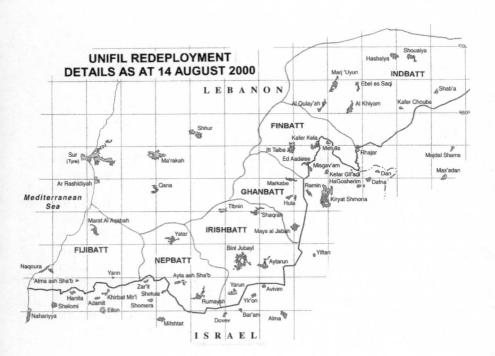

UNIFIL REDEPLOYMENT
DETAILS AS AT 14 AUGUST 2000

BREAK FOR THE BORDER

CAPT CAIMIN KEANE

From early March 2000, when the officers of the 87 Irishbatt formed up for initial briefing at UNTSI, every brief led us to believe that this was going to be a ground breaking and memorable six-month tour of duty. For those of us who had not been overseas before this just added to the intrigue. Our intelligence briefs had told us that the politicians had set a date in early July for Israeli withdrawal. However, all sorts of rumours abounded as to when and how it would actually happen and of course the knock-on effect it would have on the battalion.

Soon after the 87 Irishbatt took over operational control UNIFIL decided that reporting of Israeli withdrawal could be done in three phases. Our task, in phase one, was to monitor the withdrawal, phase two was the verification process, and phase three would involve redeployment.

The speed of the withdrawal surprised everyone including the Israelis themselves. As the eventual withdrawal date of 22 May approached the attacks on the resistance by the DFF compounds intensified. In response, the scale of the IDF/DFF retaliation increased dramatically, leading to many dangerous moments for Irishbatt personnel. As we were monitoring the abandoning of DFF and IDF posts and the withdrawal of IDF and DFF troops on 22 May, we knew we had an interesting and unique time ahead.

Irishbatt immediately starting patrolling the towns in the former ICA, in order to fill any vacuum that may have been left after the IDF withdrawal. Early on 23 May, the day after the withdrawal of IDF from the Irishbatt area, A Company recorded a first when Comdt Peter Cooney (OC A Company) led a foot patrol into Kunin, a village in the former ICA, in order to confirm Israeli withdrawal from the area. The reception the UN peacekeepers received from the local population was very warm to say the least. Meanwhile, the verification team under the command of Brig Gen James Sreenan (Deputy Force Commander) and Mr Terje Roed-Larsen (UN Special Envoy) was working very hard verifying the withdrawal under the spotlight of the world's media. They made good progress but there were many delays due to disagreements over the withdrawal line, known as the Blue Line. The various violations of the border were being dealt with and the Blue Line was beginning to take shape leading to high expectations that redeployment was imminent.

From 24 July, A Company was put on one hour's notice to deploy into the former ICA. The deployment was sketchy, as the delicate details of the Blue Line were still being finalised by all the parties involved. Finally, at 0300hrs on 28 July, Comdt Cooney received the order that A Company was to send a platoon into a position south of the Israeli/Lebanese Armistice Demarcation Line of 1949.

I could hardly believe my ears when I answered the field phone in my room in Al Yahun. Comdt Cooney explained that I would be leading a platoon* through Rosh Haniqra, across the border to occupy a position in Israel! The platoon rendezvous was in battalion HQ in Camp Shamrock and consisted of a section from A Company and a section each from B and C Companies. At 0430hrs, we departed for the border still unsure of the reception we would receive in Israel.

The excitement was palpable as the significance of our mission sunk in. At the border, Comdt Cooney gave me a final brief. I was then introduced to my escort, Major Herve Collet from France serving with Observer Group Lebanon and Capt Durak, a Polish officer who was to provide engineering support for the mission.

At 0600hrs, we crossed into Israel and preceded to Boundary Pillar 18, a contentious border position situated south-west of the village of Yahun. After receiving more then one curious glance at our three SISU armoured personnel carriers, we journeyed through the town lands of northern Israel and arrived at our position at 0750hrs. I was surprised to find that in fact it was a former IDF position, which had recently been bulldozed. To gain access to the site, we had to bulldoze our way through another IDF position's perimeter fence and defensive mound. At 0835hrs, I deployed our SISUs to give cover in all directions and the UN flag was raised. Post 6–50 was now operational.

It was now 'all hands on deck' as we secured the area and our Polish friends began bulldozing a platform for our new post. As midday approached, with a well-timed heat wave with blazing temperatures of up to 45 degrees celsius, I received an order from Brig Gen Sreenan to physically man the Blue Line.

It must have been a sight as the force commander flew over post 6–50 with senior Lebanese officers to see Irish troops and three SISUs manning the exact position of the Blue Line in this particularly contentious area.

Soon after, Lt Col Chris Moore (OC 87 Irishbatt) and Comdt Cooney arrived with much needed supplies and tentage. Later that day, the Polish bulldozer operator detonated an antipersonnel land mine as he worked to build a defensive mound around the position. Thankfully, nobody was injured, but it certainly had a positive effect on the concentration levels of the Irish and Polish troops who were working in the energy-sapping heat.

After such a demanding day, sleep was not to be hard found during guard shifts. The next morning, Lt Col Moore and Comdt Cooney arrived again, this time with an impressive 18-vehicle convoy. The Irish engineering and signals platoon commanders, Capts Tim Hehir and Cathal O'Donnell and their platoons went to work to install communications and other facilities. To their credit, by 1715hrs that evening, they had transformed post 6–50 into a self sufficient and reasonably comfortable post having provided for all our basic requirements.

Meanwhile, Ukrainian engineers were carrying out another important aspect of the operation. They were steadily making progress through the minefields north of post 6–50 in order to clear supply routes from Lebanon. At 1216hrs on Monday 14 August, another memorable moment occurred. A Ukrainian mine thrasher appeared from the dead ground to our north and drove along the fence, which marked the former Israeli border. The Ukrainian Lt Col in charge of the mine clearing operation said afterwards that it reminded him of his father's story of witnessing the link up of the Soviet army and the US forces at the Elbe in 1945.

One week later, my platoon was relieved by an A Company platoon led by Lt Liam Kiely. So, it was back to company HQ at Al Yahun for myself and the members of the platoon for a much needed shower and rest. We brought with us some great memories of an historic and groundbreaking operation, delighted that Irishbatt had been tasked with establishing the first new position in the former ICA. UNIFIL and Irishbatt redeployment had begun.

* The platoon consisted of the following personnel:

A COMPANY	B COMPANY	C COMPANY
Capt Caimin Keane	Sgt Seán Reilly	Cpl Tony King
Cpl Brian McCormack	Cpl Kevin Byrne	Cpl Tommy Smith
Cpl Noel Connell	Cpl Seamus Byrne	Cpl Des Breen
Cpl John Doyle	Pte Ronan Fahy	Pte David Ryan
Cpl Mark Singleton	Pte Pauric McDonnell	Pte Brian Harte
Pte Finbarr Rush	Pte Gavin Egan	Pte John Siggins
Pte Andy Rush	Pte Laurence Power	Pte Anthony McCormack
Pte Declan Lynch	Pte Philip Loughman	Pte Declan Gumley
Pte Anthony Cole	Pte John Jago	Pte Mark Sheridan
Pte Francis Meehan	Pte Kevin Mooney	Pte Niall O'Keeffe
Pte Dean Scully	Pte Cormac Carr	Pte Alan Conroy
Pte Brian Poole		

2001

EXERCISE BEKAA VALLEY

LT COL DAVE ASHE

Last summer Brig Gen James Sreenan (Deputy Force Commander UNIFIL) and I raised the possibility of Irishbatt undertaking training on Lebanese army facilities, should the operational situation remain stable, and the idea of a 'shoot' was raised by Capt Tom Ryan.

An application was made to UNIFIL HQ and permission was granted pending the availability of a suitable range. Various ranges within the UNIFIL AO were assessed. The old Nepbatt range was examined, but was found to be unsafe due to the construction of several new houses in the area. Then the MIO discussed the matter with the Lebanese army who responded positively and suggested their range in the Bekaa Valley.

Comdt Michael Gannon (Bn Ops Offr) was appointed as OIC exercise in January and began planning. A number of recces were carried out by the operations staff in conjunction and all aspects of the proposed battalion shoot were given careful consideration. All elements then began preparing for their respective tasks and roles.

The BMR accounted for the vast majority of crews and firers (120mm mortars, 81mm mortars, AML 90s, SISU mounted HMG) while the infantry companies readied the 84mm ATk and the HMG crews. Sgt Charlie Stone (Arty Tp Sgt) did trojan work on the refresher instruction and Sgt Niall Rennicks looked after the cavalry gunnery instruction.

On Sunday 22 April, all ammunition was loaded onto Pollog Drops vehicles. AML 90s were prepared for the journey and all mortars were packed and loaded onto transport and the initial convoy from the battalion left at 0600hrs the following morning while the main body departed from Camp Shamrock two hours later. The route brought both convoys through Ghanbatt and such villages as Shaqra, Houle, Metulla and Marjayoun and then through Indbatt. From there, it was on up the winding roads to the Bekaa Valley that unfolded towards the range near Baaleck.

Both convoys reached the range in good time, considering they were in the midst of a sandstorm. The terrain was extremely chalky and tested the specialist logs skills to the limit. The howling wind made tent erection a nightmare and the dust played havoc with the cook's work. However, base camp simply had to put in place for a two-night stay. Cooking facilities, tents accommodation, ablutions, including showers, electric power and secure storage were provided. Simultaneously, preparations began on the firing points for the first phase of firing.

Capt Johnny Mills was co-ordinator of the battalion shoot. Firing was divided into phases. The first day consisted of three independent shoots – a mortar shoot (120mm and 81mm) controlled by Lt Ray Kane, a cavalry shoot (AML 90s and SISU-mounted HMG) controlled by Lt Micheál Connelly and an infantry weapons shoot (HMG and 84mm ATk) controlled by Lt Steve Morgan. This phase took three hours to complete and it served as a good starting point. After firing was complete, all crews returned to the base camp and were glad to see it fully operational.

The main event took place on the Tuesday. The intention was to co-ordinate a combined shoot utilising all weapons. To achieve this, an exercise scenario was created which focused around one of the current roles of the battalion within its AO, the reinforcement of a patrol base.

Two BMR mobile security groups consisting of an AML 90 and a SISU APC, with 84mm ATk and HMG crews were called in to deal with the situation. Mortar smoke was delivered on call by artillery to cover the armoured advance to the firing point. At the firing point AML 90s deployed on the flanks while the ground elements, with three 84mm Atk and three HMG crews, under the watchful eyes of Sgts Colm Spellman and Declan Madden, deployed from the APCs and immediately went into action. When all personnel were in position, the artillery switched from smoke to high explosive and neutralised their specific targets. The armour and ground crews picked out and destroyed targets within their respective arcs of fire.

In all, this scenario was conducted four times, with weapons, vehicles and crews rotating to maximise the experience. As the exercise was repeated, it was visible to all that the skill and confidence levels grew immensely. Crew reaction drills, armoured vehicle tactical driving; firing accuracy, deployment drills and timings all improved.

The final phase of the shoot was the night exercise that began at 2000hrs with artillery illumination, dramatically lighting up the range and providing all crews with an excellent view of their targets. The illumination continued for the AML 90s and APC HMGs. Both the 120mm and 81mm mortars fired separately for safety reasons. The 84mm ATk provided illumination for the 84mm ATk HE and the ground HMGs. The AML 90s then operated in darkness using their highly efficient NVE laser system. Not a single miss was recorded.

The shoot was an extremely beneficial training exercise. It provided the incentive for 88 Irishbatt crews to train with a clear and definite goal in mind. The depletion of ammunition stocks, held in reserve in Lebanon, was a factor, which was considered carefully. With Irishbatt withdrawing by the end of 2001, it was essential to commence stock reduction. Storage conditions in this climate dictate that most types of ammunition will not be suitable for return to Ireland anyway so they would have to utilised or destroyed *in situ*. With these factors in mind ammunition for firing was checked and prepared by the ordnance section, Comdt Larry Devaney, Sgt Pat Leahy, Sgt Paul Kiernan, Sgt Liam Lynch, Sgt Paddy Sludds and Cpl Aidan Mullins.

While the conduct and planning of this shoot did take a large collective effort, nobody doubted that it was well worthwhile. The cavalry, artillery and infantry personnel had never previously experienced such closely co-ordinated firing. Realistic combined training such as this proved to be extremely beneficial and valuable to all involved. The utilisation of APC drills together with live firing ensured that a realistic scenario was developed. The exercise, as a whole, has highlighted some interesting results:

Firstly, a large open range, such as this, afforded us the flexibility to incorporate a high degree of realism, together with the tactical deployment of armour and infantry into the live firing practices.

Secondly, the infantry battalion, such as is deployed in Lebanon, affords the security, the structure, and the integral specialist skills necessary for the conduct of such an exercise. This exercise realistically combined all the elements of combat support and combat service support. It involved convoy movement, base camp construction, troop and armour deployment as well as the application of the command and control function.

Thirdly, personnel of this battalion have, on a round-the-clock basis, been operating in APCs in a highly operational situation along the Blue Line. These patrols, in heavily mined areas, together with the new found experience of the battalion shoot in the Bekaa Valley makes them one of the most highly trained infantry battalions for some time and will be a very valuable asset when we introduce the new Mowag APCs in 2001.

And lastly, it served to remind us all of the standard of training which will be expected of the Defence Forces in the future when we serve on new overseas missions.

2001

GOODBYE TO 'THE HILLS'

SGT TERRY MCLAUGHLIN

Travelling down through Lebanon in May 2001, after what seemed like an interminable journey from Dublin, one phrase kept coming to mind; 'the more things change, the more they stay the same'. My last trip was with 73 Irishbatt in 1993 and I had heard of all sorts of changes since the unilateral withdrawal by the Israeli Defence Forces from south Lebanon in May 2000. Yet here I was, looking out of the window of a UN bus at the same greeny-brown hills, caught in that no-man's land between winter and the onset of the searing heat that I had experienced on two previous summer trips with UNIFIL. I knew that within weeks the green would largely have disappeared and the land would mostly appear dry, dusty and barren.

The roads had not changed a lot either. Admittedly the road from Beirut to Sidon was as good a stretch of motorway as you would get anywhere, and the first few miles from Sidon towards Tyre was on the start of a fine new road under construction. But after Tyre it was the same old story – pot-holed, dusty roads with few definable edges and often wide enough for only one vehicle. Added to that there were numerous road works underway that have since made driving any-where near the Irish AO a nightmare. And the drivers? ... No change there, still half-mad, or 'majnoon' if you prefer the Arabic term. One thing was noticeable, the amount of women drivers. There was a time not too long ago when you would hardly see a woman behind the wheel in south Lebanon, particularly women in full black Muslim outfits.

The villages showed little outward signs of change either. The streets in many are still too narrow for a bicycle to pass through with any comfort let alone a large UN vehicle. The usual mixture of women in western dress, and women in various states of Islamic outfit, from those totally covered in black with only their eyes showing, to the more colourful, but still modestly clad, with arms, legs and hair covered. There were plenty of men with full beards, elderly men and women in traditional outfits, and crowds of children and dogs playing in the streets. But indeed there was change. The road works are part of ambitious water and telephone projects underway which will eventually, or so the plan goes, greatly improve the quality of life in villages such as Kafra, Haddathah, R'shaf and Bint Jubayl.

The throngs of people in the villages and the proliferation of motor-cars are also evidence of an increasing population as people return to the area, some from Beirut and places to the north and some from much further afield such as Australia or Germany. The number of houses under construction is almost as astonishing as their size and design. Huge, palatial, mansions with spiralling, unsupported concrete staircases; intricately designed balconies, arches, and pillars; and each house as individual as its builder – not for the Lebanese the uniformity, and let's face it, the drabness, of the European housing model. Taken together these changes are a sign of growing confidence that there really may be a chance of peace at last.

Moving into the UNIFIL AO and the first really significant sign of change from a military point of view came when we passed through Nepalese positions, which were either closed, or, if manned, did not have checkpoints in operation. The same applied as we passed through the first Irishbatt position, 6-48 in Tibnin East. The post had become the location for the MP section and the checkpoint was no longer in operation. Indeed there were no checkpoints in place throughout the Irishbatt AO.

The next major surprise came that night standing at the highest point in Camp Shamrock. There were lights everywhere, house lights and street lights: each village was like a cluster of diamonds lying on black velvet – Tibnin, Haddathah, Ayta Jabal (formerly Ayta az Zutt), Bayt Yahun, Bra'shit – and between the villages the lights of hundreds of other houses could be seen. This might not seem an unusual nighttime scene for an Irish person but anyone who has served in Lebanon over the years will tell you that south Lebanon at night used to be a dark and sinister place. There were much fewer lights in the villages and even less in outlying areas. Even then, total blackouts were a regular occurrence in the area, particularly if a resistance attack on one of the DFF compounds was expected.

Paradoxically, the ridge-line formerly occupied by the DFF was in darkness. Whereas before the lights of the compounds burned constantly, now the only lights to be seen were from the Irish positions on Hill 880 and the Black Hole. In a short space of time, things had changed dramatically for Irishbatt. The old DFF compounds lay abandoned and dejected each with a Hizbullah flag flying from its parapets and a large sign near its entrance. These signs carry a record of the position's history in pictures and words (Arabic and English), telling of the number of resistance attacks launched against it and the number of casualties on both sides. These compounds are now major tourist attractions for people from far and near, despite the fact that the areas surrounding them are still heavily mined and the compounds themselves are believed to be full of unexploded ordnance and booby-

208

traps. Although they are dilapidated and deserted, the compounds can still cause the hairs to stand on the back of your neck, particularly driving past them at night as they sit sightless and brooding, silhouetted against the sky-line.

The AO had expanded right up to the Blue Line (the UN-monitored line which is based on the old Armistice Line of 1949) now separating the countries of Israel and Lebanon. Places that Irish peacekeepers had mostly only known by name, such as Bint Jubayl and Kunin, as well as places that many had never heard of, like Yahun, Aytarun and Blida, were now all part of the Irish AO. Three Blue Line positions were constructed, 6-50 (near Yahun), 6–51 (on the outskirts of Blida) and 6–52 (to the south of Marun ar Ras) and occupied at platoon strength by Irishbatt. Checkpoints and OPs in the old positions became redundant almost overnight as the focus of attention moved south to the Blue Line.

The Blue Line is marked with a series of verification points known as BPs (boundary pillars), with BPs 17 to 29 falling within the expanded Irishbatt AO. Patrolling became the order of the day, mainly in armoured vehicles, although some foot patrolling was still required to check some of the intermediate positions between the BPs. These patrols were carried out by Irishbatt from the establishment of the Blue Line and will carry on right up to the time that Irishbatt ceases to be operational in October 2001. Although the situation in south Lebanon remained generally calm, the Blue Line patrols were also tasked with visiting all the villages on their routes and setting up static OPs in order to maintain a presence and reassure the local population in the AO.

During 2001, a major reorganisation of UNIFIL took place with the Finnish and Nepalese battalions withdrawing in the summer and the Irish scheduled to leave by November, with the areas of operation of these units being handed over in stages to the Indian, Fijian and Ghanaian battalions respectively. This streamlining of, and thinning out of, UNIFIL is being carried out with the approval of the Lebanese government although it is not unanimously supported. Indeed, it was the subject of a major disagreement between Prime Minister Harare and Speaker of the House of Parliament Nabbih Berri and leader of the Shia Amal movement, who vehemently opposes any reduction in the international force.

Certainly, for the Irish battalion it seems time to pull out. After twenty-three years, during which 45 members of the Defence Forces lost their lives, the situation has changed operationally to such a degree that there no longer seems to be a sense of purpose. Apart from some minor incidents, everything has become routine. In comparison to previous years, there has been little activity to report. 'Groundhogs' (taking to the bunkers when shelling was taking place) have so far been confined to exercises and a couple of occasions when Hizbullah anti-aircraft guns fired a few token salvos at Israeli warplanes violating Lebanese airspace. These rounds, which posed no threat to the warplanes flying high above, exploded high in the air, but directly above two Irish positions, leading to 'Groundhog' being called as a precaution.

Reports of shooting are rare throughout the UNIFIL AO, with the exception of Indbatt, where the disputed Chebaa Farms lies. This is a relatively remote disputed area in the foothills of Mount Hermon. The area was taken from Syria by Israel during the Arab-Israeli wars and is considered by the UN and Israel to lie outside Lebanese territory, and therefore is on the Israeli side of the Blue Line. However, both Syria and Lebanon claim that the area was originally Lebanese land. As a result Hizbullah and other resistance groups have vowed to 'liberate' the area and have carried out a number of operations in the area, the most serious of which led to the kidnapping in October 2000 of three Israeli soldiers who are still held by Hizbullah.

This brings us to the very difficult task of trying to estimate how things will fare out for Lebanon over the coming years. The Chebaa Farms certainly has the potential to renew conflict in the area. Soon after the first Hizbullah attacks, Israel stated that it would hold Syria responsible for any further attacks and would respond against Syrian positions in Lebanon. True to their word, Israeli jets struck Syrian anti-aircraft positions in the Bekaa Valley after subsequent attacks on Israeli compounds in the Chebaa Farms. Following such an incident in July, Syrian leader Bashir Assad warned that his forces would no longer adopt the policy of not responding to Israeli attacks, thereby raising the spectre of escalation in the region once more.

This is the crux of the problem for Lebanon. It is a small country trapped between two powerful, mutually hostile neighbours, who are still technically at war with one another. Syria will have a big say in Lebanon's future. The current government in Beirut is strongly pro-Syrian, although there are vociferous anti-Syrian elements in the country. Since Haffez Assad's intervention in the Lebanese civil war in 1978, Syria has to all intents and purposes controlled northern Lebanon, with up to 40,000 of its troops stationed in the country. Without Syria's tacit approval Hizbullah access to training, equipment, and finances – all stemming from Iran – would virtually disappear.

Although Damascus withdrew its troops from many areas of Lebanon, including Beirut, in July 2001, it still maintains a substantial presence and the feeling is that the troops who left 'have not gone very far'. Judging in which direction Syria will attempt to push Lebanon is not easy. The country's new leader, Bashir Assad, is still a relatively unknown quantity. On the one hand he appears to want to bring Syria in from the cold towards greater acceptance by the US and the other western powers but at the same time he must have an eye towards public opinion in the Arab world which generally seeks strongly anti-Israeli leaders.

There is also the matter of the Israeli-occupied Golan Heights to consider. Added to all of this Bashir has to ensure the continuation of his own leadership. The key figures in his father's regime are still in place, and for as long as they remain friends and advisers of the new president it is hard to see how Syria's policy of using Lebanon to keep the heat on Israel will differ greatly from policy in the past.

Israel is the other country whose actions will to a large extent dictate Lebanon's future. Israeli actions are viewed with a high degree of suspicion and cynicism, particularly in south Lebanon. The Lebanese point to what they see as illegal diversions of water sources during the occupation, and the continued pumping of water from the Wazani river in the disputed town of Rhajar. The large number of over-flights by Israeli jets is also cited as a sign of Israel's disdain and contempt for Lebanese sovereignty and as an indication of continuing intelligence gathering by the Israelis for future operations against Lebanon if they feel the situation warrants such action.

Potential for flash-points along the Blue Line is high, not only in the Chebaa Farms area but also in areas such as the Sheikh Abbad tomb site and Metulla, where large groups of Lebanese often congregate to throw stones at Israeli positions only yards away. Since the withdrawal, Israeli soldiers have been restrained in their response to such activities but warning shots have been fired and on a couple of occasions protesters placing flags on the border fence have been fired on. Israel's response to any serious resurgence of conflict along its northern border would be hard to predict. The greatest fear for those who lived for so many years with the occupation is of a reoccupation, but in this writer's opinion that would be an unlikely scenario.

The Israeli Defence Forces and their allies received a bloody nose in the ICA over the last ten years of the occupation and their departure from Lebanon in 2000, while not a rout, was certainly not a dignified withdrawal. Added to that, the requirements stemming from the ongoing problems within Israel would make it unlikely that the IDF would wish to commit scarce extra manpower to their already heavily fortified northern border. Having so recently extricated themselves from the quagmire that southern Lebanon had become for the IDF it is hard to imagine that they would be liable to rush back in. More likely would be punitive air strikes against economic and resistance targets within Lebanon, and given Lebanon's fragile and depressed economy these could be devastating.

Then there are the internal problems facing Lebanon. There are still tensions between the Muslim and Christian communities, although it must be said that in many villages the two communities have lived together without a problem for many years. However, in some areas, there is deep mistrust and any incident has the potential to increase sectarianism to dangerous levels. Memories of the civil war are still fresh and the effects of it can still be seen in the many bullet-riddled buildings that still remain in Beirut. There are also at least 300,000 Palestinians (the highest estimates actually double this figure) living in refugee camps in Lebanon. At the moment, their movements are heavily restricted, with some camps virtually surrounded by the Lebanese army. The attitude of the Lebanese authorities to the Palestinians is an indication of the fear of destabilisation posed by their presence, particularly while the Second Intifada continues in the West Bank and Gaza. There is no doubt that many difficulties and problems lie on the horizon for Lebanon, and unfortunately most are beyond the country's control. As before, Lebanon's future will depend largely on the actions of its powerful neighbours, another small country caught up in international power games.

However, one thing is certain, come what may, the Lebanese people will find a way to survive as they have done for centuries. They are a resilient people, inured to hardship, and stoical by nature. The land in the south is hard and unyielding and anything taken from it is hard won. The men and women who earn their living from such land do not give in easily. Any one who doubts this has not seen them over the years rebuilding houses days after they have been hit by shells, or even, in the aftermath of the bombardments unleashed during the Israeli operations Accountability (1993) and Grapes of Wrath (1996), when they literally rebuilt whole villages.

Whatever the future holds for Lebanon, Irishbatt will not be a part of it. After twenty-three years, it was time to go. Many critics of UNIFIL accused the mission of being ineffective. Certainly, it was unable to obtain the withdrawal of the IDF until Israel decided to leave of its own accord, but it never had the equipment, manpower, nor, more importantly, the mandate to force the IDF out. UNIFIL did what it could and personnel from all contingents paid the ultimate price in trying to bring peace to southern Lebanon – 45 of them from Ireland.

The best judges of the role played by the Irish battalions down through the years are the local population, and they have said on many occasions that if it wasn't for Irishbatt's presence the area would have become virtually uninhabitable. Irishbatt had become so much a part of the landscape that right up until the day that 89 Irishbatt pulls out, many of the locals will refuse to believe that it will actually happen.

Almost half of the populations of Tibnin, Haddathah, Haris, Ayta az Zutt, Bra'shit, R'shaf and Shaqra, were not even born when the first Irish troops arrived in Lebanon. Among many of the local population English is spoken with a heavy Irish brogue and some can even muster a few phrases 'as Gaeilge'. Similarly, a large proportion of the Defence Forces have never known a time when there was no Irish battalion in Lebanon, and more than a few have a smattering of Arabic words and phrases that they picked up over the years. A bond has been formed over two decades which may last for much longer, and without doubt any future news about Lebanon will be followed avidly in hundreds of Irish homes.

As we pull out of Camp Shamrock for the last time, I think many of us will share the locals' sense of disbelief. Can this really be the end? Although everyone will be delighted to be going home there will also be an underlying sense of sadness and the recognition that a major chapter in the history of the Irish Defence Forces is drawing to a close.

Football final, Irishbatt = 2, Nor Maint Coy = 0

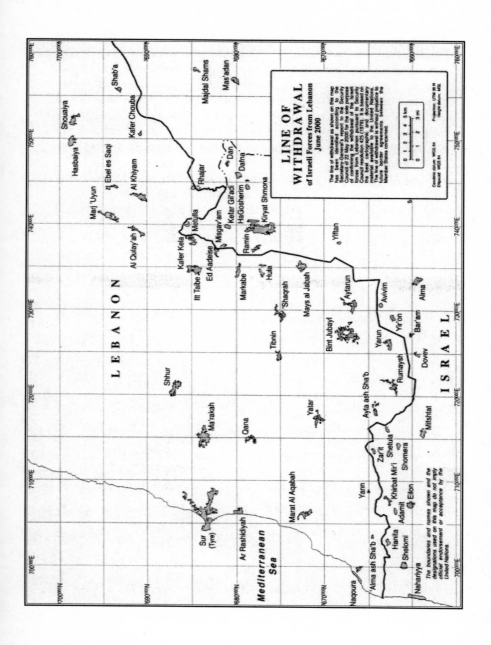

LINE OF
WITHDRAWAL
of Israeli Forces from Lebanon
June 2000

The line of withdrawal as shown on this map
has been delineated according to the
Secretary-General's report to the Security
Council of 22 May 2000 for the sole purpose
of confirming the withdrawal of the Israeli
forces from Lebanon pursuant to Security
Council resolution 425 (1978). It is based on
the best cartographic and documentary
material available to the United Nations.
The line of withdrawal is without prejudice to
future border agreements between the
Member States concerned.

Geodetic datum: WGS 84   Projection: UTM 36 N
Ellipsoid: WGS 84   Height datum: MSL

0 1 2 3 4 5 km
0   1   2   3 mi

LEBANON

ISRAEL

Mediterranean
Sea

Shab'a
Shouaiya
Hasbaiya
Kafer Chouba
Majdal Shams
Mas'adan
Ebel es Saqi
Al Khiyam
Marj 'Uyun
Rhajar
Dan
Dafna
Al Qulay'ah
Kafer Kela
Metulla
Misgav'am
Kefar Gil'adi
HaGosherim
Kiryat Shmona
Itt Talbe
Ed Aadelse
Ramin
Yiftan
Markabe
Hula
Shaqrah
Mays al Jabah
Aytarun
Avivim
Alma
Tibnin
Bint Jubayl
Yarun
Yir'on
Bar'am
Dovev
Shhur
Ma'rakah
Qana
Yalar
Rumaysh
Ayta ash Sha'b
Miftshtat
Marat Al Aqabah
Yann
Zar'it
Khirbat Miri
Eilon
Shetula
Shomera
Sur
(Tyre)
Ar Rashidiyah
Hanila
Adamit
Shelomi
Alma ash Sha'b
Naqoura
Nahariyya

The boundaries and names shown and the
designations used on this map do not imply
official endorsement or acceptance by the
United Nations.

214

2001

IN THE SERVICE OF PEACE
A REFLECTION

SGT PAT MCKEE

I was a late convert to overseas service and had not experienced the great adventure until 1985, by which time the mission was already over seven years in existence. Having listened to the stories about Lebanon, and fed up with constructing theories of my own, I took the plunge and was selected for service with the 12th Irish Component in Naquora – that other Lebanon, that paradise of white roofs attached to the Mediterranean Sea.

My appointment was Sergeant Clerk to COMIRCON. The holder of this appointment at the time was Colonel W. V. MacNicholas. I quickly settled into the existence of life on the edge of the 'Enclave'. My first impressions – war, what war? This was home from home.

It was some weeks before I finally crossed 'Charlie Swing Gate' (the crossing dominated by the DFF compound on the coastal road) and made my way to Irishbatt's area of operations. I thought that life in the AO couldn't be that different. After a flying visit to some of the soldiers from Collins Barracks Cork who were serving in the village of Haddathah I quickly realised that there was no comparison to be made between the job I was doing and what these men were doing in Irishbatt.

I asked a local man what his life was like since the UN had come to south Lebanon. His dark patient eyes said more than words could – the return of his dignity as a man, and his self-respect. These concepts, he said, were needed, just like food, to sustain the soul. What a learning experience that summer was.

It wasn't until 1988 that I decided to volunteer for another tour of duty and I was selected for service with Headquarters Company, 64 Irishbatt, as acting company sergeant with title of chief clerk. The commanding officer was Lt Col Pat McMahon, and the maturity and experience of the officers and senior NCOs, combined with the evident enthusiasm of the younger soldiers, made the 64th a good battalion in every respect. We arrived in Lebanon in October 1988 and settled down to the tasks at hand.

Operationally it was a difficult tour and our real problems began with the capture of Jiwad Kasfi in December. He was taken by the Israeli-backed General Security Service, who had used Irishbatt routes to make the arrest. Irishbatt quickly became the fall guy and a dismal Christmas was spent with the hatches battened down and the gates locked, and armour with everything in the same way 'fish goes with chips'. In retrospect, I suppose it was inevitable that Irish lives were going to be lost – eventually.

Threats had been issued and they were taken seriously. Position 6-48 at Tibnin East came under heavy fire. A car had entered the CP and then abducted three soldiers at gun-point. Afterwards Amal negotiated their release down in the city of Tyre.

Then on a beautiful Friday morning at the end of February the staccato rattle of a heavy machine gun broke the silence. A DFF man from the Haddathah compound had opened fire and raked the main street of the village. Pte Michael McNeela died in an instant, hit in the chest by a heavy calibre bullet.

After Patrick's Day had come and gone we thought we were going to go home only missing one. The bang when it came shook the very buildings we were standing on and the pall of smoke rising towards the sky took with it the lives three young Irish soldiers: Corporal Fintan Heneghan, Private Mannix Armstrong and Private Thomas Walsh. One of my lasting memories of 64 Irishbatt was listening to the lament played by a lone piper, as he stood at the top of the guardroom in Camp Shamrock – playing out of camp, out of Lebanon, and out of our lives, those three brave men, heroes, soldiers of peace. Things were never the same after that.

Later I was selected again for service with the 68 Irishbatt as one of two operations sergeants. It was a busy but rewarding appointment. Lt Col Colm Mangan was the battalion commander and Comdt Frank Burns was the operations officer.

A memory here is standing outside the briefing room each morning and watching the daily ritual of officers rushing to be seated before the CO left his office, made that right turn at the bottom of the steps, and then made his way to the briefing room: 'Good morning gentlemen, please be seated'. Duty officer behind the podium, ops NCO pointer at the ready, and we're away – another day in the life of Irishbatt. We won every single inter-contingent competition that trip.

I again served with UNIFIL as part of 72 Irishbatt. Not long after arriving I found myself high above the village of Tibnin standing among the broken battlement of Castle Toron, the medieval Crusader fortress built by the Templar Knight Godfrey de Bouillon in the twelfth century to guard the route from Beaufort to Tyre against the enemies of Christ.

I surveyed the skyline and let my gaze pause at each village, when the 'crump' of an explosion, and the tell-tale pall of smoke, drew my attention eastwards to the impoverished village of Houle. Another road-side bomb perhaps? Such was 'life', if you want to call it that, for the people of Southern Lebanon. But why was I back here again? I tried all the headings – money, curiosity, fear? I settled for comradeship and those things that made me what I am – a soldier.

Overseas service has taught me many valuable lessons. It was a privilege to be part of something so worthwhile, even if at times the 'value' in it was hard to see. And I will forever be proud of what we achieved in a hardest calling of all – working in the service of peace.

UN cap-badge

ROLL OF HONOUR

Pte Finbarr Moon	43 Irishbatt	4 Inf Bn	25 August 1978
Cpl Thomas Reynolds	44 Irishbatt	2 Grn S&T	24 December 1978
Pte Philip Grogan	HQ UNIFIL	28 Inf Bn	10 July 1979
Pte Stephen Griffin	46 Irishbatt	1 Fd Engrs	16 April 1980
Pte Thomas Barrett	46 Irishbatt	4 Inf Bn	16 April 1980
Pte Derek Smallhorne	46 Irishbatt	5 Inf Bn	18 April 1980
Sgt Edward Yates	47 Irishbatt	2 Cav Sqn	31 May 1980
Cpl Vincent Duffy	47 Irishbatt	6 Fd Sigs	18 October 1980
Pte John Marshall	48 Irishbatt	6 Fd S&T Coy	17 December 1980
Coy Sgt James Martin	HQ UNIFIL	4 Grn MP Coy	10 February 1981
Pte Hugh Doherty	49 Irishbatt	28 Inf Bn	27 April 1981
Pte Niall Byrne	49 Irishbatt	6 Inf Bn	23 June 1981
Pte Gerard Hodges	50 Irishbatt	CTD S Comd	20 March 1982
Comdt Michael Nestor	UNTSO	Mil Col	25 September 1982
Pte Peter Burke	52 Irishbatt	5 Inf Bn	27 October 1982
Cpl Gregory Morrow	52 Irishbatt	2 Inf Bn	27 October 1982
Pte Thomas Murphy	52 Irishbatt	2 Inf Bn	27 October 1982
Cpl George Murray	55 Irishbatt	2 Grn MP Coy	09 October 1984
Tpr Paul Fogarty	59 Irishbatt	1 Tk Sqn	20 July 1986
Lt Aengus Murphy	59 Irishbatt	AAS	21 August1986
Pte William O'Brien	60 Irishbatt	6 Inf Bn	06 December 1986
Cpl Dermot McLoughlin	60 Irishbatt	28 Inf Bn	10 January 1987
RSM John Fitzgerald	HQ UNIFIL	1 Fd Arty Regt	24 February 1987
Cpl George Bolger	61 Irishbatt	12 Inf Bn	29 August 1987
Gnr Paul Cullen	62 Irishbatt	2 Fd Arty Regt	17 March 1988
Pte Patrick Wright	63 Irishbatt	27 Inf Bn	21 August 1988
Pte Michael McNeela	64 Irishbatt	27 Inf Bn	24 February 1989
Cpl Fintan Heneghan	64 Irishbatt	1 Inf Bn	21 March 1989
Pte Thomas Walsh	64 Irishbatt	28 Inf Bn	21 March 1989
Pte Mannix Armstrong	64 Irishbatt	28 Inf Bn	21 March 1989
Sgt Charles Forrester	65 Irishbatt	2 Fd Arty Regt	21 May 1989
Comdt Michael O'Hanlon	66 Irishbatt	HQ C Comd	21 November 1989
Cpl Michael McCarthy	70 Irishbatt	4 Inf Bn	15 November 1991
Cpl Peter Ward	71 Irishbatt	6 Inf Bn	29 September 1992
Cpl Martin Tynan	72 Irishbatt	Depot MPC	13 December 1992
CQMS Declan Stokes	HQ UNIFIL	Mil Col	14 June 1993
Armn Stephen O'Connor	73 Irishbatt	Air Corps	03 October 1993
Sgt John Lynch	HQ UNIFIL	C Comd	06 August 1997
Pte Kevin Barrett	84 Irishbatt	28 Inf Bn	18 February 1999
Pte William Kedian	85 Irishbatt	1 Inf Bn	31 May 1999
Tpr Jonathan Campbell	85 Irishbatt	4 Cav Sqn	05 September 1999
Pte Declan Deere	86 Irishbatt	3 Inf Bn	14 February 2000
Pte Brendan Fitzpatrick	86 Irishbatt	3 Inf Bn	14 February 2000
Pte Mathew Lawlor	86 Irishbatt	3 Inf Bn	14 February 2000
Pte John Murphy	86 Irishbatt	3 Inf Bn	14 February 2000

Missing in Action

Pte Kevin Joyce   48 Irishbatt   1 Inf Bn   27 April 1981

NOTES

BACKGROUND TO THE BATTLE OF AT TIRI

1.The text of the communique dated 10/2/80 was issued by the Irish Government Information Service.

2. *Ma'ariv* (Israeli daily newspaper), 12/2/80.

3.*The Irish Times*, 18/2/80.

4. Document S/13994 of 12/6/80, para 32.

5. In conversation with an Irish officer serving with UNIFIL at the time.

6. Report by Robert Fisk, *The Times* (UK), 23/24/5/80 – see sketch map attached.

7. Document S/13888 of 11/4/80 and additional docs dated 16/4/80 and 18/4/80. See also Doc. S/113994 of 12/6/80, paras 44-52; R. Smith, *Under the Blue Flag*, p. 218-226; *Dáil Debates*, Vol. 319, 16/4/80, p. 1257-1274; and *Kessings Contemporary Archives*, Vol XXVII pp. 30919-30944.

8. Pte Stephen Griffin and a Fijian soldier were killed. Several others were wounded. A militia man was also killed and at least three others were wounded.

9. *Jerusalem Post*, leading article 8/4/80; *The Times*, UK, 9/4/80; and *Kessings Contemporary Archives*, Vol XXVII, pp. 30919-30921.

10. S/13994, *op. cit.*, para 51.

11. In conversation with an Irish officer serving in the area at the time.

12. *The Times* (UK), 10/4/80.

13. Hurst, David, *The Guardian*, 10/4/80.

14. Goodman, Hirsh, *Jerusalem Post*, 14/4/80; and S/13994 para 51.

15. S/13947 para 47. Pte O'Mahony was shot and wounded. Pte Barrett and Pte Smallhorne were killed.

16. UN Press Release SG/SM 2908 21/4/80. The Secretary General also stated that 'this execution of members of a peacekeeping force is without precedent in the history of this most essential activity of the United Nations'.

17. *Jerusalem Post*, 20/4/80 and *The Irish Times*, 22/4/80.

18. *The Irish Times*, 22/4/80.

19. *Ibid.*

20. *Jerusalem Post*, 20/4/80.

21. *Ibid.*, 25/4/80.

22. Document S/13900 of 18/4/80 and SCOR 2217 Mtg Para15, 18/4/80.

23. *Ibid.*

24. This was adopted as Resolution 467 (1980) of 24/4/80.

25. *Ibid.*, para 2(b) and 2 (d).

26. Carter, J., *Keeping Faith*, Collins, London 1982., pp. 368-369.

27. SCOR Mtg 24/4/80.

28. Conversation with troops serving with UNIFIL at the time, and *The Irish Times*, 2/5/80.

29. *The Irish Times*, 2/5/80 in which Irish troops serving in Lebanon are reported to be gravely disappointed with Mr Lenihan's statement.

30. *The Irish Times*, 3/5/80.

31. S/13921, para 5.

32. Iandau, David and Anan Safadi, Anan, 'A Reassessment of Relations', in *Jerusalem Post*, 2/5/80, p. 16.

33. *The Irish Times*, 7/5/80.

34. McDonald, F., in *The Irish Times*, 23/4/80; *The Irish Press*, 2/5/80; *The Times* (UK), 28/5/80; *The Irish Times*, 26/5/80; and *Hibernia*, 3/7/80.

35. McDonald, F., *The Irish Times*, 23/4/80.

36. *Ibid.*

37. Doc. S/12611 of 19/3/78, para 4 (d).

38. *Dáil Debates*, Vol. 320, No. 7 8/5/80, p. 1144.

39. Doc. S/13888 of 11/4/80, para 12.

40. Resolution 467 (1980), para 6.

41. Doc. S/13921 of 2/5/80.

42. Doc. S/13994 of 12/6/80, para 69.

43. *Ibid.*

44. In conversation with senior Irish officer serving with UNIFIL at the time.

45. The IDF and Major Haddad had for some time proposed that Irishbatt be redeployed or withdrawn altogether from UNIFIL. After At Tiri the pressure for such a move was intensified. When the Nepalese contingent withdrew in late 1980 it looked as if the Irish would replace them in the more mountainous sector of operations. The proposal was strongly resisted by Ireland. Such a move would have been seen as giving in to outside pressure and could have boosted the campaign to discredit the Irish. The Force Commander decided against redeployment.

46. Doc. S/14296 of 15/12/80.

47. Doc. S/13301 of 7/5/79 and Doc. S/14296 of 15/12/80.

UNIFIL – An Interim Analysis

1. *Time* Magazine, 27 March 1978. The raid had been the subject of considerable adverse comment in the Israeli press.

2. SCOR 2071 Mtg., 17 March 1978.

3. SCOR 2072 Mtg., 18 March 1978.

4. SCOR 2074 Mtg., 19 March 1978

5. Tueni, Ghassan, *Une guerre pour les autres*, Jean Claude Lattes, Paris 1985, pp. 200–204. Mr Tueni was Lebanon's ambassador to the UN at the time.

6. SCOR 2074 Mtg., *Op cit.*

7. Carter, Jimmy, *Keeping Faith: Memoirs of a President*, Collins, London 1982. See also Reich, B. and Hollis, R. 'Peacekeeping in the Regan Administration' in *Peace Making in the Middle East – Problems and Prospects*, P. Marantz and J. Gross (Eds), Croom Helm, London 1985, pp.. 133–155.

8. Azar, Edward E. and Shnayerson, Kate, 'United States – Lebanese Relations: A Pocketful of Paradoxes' in *The Emergence of a New Lebanon, Fantasy or Reality*, Praeger, New York 1984, pp. 219–275.

9. Kissinger, Henry, *Years of Upheaval*, Weidenfeld and Nicolson, London 1982, p. 792 and *passim;* Cruise O' Brien, Conor, *The Siege: The Saga of Israel and Zionism*, Weidenfeld and Nicolson, London 1986, pp. 400–403 and *passim.*

10. *Kessings Contemporary Archives*, Vol V, p. 22956, 2 November 1979.

11. *Kessings Contemporary Archives*, Vol VII, p. 30874, 22 May 1981.

12. *Kessings Contemporary Archives*, Vol XXIX, p. 32412, September 1983, Vol XX, p. 33691, June 1985; Vol XXI, pp. 34074–34079, December 1985 and *International Herald Tribune* 14/15 February 1987, pp. 1, 5.

13. Jordan, Hamilton, *Crisis: The Last Year of the Carter Presidency*, New York, G. P. Putman's Sons, 1982; *Peace Making in the Middle East – Problems and Prospects, op cit*, pp. 133–134.

14. Rikhye, Indar J., *The Theory and Practice of Peacekeeping*, Hurst and Company, London, 1984, p. 109.

15. *Dáil Debates*, Vol. 306, No 4, 9 May 1979 pp. 395–613, esp. Dr G. Fitzgerald, pp. 599–604.

16. *The Blue Helmets*, A Review of United Nations Peacekeeping, United Nations, 1985, p. 116.

17. Security Council Document S/12611 dated 19 March 1978 was approved by Security Council Resolution 426 (1978) dated 19 March 1978.

18. *The Peacekeepers Handbook*, International Peace Academy, 1984, chapters 2 and 3, especially pp. 33–35.

19. GAOR, 15th session

20. Report of the Secretary General on UNIFIL, S/17965, 9 April 1986, para 51.

21. SCOR 2074 Mtg, *op cit.*

22. SCOR, S/PV 2681, 18 April 1986, pp 6–10.

23. Freeman, Robert O., *Soviet Policy toward the Middle East since 1970*, third edition, Praeger, New York, London, Sydney, Toronto, 1982, and also by the same author 'The Soviet Union and a Middle East Peace Settlement: A Case Study of Soviet Policy during the Israeli Invasion of Lebanon and its Aftermath' in *Peace Making in the Middle East – Problems and Prospects, op. cit.*, pp. 156–198.

24. Freeman, Robert O. in *Peace Making in the Middle East – Problems and Prospects, op. cit.*, p.

165.

25. *The Blue Helmet, op. cit.,* p. 110.

26. Interview between Lt Gen Erskine and the author, February 1986.

27. Security Council Document, S/12845 dated 13 September 1978, paras 36–38; *The Blue Helmets, op.cit.,* p .116.

28. The text of the agreement is given by Walid Khalidi, *Conflict and Violence in the Lebanon: Confrontation in the Middle East, Harvard Studies in International Affairs,* No. 38, Harvard, 1979, pp. 185–187.

29. S/12845, *op. cit.,* para 37.

30. Interview with Lt Gen Erskine, February 1986.

31. Tueni, G., *op. cit.,* pp. 203–204.

32. Security Council Document, S/12929 dated 18 Nov 1978, para 18.

33. S/12620 Add. 5, *op. cit.,* paras 15–17.

34. *Ibid.*

35. Security Council Document, S/12736, letter dated 13 June 1978 from the representative of Israel to the Secretary General. For the Secretary General's description of the 'accommodation' reached with the PLO see Security Council Document S/12845 dated 13 September 1978, paras 29–42.

36. See the reports in *The Irish Times,* 8 June 1978 and 19 June 1978.

37. Security Council Document, S/12840 letter dated 5 September 1978 from the representative of Lebanon to the Secretary General paras 5 and 6.

38. Security Council Document, S/12840, letter dated 8 September 1978 from the representative of Israel to the Secretary General.

39. *The Blue Helmet, op. cit.,* pp. 130–132.

40. *The Peacekeepers Handbook, op. cit.,* p. 22.

41. Article 47 of the UN Charter provides for the establishment of a military staff committee. No agreements have been concluded to place armed forces at the disposal of the Security Council under Article 43 to date. Nor has the committee been involved in Peacekeeping operations. See D. W. Bowett, *United Nations Forces, A Legal Study of United Nations Practice,* Stevens, London, 1964, pp. 12–18 and *passim.*

42. In 1965, the General Assembly decided to establish a special committee on peacekeeping. Much progress has been made in drawing up an agreed set of principles to govern peacekeeping operations, however disagreement remains in certain key areas. See Special Committee on Peacekeeping Operations: a comprehensive listing under specific headings of concrete proposals received, and a description of progress made to date. UN General Assembly Document A/AC. 121/L18 of 23 January 1973, and Special Committee on Peacekeeping Operations 1976 (Doc A/31/337).

43. *New York Times,* 19 December 1983.

44. See the interview with former US ambassador to Syria, Talcott Seelye, in *Monday Morning Magazine,* Vol X, No. 433, week of 26 October–1 November, 1981 pp. 44–53. In the interview, Mr Seelye advocates, *inter alia,* a much stronger recognition of the role of Syria in Middle East affairs.

PLACENAMES IN SOUTH LEBANON

1. I am indebted to Comdt T. Sweeney, Southern Command, for his researches and calculations on this and other sites.

2. For a more detailed account of the prehistory of the Levant, two papers are recommended: (a) 'The Phoenicians and the Levant' by Benjamin Mazar, *Israeli Exploration Society Journal,* 1986; (b) 'Phoenicia and the Phoenicians' by James D Muhly, *Israeli Exploration Society Journal,* 1984.

3. For an interesting evaluation of early mapping, especially that of the Palestinian Exploration Fund, Ian W. J. Hopkins' 'Nineteenth century maps of Palestine: dual-purpose historical evidence' (published in *Imago Mundi,* 1968) is recommended.

4 .'Al Junub' is the dismissive name given to south Lebanon. It means 'The South'.

5. An earlier form of Lt Col Travers' article originally appeared in *Decoding the Landscape,* edited by Timothy Collins, and published by The Centre for Landscape Studies, Social Sciences Research Centre, University College Galway.

1. Since its inception in 1985 the security zone expanded to encompass almost 850 square kilo-metres of desolate Lebanese mountainside extending inland for 70 km from the Mediterranean eastwards to the Golan Heights and Mt Hermon, and then running north-east to the Syrian border including the thumb-shaped salient around the moun-tain-top Christian town of Jezzine.
2. Iranian News Agency (IRNA)/UNIFIL *Daily News Summary*, 16/9/95 No. 2 [195].
3. *Jane's Intelligence Review*, October 1997, p. 459. Ed Blanche offers a different sequence of events and claims that Kassir and Badran were killed later that morning when a series of road-side bombs were activated by a signal from an IAF drone hovering overhead.
4. UNIFIL *Daily News Summary*, 4/8/97, No. 1 [158].
5. Israel television, 4/8/97; UNIFIL *Daily News Summary*, 8/8/97, No. 1. [162].
6. UNIFIL *Daily News Summary*, 29/8/97, No. 1 [178].
7. Rudge, David, 'IDF soldiers die in brush fire', *Jerusalem Post*, 29/8/97, p. 1.
8. *Jerusalem Post*, 29/8/97, p. 15.
9. *Jerusalem Post*, 1/5/97, p. 12.
10. Commentary by Ephraim Sneh in *Ma'ariv*, 19/8/97.
11. *Monday Morning Magazine*, Vol. XXVI, No. 1287, 25/8/97, p. 6.
12. *Haaretz*, 26/8/98; UNIFIL *Daily News Summary*, 27/8/97, No. 1 [176]. General Lahd ad-mitted that he had ordered the shelling of Sidon. He did not explain how he had achieved this level of independent action given that the IDF share a joint operations headquarters with him in Marjayoun.
13. The 'Katyushka' rocket used by Hizbullah in 1997 are Iranian-manufactured 122mm BM–21 projectiles with a range of 22 km. Israeli sources also believe that Hizbullah now also possess a quantity of North Korean made 240 mm rockets with a range of 44 km which if true would make the affluent port city of Haifa a reachable target (Source: *Jane's Defence Weekly*, 3/9/97, p. 33/34. See also *Jane's Defence Weekly*, 10/7/96, p. 3).
14. *Haaretz*, 16/10/97 – the senior IDF officer in Marjayoun is of brigadier rank.
15. Technically correct but Jezzine was certainly within Israel's 'area of influence'.
16. UNIFIL *Daily News Summary*, 19/8/97, No. 1 [168].
17. IDF sources confirmed that 45 rockets impacted in Israel at 12 different locations.
18. Eyewitness account from Comdt Niall Cremen, a senior Irish officer serving at UNIFIL HQ in Naquora, who was travelling in the border region at the time.
19. Irishbatt Increp. No. 1. of 19/8/97.
20. UNIFIL *Daily News Summary*, 20/8/97, No 1 [170].
21. *Ibid*.
22. UNIFIL *Daily News Summary*, 25/8/97, No. 1 [173].
23. *Ibid*.
24. *Haaretz*, 24/8/97.
25. UNIFIL *Daily News Summary*, 8/9/97, No. 1 [173]. NIFIL. **[??]**
26. See also Foreign Report No. 2463, 11/9/97.
27. 'Double Agent lured soldiers to death in Lebanon', Robert Fisk, *The Independent*, 17/9/97.
28. Al Hayat, *Jerusalem Post*, 5/10/97.
29. MK = Member of the Knesset.
30. *Haaretz* and UNIFIL *Daily News Summary*, 10/9/97, No 1 [190].
31. Channel 2 television (Israel)/UNIFIL *Daily News Summary*, 11/9/97, No 1 [190].
32. Iranian News Agency (IRNA)/UNIFIL *Daily News Summary*, 16/9/97 No. 2 [195].
33. 'An Interview with Hizbullah', *Jane's International Defence Review*, Vol. No. 30, October 1997.
34. *Monday Morning Magazine*, Vol. XXVI, No. 1291, 22/9/97, p. 10.
35. UNIFIL *Daily News Summary*, 15/9/97, No. 1 [193].
36. *Jane's Intelligence Review*, October 1997, p. 460.
37. *Jane's Foreign Report*, 6/11/97; UNIFIL *Daily News Summary*, 12/11/97, No. 1. [237].
38. UNIFIL *Daily News Summary*, 25/11/97, No. 1 [246].
39. Middle East television 12/11/97; UNIFIL *Daily News Summary*, 13/11/97, No. 1 [238].
40. General Levine had made his original remarks at a brigade commanders' course and a reserve officer attending had passed the information to a third, who in turn leaked the story to the press. (See *Jerusalem Post*, 8/12/97).

41. *Haaretz*, 30/11/97; UNIFIL *Daily News Summary*, 1/12/97, No. 1 [249].
42. *Yediot Ahronot*, 26/11/97; UNIFIL Daily *News Summary*, 27/11/97, No. 1 [248].
43. UNIFIL *Daily News Summary*, 2/12/97.
44. *Daily Star*, 4/12/97; UNIFIL *Daily News Summary*, 5/12/97, No. 1.
45. *Daily Star*, 9/12/97; UNIFIL *Daily News Summary*, 10/12/97, No. 1 [256].
46. *Haaretz*, 5/12/97.
47. Cockburn, Patrick, *The Independent*, 18/12/97; UNIFIL *Daily News Summary*, 19/12/97, No. 1 [263].
48. 'The Tragedy Continues' – *An Cosantóir (Irish Defence Journal)*, April 1998, p. 20.
49. UNIFIL *Daily News Summary*, 26/6/98, No. 1 [138].
50. 'Israel's Vietnam' – *An Cosantóir (Irish Defence Journal)*, March 1998, p. 6.
51. UNIFIL *Daily News Summary*, 29/6/98, No. 1 [139].
52. *Ma'ariv*, 28/6/98.
53. UNIFIL *Daily News Summary*, 8/7/98, No. 1 [[145].
54. *An Nahr*, 6/7/98; UNIFIL *Daily News Summary*, 8/7/98, No. 1.
55. *The Daily Star* (Beirut), 4/8/98; UNIFIL *Daily News Summary*, 5/8/98, No. 1 [165].
56. *Jane's Intelligence Review*, August 1997.
57. *The Daily Star* (Beirut), 4/8/98; UNIFIL *Daily News Summary*, 5/8/98, No. 1 [165].
58. UNIFIL *Daily News Summary*, 28/8/98, No. 1.
59. UNIFIL *Daily News Summary*, 17/6/99, No. 1 [125].
60. UNIFIL *Daily News Summary*, 21/8/98, No. 1 [147].
61. *Ibid.*, p. 2.
62. Kampeas, Ron, 'Netanyhu hits Lebanon hard', Associated Press Jerusalem, 25/6/99.
63. RUSI *Newsbrief*, October 1998, Vol. 18, No. 10, p. 77/78.